Digital Media
and Innovation

For Casey

and Rod Rightmire, mentor, friend, and colleague

SAGE was founded in 1965 by Sara Miller McCune to support the dissemination of usable knowledge by publishing innovative and high-quality research and teaching content. Today, we publish over 900 journals, including those of more than 400 learned societies, more than 800 new books per year, and a growing range of library products including archives, data, case studies, reports, and video. SAGE remains majority-owned by our founder, and after Sara's lifetime will become owned by a charitable trust that secures our continued independence.

Los Angeles | London | New Delhi | Singapore | Washington DC | Melbourne

Digital Media and Innovation

Management and Design Strategies in Communication

Richard A. Gershon

Western Michigan University

Los Angeles | London | New Delhi
Singapore | Washington DC | Melbourne

FOR INFORMATION:

SAGE Publications, Inc.
2455 Teller Road
Thousand Oaks, California 91320
E-mail: order@sagepub.com

SAGE Publications Ltd.
1 Oliver's Yard
55 City Road
London EC1Y 1SP
United Kingdom

SAGE Publications India Pvt. Ltd.
B 1/I 1 Mohan Cooperative Industrial Area
Mathura Road, New Delhi 110 044
India

SAGE Publications Asia-Pacific Pte. Ltd.
3 Church Street
#10-04 Samsung Hub
Singapore 049483

Acquisitions Editor: Matt Byrnie
Editorial Assistant: Janae Masnovi
Production Editor: Veronica Stapleton Hooper
Copy Editor: Pam Schroeder
Typesetter: C&M Digitals (P) Ltd.
Proofreader: Susan Schon
Indexer: Jeanne R. Busemeyer
Cover Designer: Candice Harman
Marketing Manager: Jillian Oelsen

Printed in the United States of America

Library of Congress Cataloging-in-Publication Data

Names: Gershon, Richard A., author.

Title: Digital media and innovation : management and design strategies in communication / Richard A. Gershon.

Description: First Edition. | Los Angeles : SAGE, 2016. | Includes bibliographical references and index.

Identifiers: LCCN 2015041624 | ISBN 978-1-4522-4141-8 (pbk. : alk. paper)

Subjects: LCSH: Mass media—Management. | Organizational effectiveness. Classification: LCC P96.M34 G47 2016 | DDC 302.23/068—dc23 LC record available at http://lccn.loc.gov/2015041624

This book is printed on acid-free paper.

16 17 18 19 20 10 9 8 7 6 5 4 3 2 1

Brief Contents

Detailed Contents

Preface

The Navarra Lectures

This book was several years in the making. It represents the direct outgrowth of a graduate course that I began teaching at Western Michigan University in 2009 entitled *Strategic Planning, Communication, and Innovation*. In this course, we look at the importance of strategic decision making and innovation with a special emphasis given to the entrepreneurs, project teams, and companies responsible for some of today's most engaging media and telecommunications products and services. This course set the foundation for much of my current research in the field of media management and telecommunications. In 2011, I was fortunate to obtain a Fulbright scholarship that took me to the University of Navarra in Spain, where I was invited to be a visiting professor. While at Navarra, I taught a similar graduate course but used the time to refine the subject matter and sketched out the basic outline for the present text. In many ways, this book could just as easily be subtitled *The Navarra Lectures*.

During my time at Navarra, I was able to successfully complete a monograph entitled "Intelligent Networks and International Business Communication: A Systems Theory Interpretation," *Media Markets Monographs, No. 12*, Universidad de Navarra Press. In this monograph, I ask the question: What makes an intelligent network intelligent? Second, how are intelligent networks used by people and business organizations? The intelligent network can be likened to the internal nervous system of an organization. Developing a set of answers to these questions became the basis for a whole host of material pertaining to digital media and photographic display, electronic commerce (EC), social networking, and artificial intelligence (AI). Part of this effort included developing a working construct that I call the Information and Telecommunications Systems (ITS) model as a way to understand the social and technological consequences of intelligent networks on people and organizations.

About This Book

This book represents a unique opportunity to look at the importance of innovation and innovative thinking to the long-term success of today's leading media and telecommunications companies. Advancements in technology, most notably the

Internet and digital media arts, are changing many of our basic assumptions regarding information, news, and entertainment content. This book takes an in-depth look at how smart, creative companies (both past and present) have transformed the business of media and telecommunications by introducing unique and highly differentiated products and services. Digital media represents the artistic convergence of various kinds of hardware and software design elements to create entirely new forms of communication expression. Digital media has transformed the business of retail selling and personal lifestyle, including EC, music and video streaming, social networking, as well as the sharing economy. Such innovations have proved to be real game changers by introducing into the marketplace a unique value proposition for the consumer.

Consider, for example, how a small, start-up company called Home Box Office (HBO) in 1972 challenged the conventional thinking of the time by introducing the concept of pay television. The principle of advertiser-supported "free" television was firmly engrained in the minds of the American public. What HBO did was change public perception about the nature of television entertainment. HBO offered a uniquely innovative service emphasizing recently released movies and other specialized entertainment that could not be found elsewhere on the general airwaves. Whereas HBO was not the first company to introduce a monthly per-channel fee service, it was the first to make it work successfully. This marked the beginning of a new business model called pay television.

Fast-forward 30 years later, and a company called Apple Computer (a one-time game changer in the field of personal computing) challenged the music industry by introducing the iPod portable music player, which relied on MP3 music file sharing software and the iTunes music store. The combination of the Apple iPod and iTunes media store created the first sustainable music downloading business model of its kind. All this came at a time when Internet piracy threatened to tear the music industry apart. The iTunes music store has redefined the way music is sold and distributed to the consumer. In 2007, lightning struck twice when Apple introduced the iPhone, an altogether new approach to smartphone technology. Both the iPod and iPhone have come to symbolize digital media in its most essential form and given shape and meaning to the principle of information exchange.

On an altogether different innovation stage, Seattle-based Amazon.com in 1994 started with online books given the large, worldwide demand for literature, the low-price points for books, as well as the large number of titles available in print. The basic idea was to create a mail-order catalog, albeit electronically, using the Internet and the power of intelligent networking. To build a substantial mail-order catalog covering books in all areas of the arts, sciences, and humanities would require an encyclopedia-like publication (if not bigger). And it would be too expensive to mail. The solution, of course, was the Internet, which is ideally suited for organizing and displaying a limitless amount of information. Two decades later, company founder Jeff Bezos presides over an EC company that has redefined online shopping for billions of people worldwide.

Another media business worthy of our consideration is the Walt Disney Company. The name Disney has become synonymous with family entertainment. The result has been an ongoing relationship with the public that began in 1923, when brothers Walt and Roy founded the Disney Brothers Cartoon Studio. Disney's signature brand has left an indelible imprint on its animated films, theme parks, and hotel stays. What is less familiar to the public is the company's creative design team known as Walt Disney Imagineering (WDI). They are responsible for building the creative set design, rides, and attractions, that are found throughout the various Disney worldwide theme parks, resorts, and cruises. Perhaps, most importantly, Walt Disney is an example of a company that has learned how to reinvent itself many times over throughout its more than ninety-year history, thereby demonstrating the ability to make innovation a sustainable, repeatable process.

What companies like these share in common is a remarkable attention to detail and a commitment to the power of a good idea. This book goes inside the creative edge and looks at what makes such companies successful. It also considers why some companies fail to stay innovative over time. Special attention is given to companies such as Eastman Kodak and Blockbuster Video. In a book entitled *Blue Ocean Strategy,* business authors Kim and Mauborgne make the argument that to create new market opportunities, innovative companies redefine the playing field by introducing an altogether new product, service, or idea. Instead of trying to outwit the competition in a zero-sum game of one-upmanship, blue ocean companies pursue the potential market space that has yet to be explored. The rules of competition are waiting to be set. In my view, that is the true meaning of the term innovation.

Acknowledgments

My time spent teaching and doing research at the University of Navarra gave me the chance to affirm that this was a book worth writing. I am grateful to my colleagues and friends at the University of Navarra for their friendship, collegiality, and warm hospitality. A special thank-you goes to Dr. Mercedes Medina, Dr. Alfonso Tabernero, and Dr. Alejandro Pardo. I also want to take a moment to acknowledge the Fulbright Foundation and the Haenicke Institute at Western Michigan University for providing the financial support that made my stay at the University of Navarra possible.

I am also grateful to several of my colleagues in the field of media and telecommunications who afforded me an opportunity to write contributing chapters to various edited works collections that they were working on. Where possible, I tried to write book chapters that had direct relevance to the mission and scope of the present book. Let me begin by thanking the following people: Dr. Alan Albarran, University of North Texas, United States; Dr. Robert Picard, Oxford University, UK; Dr. Yu-Li Liu, National Chengchi University, Taiwan; Dr. Mike Friedrichsen, Institute for Media Business, Germany; Dr. Zvezdan Vukanovic, University of Donja Gorica, Montenegro; Dr. Paulo Faustino, Porto University, Portugal; Dr. Fu-Lai Tony Yu, Hong Kong Shue Yan University, Hong Kong; Ho-Don-Yan, Feng Chia University, Taiwan. There are several people on the executive board of the Information and Telecommunications Education and Research Association (ITERA) whose comments and suggestions have made this book immeasurably better. My thanks to Steve Wildman, Michigan State University; Mike Bowman, Murray State University; Ray Hansen, Purdue University; and my colleagues on the executive board of ITERA for helping me to better understand the principles of intelligent networking.

A special thank-you goes to Leigh Ford, Mike Tarn, Dennis Simpson, Keith Hearit, and my colleagues at Western Michigan University for their continuous support and friendship. They allow me to do what I love doing best—teaching. I am also grateful to the senior administration at Western, whom I consider to be both colleagues and friends. They have given me encouragement and support to engage the university in a number of special projects on campus. My thanks to Dr. John M. Dunn, President, Dr. Tim Greene, Provost and Vice President for Academic Affairs, and Ms. Jan VanDerKley, Vice President for Business and Finance. There are, of course, friends and family along the way who provide continuous support and encouragement in a variety of ways. I want to take a moment to thank Peter Gershon and Carol Levin.

I am indebted to the editorial staff at Sage for helping to make this project possible. In particular I want to thank Matthew Byrnie (my editor) for his strong encouragement and belief in the value of this project. A special thank-you goes to Janae Masnovi, senior editorial assistant, who was critical to the project's success. I also want to take a moment to thank the Sage production staff, including Veronica Stapleton Hooper and Pam Schroeder, for their invaluable assistance in the production of this work. There were several occasions where they worked their magic and smoothed out the rough edges of a table, figure, or jumbled paragraph. More importantly, they made this project look whole.

Finally, the most important thank-you goes to my wife Casey for her continuous love and support. From North Carolina adventures to Nordic walking along the Lake Michigan coastline, I so appreciate her grace, wisdom, and sense of humor. She is my North Star. And to my son Matthew, who is learning to be a chef; Brook, who is learning to be a hair stylist; and of course my grandson, Oliver, whose deep-seated fascination with Spiderman makes the adventure all the more fun . . .

Richard A. Gershon
Western Michigan University

About the Author

Richard A. Gershon, PhD (Ohio University, 1986), is professor and co-director of the Telecommunications & Information Management Program at Western Michigan University, where he teaches courses in media management and telecommunications. He is the author of *Media, Telecommunications & Business Strategy,* 2nd ed. (2013) and *The Transnational Media Corporation: Global Messages and Free Market Competition,* winner of the 1998 book of the year sponsored by the National Cable Television Center. Dr. Gershon is a Fulbright scholar, having held visiting appointments at the University of Navarra, Spain, and Nihon University, Japan.

Dr. Gershon has twice been selected for national teaching honors, including the Steven H. Coltrin Professor of the Year Award (2000) by the International Radio & Television Society (IRTS) and the Barry Sherman Award for Teaching Excellence (2001) by the Management and Economics division of the Association for Education in Journalism and Mass Communication (AEJMC). In 2007, he was the recipient of the Distinguished Teaching Award at Western Michigan University. Dr. Gershon is a founding member of the Information and Telecommunications Education and Research Association (ITERA), where he served as the organization's first president.

Dr. Gershon currently serves on the executive board of the Western Michigan University Faculty Senate. He has twice chaired the Campus Planning and Finance Council and has been directly involved with a number of strategic planning and design efforts across campus. In addition, he serves on the WMU athletic advisory board.

Dr. Gershon welcomes you to visit him at his website http://www.rgershon.com

CHAPTER 1

Innovation and the Power of a Good Idea

If I have seen further it is by standing on the shoulders of giants.

—Sir Isaac Newton

There is one thing stronger than all the armies in the world, and that is an idea whose time has come.

—Victor Hugo

Introduction

The lessons of business history have taught us that there is no such thing as a static market. There are no guarantees of continued business success for companies regardless of their field of endeavor. In 1942, economist Joseph Schumpeter introduced the principle of *creative destruction* as a way to describe the disruptive process that accompanies the work of the entrepreneur and the consequences of innovation. In time, companies that once revolutionized and dominated select markets give way to rivals who are able to introduce improved product designs, offer substitute products and services, and/or lower manufacturing costs.[1]

The resulting outcomes of creative destruction can be significant, including the failure to preserve market leadership, the elimination of a once highly successful product line, or in the worst-case scenario, business failure itself.[2] The history of media and telecommunications is replete with examples of companies that were once high flyers (the best of the best) but who failed to plan for the future. Companies with iconic names like Eastman Kodak, Blockbuster Video, and BlackBerry wireless, to name only a few, have been greatly reduced or are no more.

Today, the international business landscape has become ever more challenging. Global competition has engendered a new competitive spirit that cuts across countries and companies alike. No company large or small remains unaffected by the desire to increase profits and decrease costs. Such companies are faced with the same basic question; namely, what are the best methods for staying competitive over time? In a word, *innovation*. This book is about the power of good ideas. It's about those business enterprises that have harnessed the power of good ideas to become real difference makers in the field of media and telecommunications.

When we use the word *innovation,* there is a tendency to think of it in present-day terms. Companies like Apple and Google are considered innovative companies. Similarly, the term *innovation* often is linked to companies that are engaged in digital media. From Sony's Akio Morita and the invention of the Walkman to Steve Jobs and the development of the iPhone, one of the goals of this book is to show the full measure of creativity and entrepreneurship both past and present. While there are numerous books on the subject of innovation (and specific corporate histories of well-known media companies), there are few books presently that are fully focused on the linkage between innovation and media and telecommunications. What has long fascinated me about the work of innovators like Walt Disney (Disney), Steve Jobs (Apple), and Jeff Bezos (Amazon), to name only a few, is the opportunity to examine how such companies and individuals create groundbreaking products and services while addressing the challenges of staying innovative over time. This book represents a unique opportunity to look at the importance of innovation and innovative thinking to the long-term success of today's leading media and telecommunications companies. Specifically, it will address four sets of questions. First, what does it mean to be an innovative media business enterprise? Second, what are the different types of media innovation, and who are some of the players who have proved to be real game changers in shaping the business of communication? Third, why do good companies fail to remain innovative over time? And fourth, how do the best companies foster a culture of innovation within their own organizational settings? This book will examine some of the people, companies, and strategies that have transformed the business of media and telecommunications.

What Is Innovation?

Renowned scholar Everett Rogers (1995) defines innovation as "an idea, practice or object that is perceived as new by an individual."[3] In principle, there are two kinds of innovation, namely, sustaining technology versus disruptive technology. A sustaining technology has to do with product improvement and performance. The goal is to improve on an existing technology or service by adding new and enhanced feature elements.[4] A computer manufacturer, for example, routinely is looking to improve on basic design elements like speed and throughput, processing power, and graphics display. For most companies, sustaining technology (or incremental innovation) is the most common form of innovation, often receiving more than 80 percent of the organization's total research and development budget.[5]

Sustaining technology is extremely important because it provides the steady and necessary improvements in product design that guard against rival product offerings. It also demonstrates a commitment to brand improvement. Such examples might include incremental improvements in Microsoft Office software or the steady progressions made in the Apple iPhone. The goal of sustaining (or incremental) innovation is to try and realize as much value as possible from an existing product or service without having to make a significant change in product design and/or a major retooling in production. By doing so, a company can preserve market share, extend brand awareness, and maintain profitability for a long period of time.

In contrast, a disruptive (or breakthrough) technology represents an altogether different approach to an existing product design and process. It redefines the playing field by introducing to the marketplace a unique value proposition. (See Table 1.1.) Consider, for example, the impact that MP3 file-sharing technology has had on the music industry. The speed and efficiency of Internet-delivered music using MP3 file-sharing software has fundamentally changed the cost structure of music recording and distribution on a worldwide basis.[6] The combination of the Apple iPod and iTunes media store created the first sustainable Internet music business model of its kind. It would redefine the way music is distributed and recorded forever more and give rise to the principle of personalized music selection. It was an absolute game changer and the quintessential example of a disruptive technology.

The Power of a Good Idea

There are any number of terms that we use in our day-to-day experience to describe the power of a good idea. Such words and phrases as *inspiration, compelling vision,* and *natural insight* are just a few of the lexicon of terms to describe that moment in time when a good idea takes hold. The best innovators have natural curiosity

Company	Disruptive Product/Service	Value Proposition
Apple	iPod and iTunes music store	Portable and customized music selection
Home Box Office (HBO)	Paying for television	Premium television programming *The Sopranos, John Adams, Game of Thrones,* and so on
Walt Disney Company	Walt Disney World Theme Parks and Resorts	Enhanced family entertainment
Amazon	Amazon.com; online shopping	Business-to-consumer e-commerce (EC)
Sony Inc. and Phillips	Compact disk (CD)	Transformed music delivery, playback, and storage; later used for information and video game delivery[7]

Table 1.1   Media Innovation: Disruptive Effects and New Value Proposition

about their environment. They are keen observers of human behavior and one's natural landscape. They are willing to juxtapose various idea combinations to see what happens.

As author Steven Johnson (2010) points out, a good idea is really a network of possibilities. A good idea spawns infinite connections and opportunities.[8] One of the important themes in this book is that the best innovators work in environments that allow them to be creative. From the original AT&T Bell Labs to the present-day Googleplex, there is a natural synergy that occurs when a project team combines talents and skills toward a common effort. A good idea has to be malleable; that is, it must be capable of adapting to various designs and configurations. As Ideo's Tom Kelley (2005) describes it, the best projects and design configurations are a collaborative effort; they never finish where they began. He characterizes it as the "magic of cross-pollination."[9]

The Serendipitous Discovery

From the original telephone to Post-it Notes, it sometimes happens that the scientist or engineer winds up creating something very different than what was originally intended.[10] As sometimes happens, the discovery is more accidental than planned. Probably, the most famous example was the invention of the telephone itself. In setting out to create the harmonic telegraph (multiple Morse code signals on a single wire), inventor Alexander Graham Bell wound up creating something far more compelling and futuristic than the original concept. Bell's extensive knowledge of sound (and sound waves) enabled him to consider the possibility of transmitting human speech electronically.[11] Both he and Elisha Gray are credited with independently having designed the first prototype devices that would later become the telephone. The telephone became the foundation for an entire system of communication that would take more than fifty years to build and require telephone exchanges (including operators, switches, and routers), long-distance lines, and assigned numbers. In time, the future AT&T would become the largest corporation in the world.

Research and Development

The words *research* and *development* are 20th-century terms that owe their beginning to the original industrial lab concept promoted by men like Thomas Edison, who built one of the first of its kind in Menlo Park, New Jersey (now called Edison in his honor). Menlo Park was home to one of America's first research and development (R&D) labs, which created products such as the phonograph and the incandescent lightbulb as well as an estimated 400 patents. The laboratory's open floor plan allowed for easy communication among Edison and his associates. The layout created an informal environment that Edison felt would foster creativity. Edison had no rules for work and no time clock. But his team worked long hours and was highly successful in their endeavors.[12] In time, other high-tech companies would one day follow suit and create their own version of the industrialized R&D lab. One such company was AT&T.

AT&T

The traditional R&D model assumes a more formal approach to research and product development. The goal is to enhance current product design as well as solve problems related to its implementation. Such R&D groups are assigned an annual budget with which to conduct research pertaining to product development as well as pure research (i.e., creating, new knowledge) that may not have immediate benefit. One of the best examples of a successful R&D model was AT&T Bell Labs, established in 1925. Bell Labs would prove to be an extremely fertile ground for the development of new and enhanced communication technology. Bell Labs had more PhD's under the roof of its 21 branches than any single university could claim in the field of engineering and turned out more than 19,000 patents since it began in 1925. As an R&D facility, Bell Labs could boast a number of firsts, including the first transistor, first laser, the first efficient communication satellite known as Telstar, early prototype designs in cellular telephones, as well as telephone switches and fiber optic communications.[13]

Bell Labs was unique for its time because it enabled its people to pursue pure research. One Bell Labs researcher described it as "managed anarchy." Pure research is an unpredictable path, with many hidden twists and curves. As so often happens, one discovery may not be useful for the moment but may eventually lead to another that is. Consider, for example, the work of Bell researcher Clinton Davisson, who won the Nobel Prize for physics in 1927 for work that revealed the nature of sub-atomic particles. His work proved that electrons can behave like a wave. Decades later, his work would be critical to the understanding of how semiconductors and lasers work. For his part, Davisson was simply trying to figure out how electrons behaved in a vacuum tube environment. Vacuum tube design was essential to AT&T's growing long-distance telephone network. It should be remembered that all communication signals suffer from problems of attenuation; that is, the signal becomes weakened over distance.[14] A typical phone signal becomes weaker as it travels over hundreds of miles. A vacuum tube helps to restore and amplify the weakened signals. But a vacuum tube has certain limitations.

Davisson's work attracted William Shockley, a young physicist from the Massachusetts Institute of Technology (MIT) to Bell Labs. Shockley headed up a group that included John Bardeen and Walter Brattain. They began doing preliminary research in the field of semiconductor design. This would require a deeper understanding of the switching and amplification of electrons. On December 12, 1943, Bell Labs physicists Shockley, Bardeen, and Brattain demonstrated the transistor: the world's first semiconductor device that could do the work of a vacuum tube.[15] The transistor would allow for more efficient transfer, switching, and amplification of electrons. The transistor provided the beginning step toward the efficient transfer of electrons and the miniaturization of that effort.

The transistor set into motion a whole host of innovation that was to touch every aspect of future communication technology, ranging from transistor radios to command and control telemetry for space flight. The transistor proved to be an important step that would lead to the development of the integrated circuit (i.e., multiple interconnected transistors on a single piece of silicon), popularly known as the computer chip.[16] The development of the transistor would win Shockley, Bardeen, and Brattain a Nobel Prize for physics.[17]

Another important discovery was in the field of wireless communication. The principle of cellular telephony was first articulated by D. H. Ring in 1947 in a technical memorandum at Bell Labs. Ring's paper, with valuable assistance from W. R. Young, referenced several critical elements, including the need for small geographical areas called cells (or areas of phone coverage), a low-powered transmitter in each cell, traffic to be controlled by a central switch, and the reuse of frequencies in different cell sites. Writing for the *Bell System Technical Journal*, W. R. Young stated that Bell's engineering teams "had faith that the means for administering and connecting to many small cells would evolve by the time they were needed."[18] On June 17, 1946, in St. Louis, Missouri, AT&T and Southwestern Bell introduced the first American commercial mobile radio-telephone service. It was simply called Mobile Telephone Service.[19] It should be noted that early design work in the area of cellular telephony was happening in other parts of the world as well, most notably Sweden and Finland. But the AT&T demonstration marked the beginning of cellular telephone communication as we know it.

Mavericks and the Power of a Good Idea

Very few entrepreneurs ever set out with the goal of becoming an entrepreneur. Rather, they are highly committed individuals who develop a deep-seated passion toward a problem or issue that they are working on. Some of the best innovation comes from the lone individual who I like to term the *maverick*. The maverick stands outside the box in terms of his/her thinking. Mavericks come in many forms. They may include those individuals who criticize deficiencies in current business processes and products. Innovators sometimes include whistle-blowers whose strong sense of right and wrong call out unethical or self-defeating business practices of the organization. And likewise, innovators can be those individuals who think up new ideas that have never been tried before. They put an entirely different lens on a problem.

Tim Berners-Lee, Great Britain

There is something to be said for the fact that good ideas often take a while to germinate. Steven Johnson refers to it as the "slow hunch." Consider, for example, the evolutionary thought process that gave birth to the principle of hypertext linking. In 1980, Tim Berners-Lee began working on a software project called Enquire that was an early version of hypertext linking and the World Wide Web concept. It was an idea that took several years to evolve. He would come back to it time and again during the next several years. In March 1989, Tim Berners-Lee, now a scientist at CERN, the European Organization for Nuclear Research, wrote a paper detailing the means by which members of the particle physics research community could easily research and share electronic documents.

At the start of the 1990s, the Internet was used primarily by the military, academic institutions, and business contractors. The primary system for communication was entirely text based, relying on basic newsgroups and remote Telnet chat sessions to send messages between users. Berners-Lee was challenged by the fact that searching for information meant having to log on to different computers with different protocol languages. As the popularity of the Internet increased, newcomers often found the arcane navigational commands a difficult task. Such would-be users had to master a complex set of computer commands and procedures before they could access the Internet. What was needed was an easy-to-use communication procedure that could link various programs.

In March 1989, Berners-Lee wrote a proposal to develop a large hypertext database with typed links. The initial proposal generated little interest. Later that same year, both he and colleague Robert Cailliau rewrote the proposal with the goal of developing a more improved navigational protocol for the Internet. The new protocol design was based on the principle of hypertext (or nonlinear text), which is the foundation of multimedia computing.[20] Lee's hypertext markup language (HTML) protocol would not require any specialized computer skills other than the ability to point and click on text or graphics. The hypertext protocol allows the user to navigate the Internet by moving from one document to another (or from one computer host to another).[21] The genius in Berners-Lee's work lay in the fact that he found a way to link documents using a common protocol rather than having to access remote databases as separate and distinct pieces of information. Tim Berners-Lee's contribution to the development of the Internet cannot be overestimated. The HTML protocol forms the basis for the World Wide Web concept.

Bill Gates, United States

Microsoft is a transnational computer and information company based in Redmond, Washington. The company was founded by Bill Gates and his childhood friend Paul Allen. Microsoft is the world's largest software company. Both Gates and Allen attended Seattle-based Lakeside preparatory school. Both Gates and Allen were the proverbial computer geeks, spending most of their spare time in the school's computer room. Paul Allen would later graduate and study computer science at the University of Washington, while Gates attended Harvard but later dropped out. In January 1975, Paul Allen read an article about the Altair 8800 microcomputer in *Popular Electronics* magazine. He showed the article to Gates, who in turn, called Micro Instrumentation and Telemetry Systems (MITS), makers of the Altair. Bill Gates offered both his and Paul Allen's services to write a version of the new BASIC programming language for the Altair. In signing the contract, Allen and Gates left Boston, Massachusetts, where Allen worked for Honeywell and Gates was enrolled in Harvard, and moved to Albuquerque, New Mexico, where MITS was located. It took them eight weeks to successfully complete and demonstrate the new software package. MITS agreed to distribute and market the product under the name of Altair BASIC.

The success of the Altair project proved to be the important catalyst that motivated Gates and Allen to form their own software company called Microsoft on

April 4, 1975. Bill Gates would serve as the company's new CEO. The company was later incorporated in the state of Washington in 1981. Microsoft soon established itself as one of America's first (and perhaps largest) producers of computer software, most notably, expanded versions of BASIC, which had become the default standard on most available personal computers (PCs) to date. The real turning point for Microsoft came in 1981, when it signed a contract with IBM to write the operating system code for the company's soon-to-be-launched IBM PC. Initially, Gates referred IBM to Digital Research (DRI), makers of the widely used CP/M operating system.[22] The discussions were unsuccessful, and IBM came back to Microsoft, which agreed to develop a new operating system. Microsoft contracted with Tim Patterson of Seattle Computer Products, and together they combined to create MS-DOS for a one-time fee of $50,000. The most important part of the deal, however, was Gate's shrewd decision to retain the copyright on the PC operating system. That decision was prescient. Gates recognized that software development would drive the burgeoning computer industry. He believed that future PC manufacturers would need equivalent operating systems, and Microsoft was well positioned to be the principal supplier.

From Microsoft's founding in 1975 until 2006, Bill Gates served as the company's chief technology strategist. He helped expand the company's range of products, including the Windows operating system as well as the Microsoft Office suite of products. As the world's leading supplier of personal computing software, Microsoft developed a reputation for being aggressive and sometimes anticompetitive.[23] Gates, himself, was generally recognized to be an impatient and demanding boss. Gates met regularly with Microsoft's senior leadership team. Firsthand accounts of these meetings describe him as verbally combative, routinely challenging his managers for perceived flaws in their approach to business strategy or mistakes made in software development and execution.[24]

What is sometimes forgotten is the important role that Microsoft (and specifically Gates) has played in helping to advance personal computing. Microsoft set the defacto standards in business computing software. By shifting the value proposition in computing to software, Microsoft commoditized the manufacture of hardware equipment, thus making personal computing accessible to the general public.[25] Microsoft, more than any company, took the mystery out of computing by transforming an industry that was once the purview of the guys in the white coats. Unlike Apple, Microsoft did not create a proprietary standard, thereby allowing all manufacturers to build computers using Microsoft software. Microsoft put a PC on everyone's desk. Microsoft built a strong, reliable operating system and set of software products that enabled millions of users worldwide to engage in computing at a cost point that greatly advanced the field of personal computing.

Ken Kutaragi, Japan

The Sony Playstation was the brainchild of an engineer named Ken Kutaragi, who was fascinated with designing an entertainment device that could combine the power of a computer workstation with high-resolution graphics. For two years,

Kutaragi operated without a sponsor until his friend, Teruo "Terry" Tokunaka, a senior executive at Sony, interceded on his behalf. Tokunaka took Kutaragi to see Sony CEO Norio Ohga to discuss his idea. Ohga was sufficiently impressed that he authorized Kutaragi to begin building a working prototype of his video game console.[26] Not everyone at Sony was enamored with the idea of video game technology. In the beginning, the senior leadership at Sony did not view themselves in the business of video game technology, which was seen as a children's toy. Worse still, companies like Nintendo and Sega were the established leaders in video game technology and software. Nevertheless, Sony's executive planning committee approved $50 million in start-up costs to allow Kutaragi and his design team to develop the basic computer chip necessary for a future video game console.

One of Sony's major challenges was to convince the larger software developers to create innovative games to support the new platform system. Sony's future success in video game technology would depend on high-quality software games. In November 1993, Sony Computer Entertainment (SCE) was created for the purpose of marketing and licensing video game consoles and titles. One of the most critical elements to the new Sony video game platform was the use of CD technology instead of the existing 16-bit cartridge. It was recognized that the CD possessed greater storage capacity than a video game cartridge and was much cheaper to produce. Sony was able to play to its own strengths as both they and Phillips Corporation were the co-inventors of the CD. On December 3, 1994, the Sony Playstation was launched in Japan with eight game titles. Sony sold some 300,000 units in the first month alone, more than three times what company strategists had expected. The Playstation was launched a year later in the United States and achieved immediate success. By 1998, Playstation had sold 33 million units worldwide and become the international leader in video game consoles. In 2000, Sony's PlayStation 2 was launched and became the best-selling console ever built.[27] In time, the Sony Playstation would become more than a video game system. It would develop into an all-inclusive broadband delivery system to the home, capable of allowing users to play games, watch television, and listen to music. The development of Playstation ultimately changed the landscape of the medium forever, becoming the foundation for gaming as we know it.

Linus Torvalds, Finland

Finland's Linus Torvalds is a computer scientist who was the principal force behind the development of the Linux operating system. In 1991, while studying at the University of Helsinki, he purchased his first PC. Torvalds was not satisfied with the computer's operating system. His PC used MS-DOS, the disk operating system designed by Microsoft Corporation. Torvalds, for his part, preferred AT&T's UNIX-based operating system that was used on the university's computers.[28] He decided to create his own PC-based version of UNIX. Months of determined programming work yielded the beginnings of an operating system known as Linux. In 1991, he posted a message on the Internet to alert other PC users to his new system and made the software available for free downloading. As was a common practice among software developers at the time, Torvalds released the source code, which meant that anyone with knowledge of computer programming could modify Linux to suit his/her own purposes. Because of their access to the source code, many programmers helped Torvalds retool and refine the software, and by 1994 the Linux kernel (original code) version 1.0 was released.

Operating systems require a certain amount of technical acumen. The original Linux OS was not as easy to use when compared to the more popular operating systems such as Windows, Apple's Mac OS, or IBM OS/2. However, Linux evolved into a remarkably reliable, efficient system that rarely crashed. In addition to Linux being free, its source code can be viewed and modified by anyone, unlike a proprietary operating system. This means that different language versions can be developed and deployed in markets that would be too small for traditional companies. Compared to Windows, Linux is more difficult to use. Linux became popular in the late 1990s when competitors of Microsoft began taking the upstart operating system seriously. Companies like Oracle, Netscape Communications, and Intel (to name only a few) announced plans to support Linux as an inexpensive alternative to Windows. What sets Linux apart from other operating systems is that it has grown to become a major force in computing, powering everything from the New York Stock Exchange to mobile phones to supercomputers to consumer devices. As an open source system, Linux is developed collaboratively; that is, no one company is solely responsible for its continuation or ongoing support. Developers from hundreds of different companies contribute to every kernel release. Companies participating in the Linux economy share research and development costs with their partners and competitors. The sharing in development costs among multiple individuals and companies has resulted in a large and efficient "free" ecosystem that is unparalleled in software design.

Three Strategic Approaches to Business Transformation

The most important inventions build on the fundamental principles set forth by others. Such companies and project teams benchmark and learn by example. At the same time, the innovator must be willing to let go of basic assumptions and consider a problem from an altogether different perspective. He/she must be open to taking risks by approaching a problem in an entirely new way. That is what truly separates the innovator from the also-ran. In this book, we will consider three major types of innovation. They include: 1) Business model innovation, 2) Product innovation, and 3) Process innovation.

Business Model Innovation

Today, innovation is about much more than developing new products. It's also about building new markets to meet untapped customer needs. Business model innovation involves creating entirely new approaches for doing business. Authors

Kim and Mauborgne (2005) make the argument that to create new growth opportunities, innovative companies must consider the unknown market space, untainted by competition. They advocate what they term a *Blue Ocean strategy* approach, whereby demand is created rather than fought over. Blue oceans denote all future industries not in existence today (i.e., the unknown market space). It describes the potential market space that has yet to be explored.[29] HBO, for example, created a demand for premium television entertainment. They changed the consumer mind that television should forever be free. Likewise, Amazon.com demonstrated the potential of electronic commerce by developing a simple and efficient way to buy books and other goods using the power of the Internet and intelligent networking. This gave rise to an altogether new business model known as EC. Both companies introduced a business model innovation that proved transformative. They redefined the competitive playing field by introducing an entirely new value proposition to the consumer.

Product Innovation

Product innovation refers to the complex process of bringing new products and services to market as well improving (or enhancing) existing ones. Highly innovative companies display a clear and discernible progression in the products they make. They force themselves to create new and better products while challenging the competition to do the same.[30] There is a natural progression in product design and development.[31] Being first to market is essential. If successful, a new product innovation will create lasting advantage while spawning a host of imitators. Consider, for example, the host of imitators that followed the launch of the original iPhone by Apple.

Successful product innovation goes hand in hand with the creative process for developing unique and original ideas. The best companies foster a culture of innovation. They recognize that the source of good ideas can come from a wide variety of people and players both inside and outside the organization, including design engineers, project teams, business units, as well as individual customers.[32] One important consideration is whether the proposed idea fills an obvious gap or niche in the marketplace. Consider, for example, the success of the EC service known as Vacation Rental by Owner (VRBO) in helping to advance vacation lodging using the power of the Internet and customer feedback. It was the right product at the right time.

Process Innovation

Business process innovation involves creating systems and methods for improving organizational performance. Davenport and Short (1990) define business process innovation as a "set of logically related tasks performed to achieve a defined business outcome."[33] Examples can be found in a variety of organizational settings and structures, including product development, manufacturing, inventory management, customer service, distribution, and delivery.[34]

The benefit of business process innovation is that it creates internal efficiencies that translate into organizational cost savings, including a better use of time, people, and resources.

A highly successful business process renders two important consequences. First, business process innovation is transformative; that is, it creates internal and external efficiencies that provide added value to the company and organization. Second, a well-designed business process sets into motion a host of imitators who see the inherent value in applying the same business process to their own organization. As an example, Dell Computers was an important innovator when it came to developing just-in-time manufacturing techniques as well as direct-to-home computer sales. Similarly, Netflix harnessed the power of the Internet in providing consumers with the ability to directly order movies online, thus creating an efficiency for the delivery of movies to the home. Both companies were game changers in the field of EC by demonstrating that one could engage in EC without the need for a bricks-and-mortar retail store.

Three-Sided Innovation

It is not uncommon that some of the best companies discussed in this book are innovative in more than one area. As so often happens, the demands of bringing a product to market may require the organization to develop a business plan as well as support systems that cut across all three areas of innovation. I call this three-sided innovation. See Table 1.2.

Table 1.2 Three-Sided Innovation			
Company	*Business Model*	*Product*	*Process*
Amazon	Electronic Commerce	Books and Later General Merchandise	Supply Chain Management System
Apple	Electronic Commerce	iTunes Music Selection and iPod Music Player	MP3 File Sharing and Distribution
Google	Key-Word Search	Internet Search	Intelligent Networking and Algorithmic Function
HBO	Advertising Pay Cable Television	Premium Television and Film Entertainment	Satellite Communication
NBC/CBS Radio and Television Network	Advertiser-Supported Radio and Television	Radio and Television Entertainment— News	Network and Affiliate Relationship

Digital Media and Innovation

Today, of course, we think of innovation within the modern-day context of digital media and the Internet. Digital media represents the artistic convergence of various kinds of hardware and software design elements to create entirely new forms of communication expression. From EC (Amazon.com and Google) to music and video streaming (Apple iTunes and Netflix), digital media has transformed the business of retail selling and personal lifestyle. Digital media is at the heart of today's communication revolution. We have entered the era of personalization, where smartphone users personalize their music listening experience and newspaper readers customize their news selection via their computer tablet.[35]

Central to any discussion pertaining to digital media is having an appreciation for the importance of convergence. For communication scholars, the word *convergence* is a fairly elastic term that has come to mean different things depending on time, application, and context. There are a number of driving forces that focus public attention on the issue, including changes in technology (most notably the Internet), business merger and acquisition activities, and the search for new market opportunities.[36] While the term *convergence* may be elastic, it shoulders an important responsibility in helping explain the ramifications of technologies and business enterprises that are jointly linked together.

Digital Storytelling and Photography

Digital media has proved to be a major game changer when it comes to storytelling. *Digital storytelling* is the art of using digital tools to tell a story. Consider, for example, what has occurred in terms of how we handle photographic display. The once iconic family photo album represented a certain way of telling one's personal family history (i.e., weddings, sporting events, vacations, etc.). The digital camera changed all that. The digital photo can be stored on a variety of media devices, including PCs, flash drives, smartphones, and computer tablets as well as being uploaded to the Internet, not to mention social media sites as well as personal or professional Web site displays. Instagram, for example, is a mobile photo and video-sharing service that enables its users to take pictures and videos, apply digital filters, and share them on a variety of social networking services, such as Facebook, Twitter, and Tumblr. All this points to the fact that the transition to digital cameras is no longer about a single product but, rather, a fundamental shift in thinking regarding visual display, storytelling, and the communication process.[37]

Digital Media Innovation and Intelligent Networking: Eight Signature Features

International business has been transformed by the power of instantaneous communication. The combination of computer and telecommunications has collapsed the time and distance factors that once separated nations, people, and business organizations.[38] We start with the assumption that the intelligent network is not one network but a series of networks designed to enhance worldwide communication for business and individual users alike.[39] What gives the network its unique intelligence are the people and users of the system and the value-added contributions they bring via critical gateway points (e.g., PCs, smartphones, tablets, etc.).[40] The intelligent network provides the electronic pathways and information repositories that make global communication possible. In this book, we consider eight signature features that help define the many ways in which digital media and intelligent networks are being used. This can be seen in Table 1.3. These eight signature features are part and parcel of what I term *digital lifestyle.*

Table 1.3 Digital Media and Innovation: Eight Signature Features	
• **High-Definition Television (HDTV)**	Provides picture quality approaching that of 35 mm film. HDTV is considered the most significant development in television technology since color television because of its remarkably improved picture quality.
• **Video Streaming**	Represents the ability to distribute video information via the Internet to one's television set, computer, or mobile device. This can include video clips (YouTube), movies (HBO and Netflix), and social media (Facebook).
• **Mobile Wireless Communication**	Suggests that users require flexibility of movement and access to the Internet anytime, anywhere. The term *smartphone* describes a new generation of cellular telephones that is highly personalized and features a variety of enhanced information services.
• **Video-on-Demand (VOD)**	Represents a category of pay television services that enables the cable, Internet Protocol TV (IPTV) or Direct Broadcast Satellite (DBS) viewer to access feature films and concerts from a large selection of titles and program categories that are hosted on a remote server. Central to this discussion is the importance of Netflix, which in 2008 demonstrated the possibility of streaming movies via a broadband cable to the home. Netflix would be a catalyst for change, opening the door for other services, including Hulu and HBO-GO.
• **MP3 File Sharing**	Is a digital audio encoding format that utilizes compression technology. MP3 is designed to greatly reduce the amount of data necessary to provide a faithful reproduction of an original recording. The power of Internet-delivered music using MP3 file-sharing software has changed fundamentally the cost structure of music recording and distribution on a worldwide basis.
• **Digital Video Recording (DVR)**	Represents the ability to record selected television programs for later viewing. A DVR set-top box includes an on-screen guide of scheduled TV programs. The value proposition for the consumer is the ability to record one's favorite programs as well as the ability to skip over commercial TV ads.

• **Cloud Computing**	The expression *putting something on the cloud* refers to the idea of storing of information and data on a remote host site. Cloud computing provides both storage as well as the delivery of information services over a virtual platform using the networking capability of the Internet. The user is able to access such services on demand. Cloud computing comes in two general forms: public (Facebook and Google Calendar) versus private clouds (internal university or hospital networks).
• **Digital Video Compression (DVC)**	Refers to digitizing and compressing video pictures so that they may be processed, stored, and distributed with greater flexibility and ease. DVC has important implications for diverse technologies and services such as: 1) HDTV; 2) Increased channel capacity on cable, IPTV, and DBS; 3) Internet video streaming; and 4) Video games.

Innovation Failure

Authors Collins and Porras (1994) make the argument that highly successful companies are those that are willing to experiment and not rest on their past success. Over time, tastes, preferences, and technologies change. Innovative companies keep abreast of such changes, anticipate them, and make the necessary adjustments in strategy and new product development.[41]

This begs the question: If strategic adjustment and innovation are such basic elements, why then don't more companies succeed at it? One of the important arguments of this book is that even the best-managed companies are susceptible to innovation failure. In fact, all companies are susceptible to innovation failure or experience decline in their ability to maintain a competitive edge. Christensen (1997) posits what he calls the *innovator's dilemma.*[42]

Specifically, a company's very success can become the root cause of its failure to stay innovative. The public quickly forgets that in the mid-1990s, Apple was less than sixty days shy of declaring bankruptcy. So too, the Walt Disney Company experienced a similar decline in their innovative prowess in the decade of the 1990s, when it chose to partner with Pixar rather than internally develop new Disney animation films, once the hallmark of the company's creativity.

Past success can sometimes make an organization very complacent; that is, they lose the sense of urgency to create new opportunities.[43] Companies, like people, can become easily satisfied with organizational routines. They become preoccupied with fine-tuning and making slight adjustments to an existing product line rather than preparing for the future. They become risk averse and engage in what MIT's Nicholas Negroponte (1995) describes as the "problem of incrementalism."[44] The history of business is filled with examples of past companies where senior management failed to plan for the future. Such companies do not anticipate a time when a substitute product (or changing market conditions) might come along and dramatically alter the playing field.

The Challenges of Business Reinvention

While most organizations recognize the importance of innovation, there is a wide degree of latitude regarding the method and approach to innovation. For some business enterprises, innovation is deliberative and planned. It is built into the cultural fabric of a company's ongoing research and development efforts. Some companies like Apple have a lengthy and structured approach to R&D. Other times, innovation is a direct response to a triggering event, that is, a sudden change in external market conditions and/or technology that forces a change in business strategy.[45]

The introduction of a new technology is the consummate triggering event that can cause any number of intended and unintended consequences on the marketplace, hence, the term *creative destruction*. One of the accompanying rules of creative destruction is that once a technology has been fully introduced, there is no going backward. There is no disinventing what one already knows how to do. Consider this the fallacy of nuclear disarmament (i.e., there may be a reduction in arms, but the core knowledge remains permanent). Thus, the real test for an established media enterprise is how to reinvent itself in light of new competitive threats and changes. We have seen this pattern time and again throughout the latter part of 20th and early 21st centuries. Table 1.4 provides a select set of examples of incumbent media enterprises and the triggering event technologies that forced business reinvention.

Table 1.4 Challenges and Solutions: Disruptive Communication and Information Technology		
Incumbent Media	*Challenged by*	*Solution*
Newspapers	Radio, late 1930s and 1940s	Became more interpretative in news approaches, expanded photojournalism coverage
Radio	Broadcast Television, 1950s	Deemphasized radio drama and comedies and focused on music (top 40 music, sports broadcasting, and so on)
Broadcast Television	Cable Television, late 1970s and 1980s	Slowly bought into cable programmers or created their own cable brands: • ABC acquired ESPN • NBC launched CNBC
Cable Television	DBS, 1990s, early 21st century	Emphasized high-speed Internet access and cable telephony
Vinyl Records	Compact Disk (CD), 1980s	All music production companies eventually transitioned to CD format
CDs (traditional music retail)	iPod, MP3 music file sharing, early 21st century	Steady transition to the EC model: iTunes, Pandora, and so on
Newspapers and Television	The Internet, 21st century	Digital news and online reading formats

SOURCE: R. Gershon, adaptation of earlier model.[46]

Consider, for example, the impact that television had on the radio industry in the 1950s. Television was developed and promoted by the same companies involved in radio. In the beginning, television was conceived simply as radio with pictures. Radio provided many of the programmatic lessons that would be later adopted by television. Thus, the programming, economic structure, and the system of regulation was patterned after radio. The once highly successful radio networks (i.e., CBS and NBC) strengthened their dominance of the industry in the 1950s by establishing a strong television presence. Many of the programs and its actors and actresses would make the transition from radio to television (some would not). Thus, famous radio programs like *Dragnet, Gunsmoke,* and the *Lone Ranger* eventually would make their way to television. All this came at a price. The radio industry began feeling the effects of creative destruction. Radio listenership steadily dropped off. The challenge for the radio industry was either to adapt or face a slow, steady demise. It took several years, but eventually radio reinvented itself strategically by playing to its natural strengths, emphasizing music formats (i.e., top 40, sports, news, etc.), becoming more mobile (radios in cars and portable radios), and employing radio station formats with more targeted audiences. This included the rise of celebrity DJ and radio personalities.[47]

It was only a matter of time before television would find itself in a similar situation with the emergence of cable television in the 1970s. Suddenly, broadcast television was feeling the tide winds of creative destruction as well. The broadcast television marketplace was no longer an oligopoly of three major networks, given the explosive growth of new cable television programming services like HBO, CNN, ESPN, and MTV (to name only a few). The upstart cable networks now had the ability to narrowcast their programming by targeting specific audiences both in terms of specialized program content as well as audience demographics. Thus was born the principle of narrowcasting. They threatened to siphon audiences away from the traditional broadcast networks, and by the 1980s cable seriously had begun to fragment the television marketplace.[48]

Discussion

Failure Is Not an Option

Change is never easy. Change is especially difficult when a new technology or start-up company is poised to displace a well-established business. Nowhere is this more evident than the impact that digital media and the Internet have had on traditional newspapers and magazines. Today, the international newspaper industry finds itself on the receiving end of creative destruction. Starting in 2008, the international newspaper industry has entered into a period of unprecedented decline Many of the world's leading newspapers have experienced overall revenue decline. Once iconic magazine names like *Newsweek, Fortune,* and *Life* have been greatly reduced or are no more. Hundreds of newspapers and magazines from around the world have shuttered their doors or gone to an all-digital format. The digital fusion of Internet news in combination with computer tablets and other mobile devices has fundamentally challenged the long-term sustainability of print media. This is creative destruction in its most essential form. Today, the question for journalists, newspaper managers, and journalism educators is the same. What business are you really in?

In this book, we will see examples of companies that have overcome the challenges of business reinvention. We will meet a select number of media companies that have learned how to make innovation a sustainable repeatable process. Their lessons and experience are fully shared with the reader. We also will encounter companies that succumbed to the devastating effects of creative destruction and have been greatly reduced or no longer exist. In the life of all business enterprises, there comes a point when such companies are challenged by the moving tides of the unexpected. How they respond to such changes determines whether they will be successful or a business that failed to adapt. This juncture represents what former Intel CEO Andy Grove refers to as a *strategic inflection point;* a time when a triggering event in the competitive marketplace requires new solutions or face the prospect of business extinction.[49] Put differently, as former National Aeronautics and Space Administration (NASA) flight director Gene Kranz once said to the members of his mission control team—responsible for the safe return of the disabled Apollo 13 spacecraft—"Failure is not an option!"

Endnotes

1. Joseph Schumpeter, *Capitalism, Socialism and Democracy* (New York: Harper & Row, 1942).
2. Richard Gershon, *Media, Telecommunications and Business Strategy,* 2nd ed. (New York: Routledge, 2013).
3. Everett Rogers, *Diffusion of Innovation,* 4th ed. (New York: Free Press, 1995), 11.
4. Clayton Christensen, *The Innovator's Solution* (Boston, MA: Harvard Business School Press, 2003), 34.
5. Tony Davila, Marc Epstein, and Robert Shelton, *Making Innovation Work* (Upper Saddle River, NJ: Wharton School Publishing, 2006).
6. Paola Dubini and Bernardino Provera, "Chart Success and Innovation in the Music Industry," *Journal of Media Business Studies* 5, no. 1 (2008): 41–65.
7. Richard Gershon, "Media Management and Innovation: Disruptive Technology and the Challenges of Business Reinvention," in *The Media as a Driver of the Information Society*, eds. A. Albarran, P. Faustino and R. Santos (Lisbon, Portugal: Media XXI/ Formal Press, 2011), 299–319.
8. Steven Johnson, *Where Good Ideas Come From: The Natural History of Innovation* (New York: Riverhead Books, 2010).
9. Tom Kelley, *The Ten Faces of Innovation* (New York: Doubleday, 2005), 68.
10. A word about Post-it Notes: a Post-it Note is a small piece of colored paper with a strip of light adhesive on the back that allows it to be temporarily attached to papers, documents, books, and a variety of other things. In 1970, 3M chemist Spencer Silver was working to develop a strong glue. Instead, he wound up creating an adhesive that wasn't very sticky. Nothing came of it for four years. But it so happens that a 3M colleague by the name of Arthur Fry was a singer in a local church choir. Fry would sometimes find

himself routinely losing his place in the church hymn book when the bookmarks he would use kept falling out. Why not try something different? Fry hit on a simple but elegant idea. He decided to coat a set of bookmarks with Spencer's glue. Now for the first time, they stayed in place yet lifted off without damaging the pages. The Post-it Note was born. In time, the Post-it Note would prove to be one of 3M's most popular office products.

11. James Mackay, *Alexander Graham Bell* (New York: John Wiley & Sons, 1997), 91–130.

12. "Menlo Park: The World's First R&D Lab," *Time Magazine,* http://content.time.com/time/photogallery/0,29307,1999191_2156979,00.html

13. Jeremy Bernstein, *Three Degrees above Zero: Bell Labs in the Information Age* (New York: Charles Scribner's & Sons, 1984), 77–107.

14. Ibid.

15. Jon Gertner, *The Idea Factory: Bell Labs and the Great Age of American Innovation* (New York: Penguin Press, 2012).

16. Ibid.

17. Jeremy Bernstein, 77–107.

18. Tom Farley and Mark Van der Hoek, "Cellular Telephone Basics: Amps & Beyond," last modified 2002, http://www.privateline.com/Cellbasics/Cellbasics.html

19. Richard A. Gershon, "Cellular Telephony," in *Encyclopedia of International Media & Communications,* Vol. 1, ed. D. H. Johnston (San Diego, CA: Academic Press, 2003), 175–188.

20. Tim Berners-Lee, *Weaving the Web* (New York: Harper Collins, 1999).

21. Gershon, *Media, Telecommunications and Business Strategy,* 247–248.

22. An operating system is the fundamental software that allows a computer to function.

23. In *U.S. v. Microsoft* (D.C. Cir. 2001), Microsoft was found guilty of engaging in anticompetitive behavior by requiring computer makers who wanted to install the company's Windows operating system to also install Microsoft's Internet Explorer and exclude the once highly popular Netscape Navigator browser. Such tying arrangements were found illegal by the D.C. Circuit Court. Microsoft was also found guilty of manipulating its application programming interfaces to favor Internet Explorer over third-party web browsers.

24. Ken Auletta, *World War 3.0: Microsoft and its Enemies* (New York: Random House, 2001).

25. "Yes, Microsoft Did Change the World More Than Apple," *Business Insider,* last modified September 8, 2011, http://www.businessinsider.com/yes-microsoft-did-change-the-world-more-than-apple-2011-9

26. Reiji Asakura, *Revolutionaries at Sony: The Making of the Sony Playstation and the Visionaries Who Conquered the World of Video Games* (New York: McGraw-Hill, 2000).

27. Richard Gershon and Tsutomu Kanayama, "The Sony Corporation: A Case Study in Transnational Media Management," *The International Journal on Media Management* 4, no. 2 (2002): 44–56.

28. UNIX is a computer operating system developed in the 1970s at AT&T's Bell Research Labs. Designed originally for internal use within the Bell system, AT&T would later license UNIX to outside parties (both academic and commercial) starting in the late 1970s.

29. W. Chan Kim and Renée Mauborgne, *Blue Ocean Strategy* (Boston, MA: Harvard Business School Press, 2005).

30. Michael Brooke and William Mills, *New Product Development: Successful Innovation in the Marketplace* (Binghamton, NY: International Business Press, 2003).

31. Gary Hamel, "The What, Why and How of Management Innovation," *Harvard Business Review* (February 2006), 72–87.

32. Brooke and Mills, *New Product Development.*

33. T. Davenport and J. Short, "The New Industrial Engineering: Information Technology and Business Process Redesign," *Sloan Management Review* (Summer 1990), 11–27.

34. Thomas Davenport, *Process Innovation* (Boston, MA: Harvard Business School Press, 1993).

35. Richard Gershon, "Digital Media Innovation and the Apple iPad: Three Perspectives on the Future of Computer Tablets and News Delivery," *Journal of Media Business Studies* 10, no. 1 (2013): 41–61.

36. Michael Wirth, "Issues in Media Convergence," in Handbook of Media Management and Economics, eds. A. Albarran, M. Wirth, and S. Chan-Olmsted (Mahwah, NJ: Lawrence Erlbaum, 2005), 445–462. See also, Alan Albarran, *Management of Electronic Media* (Belmont CA: Wadsworth, 2010).

37. Yue-Ling Wong, *Digital Media Primer* (Upper Saddle River, NJ: Pearson Prentice-Hall, 2009).

38. Manuel Castells, *The Rise of the Networked Society, the Information Age: Economy, Society and Culture,* 2nd ed. (Oxford, UK: Blackwell, 2000).

39. Eli Noam, *Interconnecting the Network of Networks* (Cambridge, MA: MIT Press, 2001).

40. Richard Gershon, "Intelligent Networks and International Business Communication: A Systems Theory Interpretation," *Media Markets Monographs. No. 12* (Pamplona, Spain: Universidad de Navarra Press, 2011).

41. Jim Collins and Jerry Porras, *Built to Last* (New York: Harper Collins, 1994).

42. Clayton Christensen, *The Innovator's Dilemma* (Boston, MA: Harvard Business School Press, 1997).

43. Michael Tushman and Charles O'Reilly, *Winning Through Innovation* (Boston, MA: Harvard Business School Press, 1997), 1–16.

44. Nicholas Negroponte, "Incrementalism is Innovation's Worst Enemy," *Wired,* April 1995, 188.

45. Thomas Wheelen and J. David Hunger, *Strategic Management and Business Policy* (Reading, MA: Addison Wesley Longman, Inc., 1998), 52–67.

46. Richard Gershon, "Digital Media Innovation and the Apple iPad: Three Perspectives on the Future of Computer Tablets and News Delivery," *Journal of Media Business Studies* 1 (2011): 41–61.

47. Christopher Sterling and John Kitross, Stay Tuned: A History of American Broadcasting (Mahwah, NJ: Lawrence Erlbaum Associates, 2002);

48. Patrick Parsons, "The Evolution of the Cable-Satellite Distribution System," *Journal of Broadcasting & Electronic Media* 47, no. 1 (2003): 1–17.

49. A. Webber, "The Apple Effect," *The Christian Science Monitor,* September 19, 2011, 26–31.

CHAPTER 2

Business Model Innovation

I do not think there is any thrill that can go through the human heart like that felt by the inventor as he sees some creation of the brain unfolding to success. . . .

—Nikola Tesla

I believe you have to be willing to be misunderstood if you're going to innovate.

—Jeff Bezos, Amazon.com

Introduction

Business model innovation involves creating entirely new approaches for doing business. Business model innovation is transformative; that is, it redefines the competitive playing field by introducing a unique value proposition to the consumer.[1] In the book *Blue Ocean Strategy*, business authors Kim and Mauborgne (2005) make the argument that in order to create new growth opportunities, innovative companies fundamentally change the business landscape by introducing an altogether new product, service, or idea. They use the metaphor of red and blue oceans to describe the market universe. *Red oceans* are all the industries in existence today (i.e., the known market space). Direct competition is the order of the day. The goal is to grab a bigger share of the existing red ocean market. In contrast, *blue oceans* describe the potential market space that has yet to be explored. Instead of trying to outwit the competition in a zero-sum game of one-upmanship, blue ocean

Author's Note: The information contained in this chapter is based on a previous chapter that was part of an edited works collection: Richard Gershon. "Digital Media, Electronic Commerce and Business Model Innovation." In *Policy and Marketing Strategies for Digital and New Media*, edited by Yu-li Liu and Robert Picard, 202–217. London, UK: Routledge, 2014.

companies pursue the soon-to-be discovered opportunities that await the entrepreneur. Competition is irrelevant because the rules of the game are waiting to be set.[2]

This chapter represents a unique opportunity to look at the importance of innovation and innovative thinking to the long-term success of today's leading media and telecommunications companies. Specifically, it will address two important questions. First, what does it mean to be an innovative media business enterprise? Second, how has business model innovation been used to transform the field of e-commerce? The term *e-commerce* (EC) represents the ability to sell goods and services electronically via the Internet. The blending of EC in combination with intelligent networking has created a vast global playing field where buyers and sellers from around the world are free to participate.[3] In this chapter, we will consider three companies that exhibit the best features of business model innovation. They include Home Box Office Inc. (HBO), Amazon.com, and Google. These companies were selected because they introduced unique business models that fundamentally changed the competitive business landscape following their respective product launches. In short, they were absolute game changers.

Why Is Innovation Important?

Innovation is important because it creates a competitive advantage for a company or organization. Successful innovation occurs when it meets one or more of the following conditions. First, the innovation is based on a novel principle that challenges management orthodoxy. When HBO introduced the principle of pay television, it was challenging the conventional wisdom of its day by promoting the belief that television was something worth paying for. Second, the innovation is systemic; that is, it involves a range of processes and methods. Amazon.com's commitment to direct-to-home sales delivery involves a whole host of supply chain management processes, including EC product display, an online ordering system, warehouse inventory management, customer service, shipping, and distribution. Third, the innovation is part of an ongoing commitment to develop new and enhanced products and services. There is a natural progression in product design and development.[4] See Table 2.1.

Business Model Innovation: Strategies and Approaches

While most organizations recognize the importance of innovation, there is a wide degree of latitude regarding the method and approach to innovation. For some business enterprises, innovation is the direct result of a *triggering event,* that is, a change in market conditions or internal performance that forces a change in business strategy.[5] Both HBO's HBO Go service and Amazon's Prime Instant Video, for example, are strategic responses to the online video success achieved by Netflix. For other companies, innovation is deliberative and planned. It is built into the cultural fabric of a company's ongoing research and development efforts. Such companies display a clear and discernible

Table 2.1 Successful Innovation: Feature Elements	
The innovation is based on a <u>novel principle</u> that challenges management orthodoxy.	**HBO:** Developed the principle of premium television entertainment **Google:** Greatly advanced information gathering on the Internet through key-word search **Amazon.com:** Established the world's first and preeminent EC business model
The innovation is <u>systemic</u>; that is, it involves a range of processes and methods.	**Amazon.com:** EC product display and online ordering system, warehouse inventory management, shipping and distribution, direct-to-home sales delivery **Netflix:** Online video rental, global inventory management, and television/film video streaming
The innovation is part of an <u>ongoing commitment</u> to develop new and enhanced products and services.	**Apple:** iPod ⟶ iTunes ⟶ iPhone ⟶ iPad

SOURCE: R. Gershon, adapted from G. Hamel, (2006).

progression in the products they make.[6] Careful planning leads the way. This can be seen in the method and approach adopted by Apple starting with the iPod portable music player and proceeding forward with the iTunes music store, iPhone smartphone and iPad digital tablet (see Table 2.1).[7] As PayPal cofounder Peter Thiel, writes,

> The greatest thing Jobs designed was his business. Apple imagined and executed definite multiyear plans to create new products and distribute them effectively. . . . Jobs saw that you can change the world through careful planning, not by listening to focus groups, feedback or copying others' successes.[8]

Successful Business Model Innovation

Successful innovation is not a guarantee of success. Rather, it is an opportunity.[9] As Hoff (2004) notes, "inspiration is fine, but above all, innovation is really a management process."[10] There are no shortcuts when it comes to innovation. Putting the right structures, people, and processes in place should occur as a matter of course—not as an exception. Early in the project design process, a successful business model innovation should address five basic questions.

1. **How will the firm create value?** This first question concerns the value proposition to the consumer. The term *value* refers to the unique or specialized benefits derived from the product or service offering.[11] What value does

the proposed product or service provide the consumer? Booking a flight and vacation on Expedia is a very different value proposition than working with a travel agent. Purchasing a set of songs via iTunes is an altogether different shopping experience than walking into a music store. From a planning standpoint, the firm starts with a clear understanding of the product or service mix. The level and type of innovation should match the company's larger overriding strategy. There should be a clear alignment of goals in terms of the proposed innovation strategy.

2. **For whom will the firm create value?** This question focuses on the competitive environment in which the firm competes. Who is the target audience for the proposed product design or service? Such considerations as audience composition, geographic location, and user technology proficiency level can have significant impacts on strategy approach, resource requirements, and the nature of the product or service that is being developed for the consumer.[12] Netflix, for example, had to consider technology skill level as one important metric when it designed its Internet-based EC service. A successful product launch presupposes a clear understanding of how one's customers are going to realistically use the proposed product or service.

3. **What is the firm's internal source of advantage?** The term *core competency* describes something that an organization does well. The principle of core competency suggests that a highly successful company is one that possesses a specialized production process, brand recognition, or ownership of talent that enables it to achieve higher revenues and market dominance when compared to its competitors. Core competency can be measured in many ways including: brand identity (Disney, ESPN, and Facebook), technological leadership (Apple, Google, and Microsoft), superior business process logistics (Amazon.com, Netflix and Dell), manufacturing and production (Samsung, LG, and Philips), and excellent customer service (Disney and Amazon.com).

4. **How will the firm make money?** The financial business model provides the inherent logic for earning profits. From Alexander Graham Bell to Mark Zuckerberg, it is not uncommon to find that some of media and telecommunication's best-known entrepreneurs are better inventors and software programmers than they are business people. The start-up of Google and Facebook are two such examples of companies that began with a good idea but didn't necessarily have a plan for how they would make money. Sometimes, the best ideas often require the business acumen of someone else to come up with a sustainable business plan that will enable such project start-ups to succeed long term.

The financial model must take into consideration the strategy rationale for making money. The ESPN cable sports network, for example, has two distinct revenue streams. First, ESPN makes money through the sale of national advertising. Second, ESPN makes money through a licensing fee arrangement, whereby it charges the cable operator (and other multichannel delivery systems) an estimated $4.50+ every month per subscriber for the right to receive the ESPN service.[13] Alternatively, when the Apple iTunes music store began, it was designed to make money for Apple via the sale of its iPod portable music players. Today, iTunes earns an estimated 20 percent for all downloaded songs.

5. **How will the firm position itself in the marketplace?** This question asks us to consider how the current or proposed business enterprise plans to position itself within its external competitive environment. Specifically, the business enterprise must determine how it plans to achieve an advantage over all would-be competitors.[14] This idea is closely related to the principle of core competency listed earlier. Consider, for example, Korea-based Samsung Corporation. Samsung has proved to be the organizational master in fast and efficient (almost military-like) production. Samsung has focused on becoming a superior manufacturer rather than original R&D. The company has learned how to manage and work through the highly volatile world of commoditized consumer electronics products. Speed is the key to all perishable commodities from mobile phones to digital television sets. As Chang (2008) points out, unless a firm comes up with its products quicker than its competitors, it is doomed to the hellish competition of commodities. Samsung Electronics has invested aggressively in product and process technology so that it can beat its competitors to market and capture price premiums before its offerings become commodities.[15]

Value Proposition

A value proposition involves creating some unique product offering or service enhancement that greatly improves the customer experience. Some notable examples of business model innovation in the field of media and telecommunications can be seen in Table 2.2. Each of the said companies developed a unique value proposition to the consumer. They were blue ocean companies in the best sense of the term. They would help set the standards for their respective areas of business commerce.

Being First-to-Market

Being first to market presents enormous opportunities for the organization that is able to establish a clear and recognized product or service before anyone else. All future competitors are faced with the task of having to compete with a well-established company possessing enormous brand recognition. This was certainly the case with companies like HBO and Amazon.com. Both companies became synonymous with their respective business model (i.e., HBO, pay television and Amazon, EC). At the same time, being first-to-market is not without its challenges. The start-up company is tasked with having to build consumer interest for a product or service that is entirely new and untested. Consider, for example, the challenges of being HBO in 1974 and convincing a skeptical American public about the value of premium TV (i.e., paying for something that was otherwise free). Similarly, imagine the challenges faced by the Sony Corporation in 1990 when it tried to persuade America's television-viewing audience about the benefits of high-definition television ten years before the general public, television stations, and regulatory structures were in place to consider it realistically.[16]

Table 2.2 Select Examples of Media and Telecommunications Business Model Innovation	
• **Apple**	Launched iTunes, the first sustainable MP3 music downloading business of its kind.
• **Amazon.com**	Created the world's preeminent EC business model for goods and services online.
• **eBay**	Helped advance electronic auctioning on the Internet; creating the world's largest customer-to-customer online marketplace.
• **Facebook**	Developed the world's preeminent social networking Internet site; helped advance online advertising.
• **Google**	Helped advance Internet key-word search advertising and developed the principle of micromarketing.
• **HBO**	Introduced the principle of pay television service.
• **Netflix**	Developed the world's most successful online video rental service.
• **PayPal**	Introduced the first online EC payment system of its kind; providing a significant alternative to checks and money orders.

Boundary Spanning

In his book, *Where Good Ideas Come From: The Natural History of Innovation,* author Steven Johnson (2010) describes what he calls "the adjacent possible":

> We are often better served by connecting ideas than we are protecting them. . . . Good ideas . . . want to connect, fuse, recombine. They want to reinvent themselves by crossing conceptual borders.[17]

The term *boundary spanning* means finding adjacent (or complementary) areas that add value to one's current business or organizational enterprise.[18] The Center for Creative Leadership defines *boundary spanning* as the ability to establish direction, alignment, and commitment across boundaries in service of a higher purpose or goal.[19] Two examples come to mind. The first example is when Starbucks Coffee saw the value of extending its coffee brand by creating a warm, convivial café environment. The second example is when Federal Express overnight delivery mail service acquired Kinko's printing (near university campus environments), thereby creating a natural synergy among copying, packaging, and overnight mail delivery. Highly innovative companies routinely are engaged in boundary spanning by exploring the natural, ancillary meeting points of other business enterprises. (See Table 2.3.)

Home Box Office, Inc.

The real move to modern cable television began on November 8, 1972, when a new start-up company named Home Box Office (HBO) began supplying movies to 365 subscribers on the Service Electric Cable TV system in Wilkes Barre, Pennsylvania. That night, Jerry Levin, then vice president for programming, introduced viewers to the debut of HBO. The feature programming for that inaugural night was a hockey game between New York and Vancouver and a film prophetically titled *Sometimes a Great Notion*. HBO was the brainchild of cable entrepreneur Charles "Chuck" Dolan, who drew up the concept for a pay television service in the summer of 1971 while aboard the Queen Elizabeth II en route to France.

From the beginning, HBO developed two important innovations that helped to promote its rapid growth and development. First, HBO introduced the principle of premium television (i.e., business model innovation). Specifically, HBO achieved what no other television service provider had accomplished to date, namely, getting people to pay for television. The principle of advertiser-supported "free" television was engrained firmly in the minds of the American public. What HBO did was change public perception about the nature of television entertainment. HBO offered a unique value proposition emphasizing recently released movies and other

Table 2.3 Boundary Spanning—Select Examples

Company	Value Proposition	Business Model	Boundary Spanning	
HBO	Premium Television Services	Pay-Supported Television	HBO Original Entertainment HBO GO HBO Video-streaming Service	
Amazon.com	Online Shopping and Direct-to-Home Delivery of Products and Goods	EC	Amazon Kindle Amazon Marketplace Amazon Web and Cloud-Computing Services Amazon Prime	
Google	Internet Search	Key-Word Search Advertising	Chrome Analytics YouTube Calendar Image	Gmail Maps Translate Scholar

specialized entertainment that could not be found elsewhere on the general air-waves.[20] While HBO was not the first company to introduce a monthly per-channel fee service, they were the first to make it work successfully. This marked the beginning of premium television entertainment. In September 1973, Time Inc. demonstrated its confidence in the young company by acquiring HBO as a wholly owned subsidiary. A year later, HBO quickly established itself as the largest pay cable program supplier in the United States. And by the start of the 1980s, HBO had become one of Time Inc.'s most successful business operations. From the beginning, HBO developed a number of strategies that helped promote its rapid growth, including the use of a monthly per-channel fee and the use of microwave and later satellite communications for the transmission of programming rather than distribution by videotape.[21] Prior to HBO, there was no precedent for the extensive use of satellite delivered programming in the United States.

HBO and the Principle of Satellite/Cable Networking

HBO's 1975 decision to use satellite communications was significant in two ways. First, it demonstrated the feasibility of using satellite communication for long-haul television distribution (i.e., process innovation). As a consequence, HBO was able to create an efficient distribution network for the delivery of its programming to cable operators.[22] Second, the development of the satellite/cable interface would usher in a whole new era of cable programmers that were equally capable of leasing satellite time and delivering their programs directly to cable operating systems, including: WTBS, 1976; ESPN, 1979; CNN, 1980; and MTV, 1981.[23] Thus was born the principle of satellite/cable networking; that is, television programming designed exclusively for cable operating systems and later direct broadcast satellite systems. The principle of satellite/cable networking would transform the business process of long-haul television distribution.[24] As cable analyst, Paul Kagan (1984) once remarked:

> Rarely does a simple business decision by one company affect so many. In deciding to gamble on the leasing of satellite TV channels, Time Inc. took the one catalytic step needed for the creation of a new television network designed to provide pay TV programs.[25]

HBO and Boundary Spanning

Today, HBO has extended its geographical boundaries worldwide and reaches an estimated 122 million subscribers in more than 151 countries worldwide. At present, HBO is faced with two major problems. HBO's current subscriber growth is flat and has been that way for several years, while growth in competing premium television services like Netflix has increased. Second, and perhaps more importantly, HBO's cable-dependent business model is no longer sustainable. At issue is the fact that there are now multiple video streaming services as well as technology options for watching premium television. HBO, in its present form, is an add-on service to basic cable television. In other words, to get HBO, the subscriber must take the operator's basic cable service first. As the cost of cable television continues to climb, it makes HBO less attractive. HBO has had to reposition its program offerings in light of the changes being made by companies like Netflix. HBO's HBO Go service, for example, is a strategic response to the online video success achieved by Netflix. However, the HBO Go service applies only to HBO-owned programming. In looking to the future, HBO is strongly committed to developing a video-streaming service that will operate separately and apart from cable and other multichannel television service providers. The future of HBO will involve transitioning to a fully functioning independent video-streaming service.

Amazon.com

Amazon.com, Inc. is an American-based EC company headquartered in Seattle, Washington. Company founder Jeff Bezos incorporated the company in July 1994. The company is named after South America's Amazon river. Today, Amazon.com is the largest EC retailer in the world. In 1994, Bezos resigned his position as vice president at D. E. Shaw, a Wall Street firm, and moved to Seattle.

He began to work on a business plan that would serve as the blueprint for what would become Amazon.com. The basic idea was to create a mail order catalog, albeit electronically, using the Internet and the power of intelligent networking. Bezos created a list of 20 products that could be marketed online. The list included books, CDs, computer hardware, computer software, and videos.[26]

Amazon.com started with online books, given the large worldwide demand for literature, the low price points for books, as well as the large number of titles available in print. At the time, no significant mail-order book catalogs existed. The reasoning was simple. To build a substantial mail-order catalog covering books in all areas of arts, sciences, and humanities would require an encyclopedia-like publication (if not bigger). And it would be too expensive to mail. The solution, of course, was the Internet, which is ideally suited for organizing and displaying a limitless amount of information. It so happens that Bezos attended the American Booksellers annual convention, where he learned that books are among the most highly databased items in the world. Most of the world's publishers have their works fully listed in CD-ROM format. Bezos reasoned that such information could be organized and put online.

Within its first two months of operation, the company was selling and distributing books in all 50 states as well as 45 countries. While the largest of America's bookstore chains might carry more than 200,000 titles, an online bookstore can offer several times that, plus it does not require the same level of warehouse space when compared to a traditional retailer.

Said Bezos at the time:

Within the first few days, I knew this was going to be huge. It was obvious that we were onto something much bigger than we ever dared to hope.[27]

From the beginning, Bezos took a careful and long-term view of his business. He did not expect to make a profit for several years. His slow-growth approach caused stockholders to complain about the company not achieving profitability fast enough to justify the level of investment. Amazon, for its part, survived the dot.com crash at the start of the 21st century and went on to achieve profitability by the end of 2001. Two years earlier, *Time* magazine named Bezos its Person of the Year, recognizing Amazon's success and contributions in helping advance the principle of EC.

> Bezos is a person who not only changed the way we do things but helped paved the way for the future. . . . E-commerce has been around for four or five years . . . but 1999 was a time in which e-commerce and dotcom mania reached a peak and really affected all of us. [28]

Today, Jeff Bezos presides over an EC company that has redefined online shopping for billions of people worldwide. The value proposition for all would-be Amazon customers is exchange efficiency, which can be translated in one of three ways: selection, convenience, and low prices. It is central to Amazon's business model and philosophy.

Amazon.com and Exchange Efficiency

The principle of *exchange efficiency* is an important concept found in management theory. It has to do with creating the optimum conditions through which a consumer can obtain a product or service. Traditional examples of exchange efficiency can be seen with speed lanes in a supermarket, thereby allowing customers to move quickly through the checkout line. Similarly, the principle of exchange efficiency can be seen with companies who once specialized in catalog shopping using a 24-hour-a-day toll-free telephone number such as L.L. Bean and Eddie Bauer, to name only a few. Today, EC has taken the principle of exchange efficiency to a whole new level in terms of retail trade and distribution.[29] Companies such as Amazon.com (books), Zappos (shoes), and Dell (computers), to name only a few, have developed a highly sophisticated supply chain management system. A *supply chain* consists of all parties involved, directly or indirectly, in fulfilling a customer request. The supply chain not only includes the manufacturer and suppliers but also warehouses, retailers, and direct delivery to the customer.[30]

Amazon and Supply Chain Management. When an order is placed on Amazon, the EC site sets into motion a kind of software road map that will enable the said purchase order to be completed by the various players who make up the supply chain. From manufacturers and wholesalers to product shipping, everyone who comprises the supply chain has access to all of the pertinent information to complete the transaction, including the customer order information, credit rating (where appropriate), order history, production status, warehousing, and distribution. To enhance product delivery, Amazon developed Amazon Prime. Part of any business-to-consumer EC model requires a mastery of cost-effective shipping and distribution. In 2005, Amazon initiated Amazon Prime, a two-day shipping service on all eligible purchases for a flat fee.

Amazon.com and Boundary Spanning

Amazon employs a multilevel EC strategy. In its formative years, Amazon focused on business-to-customer EC. The challenge was to become more fully diversified in terms of product and service offerings. In time, they incorporated customer reviews and leveraged such information as a way to sell more products and services as well as improve the customer experience. Amazon is a highly innovative company and has adopted the principle of boundary spanning in three specific ways. Each area is a natural extension of what Amazon already does.

Amazon Marketplace. Amazon has also greatly expanded its third-party marketplace, where merchants all over the world can set up their own virtual stores on Amazon.com and sell their products alongside Amazon's—all the while leveraging Amazon's large customer base and credit-card-processing capabilities. Both retailers and individual sellers utilize the Amazon.com platform to sell goods. Large retailers like Nordstrom and Target use Amazon.com to sell their products in addition to selling them via their own Web sites.

Amazon Web Services. This is a collection of cloud-computing services offered by Amazon via the Internet. The expression *putting something on the cloud* refers to the idea of storing information and data on a remote host site. Amazon's most daring strategy is its foray into business-to-business services. In recent years, Amazon has greatly expanded its cloud computing services by leasing out server capacity in its large data centers around the world so that small businesses do not have to make large, up-front investments in computing infrastructure.

Amazon Kindle. In November 2007, Amazon launched its Amazon Kindle; an e-book reader. Today, most analysts agree that Amazon probably sold its original Kindle hardware at breakeven or at a small loss to subsidize media sales. With the original Kindle, Amazon pioneered the sale of digital books and as a result owns more than 90 percent of their distribution. By July 2010, Amazon e-book sales for its Kindle reader outnumbered sales of hardcover books for the first time ever. In September 2011, Amazon announced its entry into the computer tablet market with the introduction of its Kindle Fire, which runs on the Android operating system.[31] The Amazon Kindle is much more than an e-reader. It represents the foundation for an entire media ecosystem. Specifically, the Kindle Fire is a computer tablet, media store, a platform for digital media sales, as well as a publishing imprint. The goal is to make all of Amazon's digital media product offerings part of the Kindle ecosystem. This includes: 1) Digital books, 2) MP3 music and software products, 3) Internet video streaming (Amazon Instant Video), 4) Software apps, and 5) Advertising. The Amazon Kindle is a decade-long investment in media planning, product design, development, and distribution.[32]

Google

Google was founded by Larry Page and Sergey Brin while they were PhD students at Stanford University. Together, they formed a unique partnership based on intellectual curiosity and competitiveness. One of toughest challenges facing the Internet at that time was the ability to organize and retrieve information from massive amounts of data. Together, Page and Brin began work on a search engine called BackRub, named for its unique ability to analyze the back links pointing to a given Web site.[33] Equally important was the development of PageRank, an algorithm that ranks Web sites in terms of search engine results. PageRank was designed to count the number and quality of links to a page and thus provides an estimate of how important the Web site is. They received encouragement from David Filo, Yahoo cofounder and fellow Stanford alum. One of the company's earliest investors was Sun Microsystem's co-founder Andy Bechtolsheim who wrote them a check for $100,000.[34] The name *BackRub* was eventually changed to *Googol* (or *Google*), a term coined by Milton Sirotta in 1938, nephew of the American mathematician Edward Kasner. Google refers to the number 1 followed by 100 zeros. It implies organizing vast amounts of information on the Internet. In September 1998, Google opened its door in Menlo Park, California. The company would later move to its current home in Mountainview, California. It didn't take long before several news media outlets including *USA Today* and *PC Magazine* began to take notice of the new start-up company. Google would establish itself as the world's most highly robust search engine.

The Launch of Key-Word Search Advertising

The launch of its key-word search advertising program in 2001 provided a unique business model that would transform Google as a major communications company. *Key-word search*, also known as *contextual advertising*, involves text-based ads and links that appear next to search engine results. The new advertising program was given the name AdWords (later changed to AdWords Select). An advertiser buys a key word or phrase from the search engine site and only pays if consumers click through to its site. An advertisement that generates a large number of hits can be considered successful in terms of promoting consumer interest.[35]

As an example, if a user were to type *Hotel Le Bristol in Paris* into the Google search bar, the ads that appear next to the search query are probably links to Booking.com and Expedia.com as well as other hotel booking companies. These advertising links are listed on the display page as well as on the right-hand portion of the search results window. These ads are ranked for presentation based on a bidding process. Bidding is competitive, with the bid range determined by the popularity of the search term. The higher the bid, the greater the likelihood that an advertiser's ad will appear on the first page of the Google search query.[36] In principle, ads are supposed to reach only those people who actually want to see them, thus providing benefit to both users as well as advertisers. More to the point, a key-word search allows an advertiser to target a message to an audience that is presumably already interested in them. Moreover, the advertiser can record the number of people who click though the advertisement. Google offers the advertiser different pricing options ranging from maximum cost per click, where the advertiser sets a prescribed limit on the number of hits they are willing to pay for, to a cost-per-click option, where the advertiser pays for only those ads that are specifically queried by the user. Key-word search advertising set into motion the principle of micromarketing, that is, advertisements that are directed toward the individual based on the user's query. It has proved to be a revolutionary Internet marketing strategy that is utilized today by a whole host of companies, including Amazon.com, Apple, and Facebook.

Google and Boundary Spanning

From its very beginning, one of Google's stated missions was to organize the world's information. This would require a very powerful set of intelligent networks to accomplish this goal. Since 2008, Google has indexed trillions of URL links. The power and networking capability of the Google search engine has proved highly adaptive and grown exponentially over time.[37] The ever-increasing amount of data has created its own unique networking effect. In keeping with the principle of network evolution, there is an automatic self-learning quality that is built into the larger network design that has engendered the development of other Google software products and services (e.g., Gmail, Google Maps, Google Earth, Google Analytics, YouTube, etc.). The more people use the Google search engine, the more powerful the network becomes. Google's multiple information capabilities have enabled the company to cross a whole host of boundaries. Over time, the Google search engine network has become greater than the sum of its parts.

Discussion

Business model innovation involves creating entirely new approaches for doing business. HBO, Amazon.com, and Google have each introduced a unique business model that has fundamentally changed the competitive business landscape following their respective product launches. Both HBO and Amazon.com were first-to-market and, thereby, established a market presence and brand recognition that would make them difficult to compete against in the future. HBO proved that there was a market for premium television services. From Blockbuster to Netflix, all of today's pay television services owe their aegis to the original premium television concept developed by HBO.

Amazon.com took the early lead in EC development. Today, the company has become the world's preeminent EC company. Many of the company's supply chain management practices have become the standard for all companies engaged in EC. To be sure, Amazon.com plus the hotel and airline industries have transitioned the general public into making online shopping a routine practice. Finally, Amazon.com, through its Kindle media ecosystem, has taken the lead in defining the future of digital books. Google, for its part, has built the most widely used search engine in the world. In developing its key-word search advertising model, the company has contributed greatly to the principle of micromarketing, a marketing strategy widely adopted by numerous EC companies. Google continues to be a major innovator by introducing a variety of software applications, most notably, YouTube, Gmail, Google Maps, and Calendar, which continue to expand the company's boundaries in multiple directions. Google is unique among companies given its willingness to explore ideas and working concepts outside its core areas of expertise. Writers A. G. Lafley and Mark Johnson (2010) refer to this as "seizing the white space." The term refers to the "range of potential activities not defined or addressed by the company's current business model."[38] Google's deep-seated commitment to experimental research can be seen in areas such as Google glasses, high-speed broadband delivery systems, driverless cars, and voice recognition systems, to name only a few.

Successful business model innovation requires a commitment to a challenging management or design issue problem. It means blue ocean thinking and a letting go of traditional ways of thinking. Business model innovation is transformative; that is, it redefines the competitive playing field by introducing an entirely new value proposition to the consumer. The real test of business model innovation is the degree to which the model is later imitated by others. Each of the said companies discussed in this chapter has been a game changer by introducing a business model approach that became the standard for others to follow.

Endnotes

1. Alexander Osterwalder and Yves Pigneur, *Business Model Generation* (Hoboken, NJ: John Wiley & Sons, 2010).
2. W. Chan Kim and Renée Mauborgne, *Blue Ocean Strategy* (Boston, MA: Harvard Business School Press, 2005).
3. Richard Gershon, *Media, Telecommunications and Business Strategy*, 2nd ed. (New York: Routledge, 2013).
4. Gary Hamel, "The What, Why and How of Management Innovation," *Harvard Business Review* (February, 2006): 72–87.
5. Thomas Wheelen and J. David Hunger, *Strategic Management and Business Policy* (Reading, MA: Addison Wesley Longman, Inc., 1998), 52–67.
6. Gershon, *Media, Telecommunications and Business Strategy*.
7. Adam Lashinsky, The *Legacy of Steve Jobs 1955–2011* (New York: Fortune Books, 2011), 10–15.
8. Peter Thiel, *Zero to One* (New York: Crown Business, 2014), 79.
9. Tony Davila, Marc Epstein, and Robert Shelton, *Making Innovation Work* (Upper Saddle River, NJ: Wharton School Publishing, 2006).
10. Robert Hoff, "Building an Idea Factory," *Business Week,* Oct. 11, 2004, 194.
11. Osterwalder and Pigneur, *Business Model Generation*.

12. Michael Morris, Minet Schindehutte, and Jeffrey Allen, "The Entrepreneur's Business Model: Toward a Unified Perspective," *Journal of Business Research* 58 (2005): 726–735)
13. Gershon, *Media, Telecommunications and Business Strategy.*
14. Raphael Amit and Christoph Zott, "Value Creation in E-business," *Strategic Management Journal* 22 (2001): 493–520. See also: Michael Porter, *Competitive Advantage: Creating and Sustaining Superior Performance* (New York: Free Press, 1985).
15. S. J. Chang, *Sony vs. Samsung: The Inside Story of the Electronics Giants' Battle for Global Supremacy* (Singapore: John Wiley & Sons, 2008).
16. John Nathan, *Sony: The Private Life* (New York: Houghton-Mifflin, 1999).
17. Steven Johnson, *Where Good Ideas Come From: The Natural History of Innovation* (New York: Riverhead Books, 2010), 22.
18. Michael Tushman, "Special Boundary Roles in the Innovation Process," *Administrative Science Quarterly* 22, no. 4 (1977): 587–605.
19. Jeffrey Yip, Chris Ernst, and Michael Campbell, *Boundary Spanning Leadership* (Greensboro, NC: Center for Creative Leadership, 2011).
20. Richard Gershon and Michael Wirth, "Home Box Office: The Emergence of Pay Cable Television," in *The Cable Networks Handbook,* ed. R. Picard (Riverside, CA: Carpelan).
21. Richard Gershon, "Pay Cable Television: A Regulatory History," *Communication and the Law* 12, no. 2 (1990): 3–26.
22. The communication satellite provides an efficient means of reaching isolated places on the Earth and is considerably less expensive than terrestrial communication links for select applications. What distinguishes communication satellites from other forms of wireless communication is its high orbital position and movement. The HBO signal, for example, utilizes East Coast and West Coast feeds to blanket the entire United States. Therefore, any cable operating system equipped with an Earth station that falls within the footprint of a satellite-fed signal and is locked on to the appropriate transponder is capable of receiving the same signal. In sum, satellite communication realizes an economy of scale; that is, cost bears no relationship to the distance involved and/or to the number of users.
23. Gershon and Wirth, "Home Box Office: The Emergence of Pay Cable Television."
24. Patrick Parsons, "The Evolution of the Cable-Satellite Distribution System," *Journal of Broadcasting & Electronic Media* 47, no. 1 (2003): 1–17.
25. Paul Kagan, remarks in the *Pay TV Guide: Editor's Pay TV Handbook* (New York: HBO Inc., 1984).
26. Richard Brandt, *One Click: Jeff Bezos and the Rise of Amazon.Com* (New York: Penguin Books, 2011).
27. H. Albert Napier, Ollie Rivers, and Stuart Vagner, *Creating a Winning E-business,* 2nd ed. (Boston, MA: Thompson, 2006), 241.
28. J. C. Ramo, "Jeffrey Bezos: 1999 Person of the Year," *Time,* December 27, 1999, http://www.time.com/time/subscriber/article/0,33009,992927,00.html
29. Gershon, *Media, Telecommunications and Business Strategy.*
30. Sunil Chopral and Peter Meindl, *Supply Chain Management,* 2nd ed. (Upper Saddle River, NJ: Pearson Prentice-Hall, 2004).
31. C. Matthews, "Will Amazon Take Over the World?" *Time.* July 16, 2012, http://business.time.com/2012/07/16/will-amazon-take-over-the-world/
32. Richard Gershon, "Digital Media, Electronic Commerce and Business Model Innovation," in *Policy and Marketing Strategies for Digital and New Media,* eds., Yu-li Liu and Robert Picard. London, UK: Routledge, (2014): 202–217.

33. Gershon, *Media, Telecommunications and Business Strategy.*

34. Ken Auletta, *Googled: The End of the World As We Know It* (New York: Penguin Press, 2009).

35. Eric Schmidt and Jonathan Rosenberg, *How Google Works* (New York: Hachette, 2014).

36. Ibid.

37. Richard Gershon, "Intelligent Networks and International Business Communication: A Systems Theory Interpretation," *Media Markets Monographs, No. 12* (Pamplona, Spain: Universidad de Navarra Press, 2011).

38. A. G. Lafley and Mark Johnson, *Seizing the White Space: Business Model Innovation* (Boston, MA: Harvard Business School, 2010).

CHAPTER 3

Product Innovation and Design

Disneyland will never be completed as long as there's imagination left in the world . . . .

—Walt Disney

Carefully watch how people live, get an intuitive sense as to what they might want and then go with it.

—Akio Morita, Sony

Introduction

Product innovation refers to the complex process of bringing new products and services to market as well improving (or enhancing) existing ones. It allows a business to develop and improve on its existing product line as well as preparing the groundwork for the future.[1] If successful, a new product innovation will create a first-of-its-kind market space. Highly innovative companies display a clear and discernible progression in the products they make. They force themselves to create newer and better products while challenging the competition to do the same.[2]

This chapter looks at the importance of product innovation and design. Specifically, it will address the following question. What are some of the distinguishing features that characterize successful product design? This chapter will consider some of the people, companies, and strategies that have transformed the business of media and telecommunications in the area of product innovation and design. Specifically, we will consider three important issues related to this topic. They include: 1) Ideation—the power of new ideas, 2) New product development, and 3) Product design. Special attention is given to three media companies: Sony Inc., the Walt Disney Company, and Apple Inc. These companies were selected because they introduced an altogether new product that fundamentally changed the competitive business landscape following their respective product launch (see Table 3.1.).

Table 3.1	Media and Telecommunications Product Innovation	
• Sony	Walkman and Compact Disk (CD)	The Sony Walkman became the first portable music playback device of its kind using audio cassettes and later CDs. The CD transformed music recording from analog-based vinyl records to digital recording on CD.
• Walt Disney Company	Animated Films and Theme Parks and Resorts	The founding of Walt Disney Studios (later renamed Walt Disney Feature Animation) gave rise to numerous award-winning children's animated films while developing many of the techniques and concepts that have become standard practices in the field of animation. The introduction of Disneyland in 1955 and Walt Disney World in 1971 set the standard for family-friendly theme park entertainment with a strong emphasis on quality design.
• Apple	Macintosh Computer and iPhone	The introduction of the Macintosh computer made personalized computing much more accessible to the general public. The Mac featured a graphic user interface (GUI) design that allowed users to interact with computers through the use of graphical icons and a computer mouse. The iPhone was the first all-in-one integrated cell phone that combines voice communication, Internet access, and music and photo storage. The iPhone set the standard for future smartphone design.

Ideation: The Power of New Ideas

What is the value of one good idea or suggestion? The principle of ideation represents the creative process for developing unique and original ideas for the purpose of advancing new product development. Ideation is the essential first step in the design process. In principle, ideation has two main stages: 1) Idea generation, where quantity and diversity of viewpoints matter, and 2) Synthesis, in which ideas are discussed, refined, and narrowed down to a small set of viable options.[3] The source of good ideas can come from a wide variety of people and players both inside and outside the organization, including design engineers, project teams, business units, as well as individual customers.[4] Walt Disney's Imagineering group, which is responsible for the design and development of Disney theme parks worldwide, makes the point that ideation is about generating ideas and staying open to any and all possibilities. "The tiniest spark of an idea is no small thing. Even if born upon the tattered edge of a paper napkin, it may well grow up to be the size of something special. Each idea is approached with minds open to any intriguing possibility. Every aspect is questioned, admired, and debated until the first sketch can take a daring leap off the napkin into larger, more defined drawings and paintings."[5]

Synthesis: Asking the Tough Questions

Part of the management challenge is learning how to work with a large assemblage of highly creative people. The task is to manage the dynamic tension between creativity and value capture. By value capture, we mean the ability to transform creative concepts into commercial realities. As Davila, Epstein, and Shelton (2006) point out, "how your organization innovates determines what it will innovate."[6] Stage two requires the ability to synthesize, that is, discuss and refine the best and most promising ideas into a working set of possibilities. This involves asking the tough questions. Synthesis is a winnowing down process. The following five questions are a type of rapid-fire test designed to help bridge the transition from concept stage into practical applications.

1. Does the proposed idea fill an obvious gap or niche in the marketplace? The most effective way for an entrepreneur to succeed in an otherwise established market is to identify an obvious gap or niche that is being underserved by the established leaders. Customers have real needs and want solutions to their problems. A clever idea is nothing more than a curiosity or experiment if nobody actually needs the resultant product.[7] Every start-up should begin as a small project, that is, capturing an underserved market. Think of it as playing along the edges.[8] Once the innovator begins to dominate a niche market, then he/she gradually can expand into complementary and adjacent markets (i.e., boundary spanning).

2. Does the idea have shelf life? Are there pending, sweeping changes in technology that could render this idea moot? Companies not on guard for changes in technology can be swept away, while competitors move ahead. Consider that the AOL-Time Warner merger was once boasted as the marriage of old media and new media. The proposed merger was conceived as a global strategy that would enable the combined company to compete head-to-head with the world's leading media companies. At issue was that AOL dial-up Internet service became quickly obsolete in the face of cable modems two years after the completion of the agreement. The AOL-Time Warner merger may well be remembered as the worst merger in U.S. corporate history, having cost the company an estimated $99 billion in losses.

3. Will the proposed idea be met with resistance both inside and outside the organization? Often, the most daring and original ideas are subject to user resistance both inside and outside the organization. Sony's Ken Kutaragi, inventor of the Playstation video game system, was initially met with a lot of resistance from the company's senior management because the idea of developing a video game system was not in keeping with their view of the Sony brand. It was viewed as a kind of children's toy.[9] Established players often become risk averse, especially when existing products and services are doing well in the marketplace. They are not prepared to dismantle an otherwise successful business. They fall victim to what Clayton Christensen (1997) refers to as the "innovator's dilemma."[10]

4. Is the idea a true stand-alone business, or is it an add-on feature? For the budding entrepreneur, it sometimes easy to mistake an add-on feature as having the same breadth and weight as a stand-alone company. As an example, a software app designed for a smartphone is a very different value proposition than a stand-alone business. Real products that are uniquely designed and fill a clear niche in the marketplace qualify as stand-alone products.[11]

5. How much funding will be needed to successfully launch the product or service? Innovators and project start-ups (both past and present) need financial backing. In the days of Guglielmo Marconi and the invention of the wireless telegraph, financial support came from his father as well as the British Post Office. For Alexander Graham Bell, financial backing came from his future father-in-law, Gardner Green Hubbard. Depending on the size and scale of the operation, the funding requirements may be accomplished by the parent company. Alternatively, project start-ups sometimes will seek the assistance of venture capital firms. Kleiner, Perkins, Caufield, & Byers, for example, provided the seed capital for company start-ups such as Amazon.com, Google, and Netflix, to name only a few. There are dozens of other venture capital firms as well. Many of history's best-known innovators like Mark Zuckerberg (Facebook), Larry Page and Sergei Brin (Google), and John Lasseter (Pixar) are not businesspeople. They were more fully focused on the creative and development side of the enterprise. Venture capital firms force a level of accountability in terms of project development goals.

New Product Development

After the proposed idea has been fully screened and tested, the real work of product development and implementation begins. New product development (NPD) represents the process of transforming a working idea into a salable product or service. It is the responsibility of the project manager to translate the product design concept into action.[12] We begin with the idea of scalability; what kinds of people and talents will be required to get the product launched? NPD requires taking a highly disciplined and organized approach to strategy execution. The project manager (and team) must deliver on the details. When new product development fails, it fails because of poor project execution.[13]

The Role of Project Teams

Strategy implementation has to do with project execution, that is, getting it done on time and on budget. In most organizations, strategy implementation begins with the development of an action plan. An action plan includes the essential steps needed to accomplish the said strategy. A successful action plan recognizes the value of designing a person's job around an outcome rather than a series of tasks. This often is best accomplished through project teams that are responsible for performing the whole process. The project team is a very specialized group because it has been formed for the specific goal of advancing a proposed strategy concept. The project team typically is headed by a project manger who is responsible for creating the system that will drive the project forward to completion.[14]

Product Design

Product design is the combined set of engineering and artistic activities that go into the creation of a product or service for the benefit of the end user. The design must balance a diverse set of requirements. It must possess the right aesthetics while being scalable enough to be manufactured and distributed in a cost-effective manner. The product designer should have a good eye for detail, including an appreciation for function, visual appearance, ease of use, and reliability. The designer works to ensure that all design specifications use materials and technology effectively and comply with all legal and regulatory requirements.

The Design Philosophy of Dieter Rams

Dieter Rams (1932–) is a German industrial designer closely associated with the consumer products company Braun and the functionalist school of industrial design. Rams believes that technology routinely offers up new opportunities for innovative design. Good product design should go hand in hand with its functionality. It should be pleasing to the user while providing practical utility.[15] In Rams's view, a product should be understandable and easy to use. Good product design should display a kind of simple elegance. It should blend in with its surroundings. Rams had a strong influence on the work of Apple's chief designer Jonathan Ive, who similarly believes that design should be as important as the product's function.

The Problem With Complicated Design. An overly complicated product design becomes an immediate barrier to its use. As an example, personal computers (PCs), during the introduction of the first versions in the 1980s, were typically accompanied with thick, highly detailed training manuals. The manuals, while well intentioned, proved very intimidating to the user who simply wanted to jump on to the computer and start using it. Implied in the manual's use was the underlying assumption that there was a correct way for using the said piece of equipment. With time and experience, manufacturers of PCs began to recognize that the technical manual was having the opposite effect. Eventually, they began to scale back the pages and substituted an internal self-help guide that enabled users to have a better first-time experience with their computer.

Similarly, the videocassette recorder (VCR) in the 1980s was a difficult piece of equipment to use, especially when it came to prerecording programs for later viewing. The ability to time shift should have been a signature feature of the VCR. Instead, the manufacturers of VCRs, at the time, made the recording function needlessly complicated. Consequently, the recording function was rarely used by the vast majority of VCR users. The design problems associated with the VCR offered up some important lessons for future manufacturers of digital video recording (DVR) equipment. By comparison, today's generation of DVR equipment combines a simple organized menu structure with ease-of-use.

Product Integrity. Dieter Rams believed that products should be made with integrity and built to last. There is no place for planned obsolescence. Such products should be honest and blend in with their surroundings. By this, he meant that a product does not attempt to manipulate the consumer with promises that cannot be kept. They are neither decorative objects nor works of art. The design should be both neutral and restrained. In sum, less is more because it concentrates on the essential aspects and is not burdened with nonessential features. Apple CEO and founder Steve Jobs would take this idea to heart when it came to future product design planning. Finally, good product design pays close attention to detail. This too, is something that can be seen in the work of the imagineers and the design work and construction found at Disney theme parks and resorts. Nothing is left to chance. Care and accuracy in the design process show respect for the user experience.[16]

Sony Corporation

The Sony Corporation is a leading transnational media corporation in the production and sale of consumer electronics, music, film entertainment, and video game technology. Throughout its more than 60-year history, the Sony name has been synonymous with great innovation. During that time, Sony introduced a number of firsts in the development of new communication products. Words like *Walkman, compact disk,* and *Playstation* have become part of the global lexicon of terms to describe consumer electronics.[17] Early on in his tenure, Sony president and cofounder Akio Morita developed the kinds of business skills that allowed him successfully to enter into foreign markets. Morita did not initially have a global strategy in mind. Instead, he tended to focus on those markets that he believed were important and where Sony's products would be readily accepted. The United States represented a first step in realizing that objective. In time, Sony would establish a foreign office in both the United States and Europe to handle the sales and service of its products.[18]

The Sony Walkman

The creation of Sony's highly popular Walkman portable music player was highly serendipitous in its origins. From 1966 onward, Sony and other Japanese manufacturers began the mass production of cassette tapes and recorders in response to a growing demand. At first, cassette tape recorders could not match the sound quality of reel-to-reel recorders and were mainly used as study aids and for general purpose recording. By the late 1970s, audio quality had steadily improved and the stereo tape cassette machine had become a standard fixture in many homes and automobiles.

It so happened that Masaru Ibuka (who was then honorary chair of Sony) was planning a trip to the United States. Despite the heaviness of the machine, Ibuka would often take a TC-D5 reel-to-reel tape machine when he traveled. This time, however, he asked Norio Ohga for a simple, stereo playback version. Ohga contacted Kozo Ohsone, general manager of the tape recorder business division. Ohsone had his staff alter a Pressman stereo cassette by removing the recording function and convert it into a portable stereo playback device. When Ibuka returned from his U.S. trip, he was quite pleased with the unit, even if it had large headphones and no recording capability.[19]

Ibuka soon went to Morita (then chair) and said, 'Try this. Don't you think a stereo cassette player that you can listen to while walking around is a good idea?'[20] Morita took it home and tried it out over the weekend. He immediately saw the possibilities. In February 1979, Morita called a meeting together that included a number of the company's electrical and mechanical design engineers. He instructed the group that this product would enable someone to listen to music anytime, anywhere. It was understood that the target market was to be students and young people and that it should be introduced just prior to summer vacation of that year. In developing a new portable music device, Morita would have to overcome two resistance barriers. The first was the notion that cassette tapes could provide good sound quality and the second was that people would be willing to wear headsets, albeit well-designed headsets, in public. As Nathan (1999) writes:

> The Walkman project was founded on Morita's certainty and determination; there was no conventional development process, and no market testing. From the outset, Morita insisted that the product must be affordable to teenagers.[21]

Akio Morita was the quintessential marketer. He understood how to translate new and interesting technologies into usable products. After rejecting several names, the publicity department came up with the name *Walkman*. The product name was partially inspired by the movie *Superman* and Sony's existing Pressman portable tape cassette machine.[22] The Sony Walkman created an altogether new market for portable music systems and unleashed an important change in consumer lifestyle. From public parks to public transportation, portable music and the wearing of headsets gave us a new way to appreciate music.

The Compact Disk

In 1975, the Sony Corporation entered into a partnership with Netherlands-based Philips Corporation to begin work on the digital recording of information onto laser discs. Sony president Norio Ohga, a former student of music, was enamored with the possibilities of digital recording. He designated a small group of Sony engineers to give the laser disc top priority. From 1979 to 1982, both teams of engineers worked together to refine the CD player. Demonstrations of the CD were made worldwide in preparation for the planned launch of the CD in October 1982.

Norio Ohga was convinced that the CD would eventually replace vinyl records given the technology's superior sound quality. At the same time, Ohga recognized that the development of the CD would meet with fierce resistance from many in the recording industry who felt threatened by CD technology. To them, the CD format was an unproven technology made by hardware people who knew nothing about the software side of the business. Worse still, the conversion to a CD format would require enormous sums of money while possibly destabilizing the entire music industry. In one product demonstration in Athens, Greece, a group of executives stood up and shouted back in unison, "The truth is in the groove."[23] On August 31, 1982, an announcement was made in Tokyo that four companies—Sony, Philips, CBS, and Polygram—would work together to introduce the first CD system. In time, the Sony/Philips CD became the defacto standard throughout the industry. By 1986, the production of music CDs had topped 45 million titles annually, overtaking records to become the principal recording format. In time, CD technology would ultimately redefine the field of recording technology and spawn a whole host of new inventions, including the portable CD music player, the CD-based video game console (i.e., Playstation and X-Box), digital video disc (DVD) and Blu-Ray DVD system.[24]

The Walt Disney Company

At the end of World War I, Walter Elias Disney returned home to the United States after having served as an ambulance driver for the American troops overseas. Prior to his enlistment, Disney trained as a commercial artist, having studied at the Kansas City Art Institute. Disney's plan, upon his return, was to pursue a career as a commercial artist.

Film Animation

In 1919, Disney formed his own animated cartoon company in partnership with artist Ub Iwerks. Despite several attempts, the four-year partnership proved unsuccessful. The company went bankrupt, and Disney left to join his brother, Roy, in Hollywood. Together, they formed the Disney Brothers Cartoon Studio in 1923. Walt Disney would be responsible for the creative side while brother, Roy, would devote himself to the business end.[25] Soon thereafter, word came from New York that a film distributor by the name of M. J. Winkler was interested in buying the rights to a series of Disney's live action cartoon reels, later to be called *Alice Comedies*. Winkler offered $1,500 per reel. Disney agreed and soon became Ms. Winkler's production partner. In 1927, Disney began developing a series of short animated films called *Oswald the Lucky Rabbit*. The series was an instant hit with the general public. However, *Oswald the Lucky Rabbit* was copyrighted in Winkler's name. As a result, Disney did not receive the recognition or commercial benefits of his creative time.[26] He would not make that same mistake twice. Thereafter, Disney made it a point never to relinquish the copyright and creative control to one of his character inventions.[27]

Disney would eventually conceive of an altogether different type of animated character. This time it was a charming and high-energy mouse named Mortimer—later shortened to Mickey. Disney drew up several sketches and together, with his brother Roy, invested their own money in the production of two Mickey Mouse films. The third Mickey Mouse film represented a major step forward with the introduction of sound. The film *Steamboat Willie* was a technological achievement and went on to become an all-time classic. Soon thereafter, Mickey Mouse became a cultural sensation, and the name Disney was firmly established in the minds of the viewing public.

The founding of Walt Disney Studios (later renamed Walt Disney Feature Animation) would give rise to numerous award-winning children's animated films. The company would develop many of the techniques and concepts that have become standard practices in the field of animation. Starting in the 1980s, Walt Disney Studios was responsible for producing an ongoing series of animated film hits, including: *The Little Mermaid, Beauty and the Beast, Aladdin, The Lion King, Pocahontas, The Hunchback of Notre Dame* and *Tarzan,* to name only a few. Several of these films, including *Beauty and the Beast* and *the Lion King* would eventually be turned into stage productions. In 2006, Disney acquired Pixar Studios for $7.4 billion. Pixar was founded by Apple CEO Steve Jobs. In 2009, Disney acquired Marvel Entertainment for $4 billion. Marvel Entertainment is the creative force behind Spider Man and X-men. Disney has become the undisputable leader in the field of animated film entertainment. It holds the cards in all aspects of animated film production.

Walt Disney Theme Parks and Resorts

Today, the Disney name has become synonymous with family entertainment. The result has been an ongoing relationship with the public that spans more than 90 years. The Walt Disney Company is the largest transnational media corporation in the world in terms of capital assets and revenue. Since its 1996 acquisition of Capital Cities/ABC, the Walt Disney Company has focused on five primary areas of entertainment, including: 1) Disney theme parks and resorts, 2) Studio entertainment, 3) Media networks (ABC Television and ESPN), 4) Consumer products, and 5) Interactive communication. The Walt Disney Company is a strong adherent to the principle of vertical integration. The company takes full advantage of its name by cross-promoting its products and services among the company's various films, theme parks, stores, and cruise ships.[28] Several of Disney's more notable animated film characters have become regular featured attractions in the company's theme parks.

The Disney Theme Parks and Resorts division is responsible for the operation of the company's six worldwide theme parks and corresponding venues. The two primary theme parks are Disneyland and Walt Disney World. Disneyland was founded in 1955 and is located on 500 acres in Anaheim, California. It features the original Magic Kingdom as well as numerous rides and attractions. Disney also owns and operates Walt Disney World located in Lake Buena Vista, Florida. It was founded in 1971. This resort features four major theme parks: the Magic Kingdom, Epcot Center, MGM Studios, and Animal Kingdom. Walt Disney is also an equity investor in Disneyland Paris (formerly Euro Disney) located in the suburbs of Paris, France, as well as Hong Kong Disneyland located on Lantau Island, 30 minutes from downtown Hong Kong. The company also has a licensing agreement with the Oriental Land Company, which operates Tokyo Disneyland located in Tokyo, Japan. Disney is currently building a Disney theme park in China's Shanghai's Pudong district. The resort is expected to open in 2016. Also included in the theme parks and resorts division is the Disney Vacation Club and Disney Cruises.

Walt Disney Imagineering

Walt Disney Imagineering (WDI) is the creative design and development team of the Walt Disney Company, responsible for the creation and construction of Disney theme parks, resorts, and major staged events worldwide. The Imagineering group was founded in 1952 to oversee the construction of Disneyland in California. The term *imagineering* was popularized in the 1940s by the Alcoa Corporation to describe the blending of imagination and engineering. It was later adopted by Walt Disney a decade later to describe the unique artistic and engineering skills that characterized the company's creative design team. Most of the Imagineering design team are based in the company's headquarters in Glendale, California. Often, members of the Imagineering group are sent on various locations around the world to work on specialized projects. Imagineering is best known for the development of Audio-Animatronics, a form of robotics featured in many Disney theme park attractions including Pirates of the Caribbean, the Haunted Mansion, and the Hall of Presidents, to name only a few. Throughout its history, the Imagineering group has been granted numerous patents in areas such as ride systems, special effects, interactive technology, live entertainment, and advanced audio systems. More than anything, it is the Imagineering group that shapes the building design, landscape, and color that is featured in all of Disney's theme parks and featured attractions. They are responsible for many of the special touches that are found throughout the various Disney worldwide theme parks and resorts.[29]

Apple

Few companies are so closely identified with the strategy, vision, and aesthetic tastes of one person. Apple is one such company and is a direct reflection of its cofounder and CEO Steve Jobs. Throughout its history, Apple has a long history of approaching product design by paying close attention to detail. This is reflected in a striving for perfection in both product design as well as looking at entirely new ways to make products more user-friendly and useful. For Steve Jobs, one way to accomplish this was to have end-to-end software and hardware control for every product that Apple makes.[30] Taking an integrated approach was a central tenant to Apple's basic design philosophy from the company's very start.

Apple Computer was formed in April 1976 by 25-year-old Steve Wozniak and 21-year-old Steve Jobs. After selling a van for some extra start-up cash, the two set up shop in the Jobs's family garage at 2066 Crist Drive in Los Altos, California, to start building computers. Steve Wozniak spent the summer of 1976 building the first prototype design for what would become the Apple I computer.[31] Steve Jobs, for his part, took the lead in establishing the company's first customer, a small retail outlet called the Byte Shop located in Mountain View, California. Together, Jobs and Wozniak were able to build and sell fifty Apple I computers that summer.[32] The ideas and early innovation techniques that emerged from the company's early start would set the foundation for building one of the world's most powerful and influential technology companies ever conceived.

Apple Computer

In 1977, Jobs and Wozniak began work on the Apple II with the help of a few technically savvy friends and classmates. It was at this time that Jobs first realized his true passion for the burgeoning computer industry. To fuel this passion, Jobs consulted with retired Intel Corporation marketing manager Michael Markkula regarding the possible future of Apple Computer. During this consultation, Markkula worked with Jobs in coming up with a solid business plan and purchased one-third of the company for $250,000.[33] That same year, Jobs and Markkula hired Michael Scott as the company's first president and CEO.[34]

The successful launch of the Apple II made Apple a highly valued company in the field of personal computing. Soon thereafter, the company began work on the Apple III. The Apple III was meant to be Apple's bold entry into the field of business computing. The Apple III was the first Apple computer not designed by Steve Wozniak.

The specifications were defined by a committee of Apple engineers to be implemented by project manager Wendall Sander. Apple wanted the Apple III finished in 10 months, but instead it took two years to complete due to extra features being added by the committee of engineers. Steve Jobs, who supervised the project, didn't help the situation.

He was very particular about some of the design features, including a specific demand that the computer not have a cooling fan because they were "too noisy and inelegant." In the end, the Apple III proved to be Apple's first commercial failure and put the company at risk. Part of the problem was due to the fact that it was very expensive, retailing at a cost ranging between $4,340 and $7,800. The launch of the Apple III got very poor reviews from the outset. The Apple III's software and hardware were highly erratic. It would sometimes crash when using the save command, causing great frustration to its users. Apple's next follow-up computer was the Lisa, named after Steve Jobs's daughter. The Lisa was targeted to business customers as well. The Lisa did not fare any better than the Apple III, having sold only 10,000 units. The one important design element that became part of the Lisa project was Apple's involvement in GUI design. In the end, the Apple III and Lisa failures would give rise to the development of the Macintosh computer.

Microsoft and Apple. Simultaneous to the release of the Apple III and Lisa computers, IBM had been developing a PC of its own whose target market was the business community. IBM, of course, was synonymous with business computing. IBM was the undisputed leader in large mainframe computers. In 1981, IBM introduced its own PC at a cost of $1,565. More importantly, the IBM PC could do more in the way of business software applications. IBM's operating system and beginning software products were being developed by a then-unknown company called Microsoft. In time, Microsoft would set the de facto standards in business computing software. By shifting the value proposition in computing to software, Microsoft commoditized the manufacture of hardware equipment, thus making personal computing accessible to the general public.[35] Unlike Apple, Microsoft did not create a proprietary standard, thereby allowing all manufacturers to build computers using Microsoft software. While Microsoft software was not as elegant as the Macintosh, it built a strong, reliable operating system and set of software products that enabled millions of users worldwide to engage in computing at a cost point that greatly accelerated the field of personal computing. Throughout their respective histories, Apple and Microsoft have had a kind of symbiotic relationship. They have been both competitors as well as innovation partners. Specifically, Microsoft has developed a number of key software products that are featured on Mac computers, including Microsoft Word and Excel, two of the most widely used programs in professional software. It should also be remembered that Microsoft rescued Apple in August 1997 with a $150 million in cash to ensure Apple's survival. This came at a time when Apple was seriously at risk of failing. Jobs had just recently returned to the now-struggling company. Dreams of revolutionizing the music and telephone industries with the Apple iPod and iPhone were still a few years away.[36]

Macintosh

The Macintosh project was begun in 1979 by Jef Raskin, an Apple employee who envisioned an easy-to-use, low-cost computer for the average consumer. He wanted to name the computer after his favorite type of apple, but the spelling was changed to *Macintosh* for legal reasons. Raskin was given the responsibility to hire a number of new engineers and designers to the team. In time, the Mac team would represent some of the most talented individuals ever to work on the same design team. Jobs left the Lisa project team and focused his full attention on the Macintosh project. In 1981, Raskin left the team due to professional differences (and personality conflicts) with Jobs.

Graphic User Interface. The Mac featured GUI, that is, a type of interface that allows users to interact with computers through graphical icons, as opposed to typing-in text-based commands (see Figure 3.1). The GUI concept was developed by Xerox

PARC laboratories. Xerox Corporation's Palo Alto Research Center (Xerox PARC) was established in 1970 for the purpose of performing R&D work in the area of business machine equipment and computing. The Mac project team was somewhat familiar with the work being done at Xerox PARC. Jobs arranged for a meeting and negotiated rights to the technology in exchange for Apple stock. Jobs and his team were able to immediately seize on the possibility of what GUI could mean to the future of personal computing.[37] To many observers, the Apple raid on Xerox PARC represents one of the great technology thefts of all time. Jobs, for his part, takes a different view, stating that what transpired was less of a heist by Apple and more of a fumble by Xerox. "They were copier heads who had no clue about what the computer could do. . . . Xerox could have owned the entire computer industry."[38]

Writer Walter Isaacson makes the point that Jobs and his team of engineers were able to take the basic design concept and greatly improve upon it in ways that Xerox could not have envisioned. The use of visual icons in combination with a computer mouse was a real breakthrough in the organizing of computer files and the manipulation of software applications.

On January 24, 1984, at the Flint Center on De Anza College's campus in Cupertino, California, Apple formally announced the Macintosh at its shareholder meeting in front of an audience so packed that large numbers of people who owned Apple stock couldn't get in at all. The introduction of the Macintosh computer would set the foundation for personal computing for an entire industry. In the beginning, the Macintosh was a commercial failure. But in time, the Mac would become more than a stand-alone computer. It would become a computing platform spawning a whole host of computer, laptop, and notebook derivatives.

Figure 3.1 Graphical User Interface of the Apple Macintosh (1984)

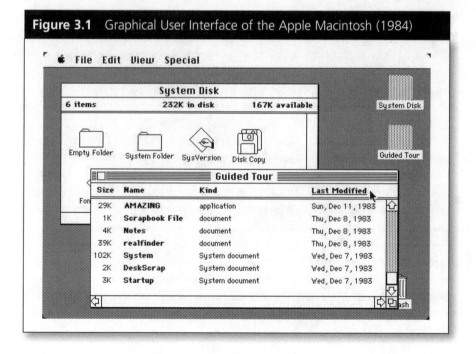

The Macintosh, like all Apple products, emphasized the importance of combining both hardware and software elements into a seamless integrated design. Today, the Mac is the only PC with a 30 plus-year history. Other than Apple, the leading computer companies of the time, Atari, Commodore, Compaq, Kaypro, and Radio Shack no longer exist. Even IBM left the PC field in 2004. The true look and feel of PCs today can be attributed to the early design features found in the original Macintosh computer.

The Apple iPhone

The Apple iPhone is a line of cellular smartphone devices designed and marketed by Apple Inc. The iPhone is designed as a multimedia platform that can support a whole host of applications, including voice communication, mobile Internet access, music playback and storage, as well as a camera and photo storage. Apple CEO Steve Jobs introduced the iPhone at the Macworld convention at the Moscone Center in San Francisco, California, on January 9, 2007. In his presentation, Jobs described the iPhone as a three-in-one device that included music, phone, and a mobile Internet connection. It is the principle of convergence made practical.

> Every once in awhile a revolutionary product comes along that changes everything. . . . Today we're introducing three revolutionary products of this class. The first one is a widescreen iPod with touch controls. The second is a revolutionary mobile phone. And the third is a breakthrough Internet communications device. Are you getting it? These are not three separate devices, this is one device, and we are calling it iPhone.[39]

Technical Design Features. The iPhone is built around the device's multi-touch screen, including a virtual keyboard and buttons. It utilizes both Wi-Fi and cellular 4G connectivity. The iPhone runs on Apple's iOS mobile operating system. The introduction of the Apple iPhone redefined mobile wireless communication by changing public perception of what a cell phone can and should be able to do. Today's smartphone should contain a number of feature elements, including: 1) Mobile Internet access, 2) Text messaging and e-mail, 3) Personal calendar, 4) MP3 music player and storage, 5) Camera and video camera, 6) Photo storage, and 7) Global positioning system (GPS) locator.

The iPhone fundamentally changed how people communicate and interact with the world. To that end, Apple has created an entire digital media ecosystem. The iPhone is managed and synced by the Apple iTunes media store. iTunes serves as the basic platform for downloading music, photos, and other software applications onto the mobile device unit. This, in turn, enables the device to be highly personalized when it comes to software applications. Since 2007, Apple has encouraged software developers to create specialized apps for the iPhone. Apple, for its part, takes a small percentage of the profits made by the apps makers. The iPhone will only run application programs approved and tested by Apple and distributed by the Apple apps store.

The iPhone Design Philosophy. Apple's design philosophy is a direct reflection of its cofounder Steve Jobs. Aesthetics in design should be as important as the product's function. From the iPhone touch screen to the Apple stores (where they are retailed), there is a commitment to simplicity in design. Apple's abiding philosophy is that such devices should be simple to the touch, display clean lines, and exercise a less-is-more quality. A second important design principle is that aesthetics in design should be as important as the product's function. Isaacson (2011) makes the point that at most companies, engineering tends to drive design. The engineers set forth their specifications, and the design team comes up with cases and displays that will accommodate them.[40] At Apple, it's often just the opposite. Design drives the engineering. For Chief Designer Jonathan Ive, the most important aspect to the iPhone experience is the display screen. The iPhone's ergonomic design and high-resolution graphics should be simple and attractive. All applications should defer to the screen.[41] Since the introduction of the Apple iPhone, other companies have introduced alternative versions to the iPhone's basic design. As the expression goes, "Imitation is the sincerest form of flattery." Companies like Samsung, Verizon, and Microsoft/Nokia, to name only a few, have introduced their own versions of smartphone designs. The iPhone (and smartphones in general) has become an integral part of today's digital lifestyle. We see this daily. As Amanda Walker (2012) writes,

> On a trip with my kids to a newly refurbished playground in San Francisco's Hayes Valley, I notice that each of the parents—myself included—are almost as busy with their mobile phones as they are playing with their kids. Whether taking pictures, texting, checking an email, tweeting, or posting a status to Facebook, these momentary distractions from the fun going on around us are the new norm.[42]

Discussion

Product innovation refers to the complex process of bringing new products and services to market as well as improving (or enhancing) existing ones. Product innovation is important because it creates a long-term competitive advantage for a company or organization. The principle of ideation represents the creative process for generating, developing, and communicating new ideas with the goal of helping to advance new product development. In this chapter, special attention was given to three major media companies and a select set of product innovation designs, including: Sony Inc. (the Walkman and CD), the Walt Disney Company (film animation and theme parks and resorts), and Apple Inc. (the Macintosh computer and iPhone).

The development of the Sony/Philips CD in 1982 redefined the field of music delivery by introducing an altogether new way of recording and playing music. The CD played on the inherent strengths of digital technology by eliminating scratches and surface noise while being able to produce a cleaner sound than was true for analog-based vinyl records. As a one-time student of music, Sony President Norio Ohga firmly supported the product's development despite a well-established music industry that was resistant to change. The CD would eventually replace vinyl records as the new standard in recording technology. As noted earlier, successful innovation leads to a progression in new products offshoots. The CD would set into motion the future development of CD-based video game systems as well as DVD and Blu Ray DVD video recording and playback.

The introduction of Disneyland in 1955 and Walt Disney World in 1971 set the standard for family-friendly theme park entertainment. This, in combination with Disney animated films, helped establish a family entertainment brand that is unparalleled. Both the theme parks as well as Disney-owned hotels, resorts, and cruises feature highly detailed design, landscaping, and period architecture. Words like *magic* and *fantasy* have become part of the Disney lexicon of terms to describe a family-friendly vacation experience. The Disney experience is driven by a strong attention to detail. One of the more interesting facts about Disney World is the 70 percent return rate of first-time Disney visitors. A 70 percent return rate says a lot about customer satisfaction and loyalty. Aside from the cities of Paris and London, Walt Disney World is the mostly highly visited tourist destination in the world.

The launch of the Apple iPhone demonstrated the first all-in-one integrated cell phone that combined voice communication, Internet access, music, a camera, and photo storage. One of the signature features of the iPhone is a meticulous attention to detail. The iPhone set the standard for personalized communication services, albeit on a mobile device. Mobility is a signature feature of today's digital lifestyle. In time, software developers would continue to create thousands of new apps that would add to the iPhone's extended reach and capability. The smartphone would later become standardized with the introduction of the Google Android application giving way to new and enhanced smartphone design by companies such as Samsung, Microsoft, and Xiaomi (China), to name only a few.

Product innovation and design have the power to redefine an industry. Successful product design balances function, value, and appearance for the benefit of the end user. Each of the companies discussed in this chapter changed the direction of an entire industry. They were blue ocean companies in the best sense of the term. They introduced an altogether new way of doing things for the consumer. What Sony, Disney, and Apple share in common is a strong attention to detail. Each product was more than a product. They became an experience for the user. Competition proved irrelevant because the rules of the game were waiting to be set. In my view, this is what it means to be a game changer.

Endnotes

1. Marc Annacchino, *The Pursuit of New Product Development* (Burlington, MA: Butterworth-Heinemann, 2007).
2. Michael Brooke and William Mills, *New Product Development: Successful Innovation in the Marketplace* (Binghamton, NY: International Business Press, 2003).
3. Alexander Osterwalder and Yves Pigneur, *Business Model Generation* (Hoboken, NJ: John Wiley & Sons, 2010).
4. Brooke and Mills, *New Product Development.*

5. The Imagineers, *Walt Disney Imagineering* (New York: Disney Enterprises, Inc., 1996), 21.

6. Tony Davila, Marc Epstein, and Robert Shelton, *Making Innovation Work* (Upper Saddle River, NJ: Wharton School Publishing, 2006), 28.

7. Farrah Detuya, "Ideation, Innovation and Creativity," *Slideshare Presentation,* June 16, 2011, http://www.slideshare.net/Farrah1978/ideation-innovation-and-creativity

8. Peter Thiel, *Zero to One* (New York: Crown Business, 2014).

9. Reiji Asakura, *Revolutionaries at Sony: The Making of the Sony Playstation and the Visionaries Who Conquered the World of Video Games* (New York: McGraw-Hill. 2000).

10. Clayton Christensen, *The Innovator's Dilemma* (Boston, MA: Harvard Business School Press, 1997).

11. Detuya, "Ideation, Innovation and Creativity," Presentation.

12. Annacchino, *The Pursuit of New Product Development.*

13. Larry Bossidy and Ram Charran, *Execution: The Discipline of Getting Things Done* (New York: Crown Business, 2002).

14. Scott Berkun, *Making Things Happen: Mastering Project Management* (Sebastopol, CA: O'Reilly Media, 2008).

15. Sophie Lovell, *Dieter Rams: As Little Design as Possible* (London, UK: Phaidon, 2012).

16. Lovell, *Dieter Rams: As Little Design as Possible.*

17. Richard Gershon, "The Sony Corporation: Market Leadership, Innovation Failure and the Challenges of Business Reinvention," in *Handbook in East Asia Entrepreneurship,* eds. Fu Lai Yu and Ho-Don Yan (London, UK: Routledge, 2014), 225–239.

18. Richard Gershon, "The Transnational Media Corporation and the Economics of Global Competition," in *Global Communication* (2nd ed.), ed. Yahya R. Kamalipour (Belmont, CA: Wadsworth, 1989), 55–78.

19. Sony Corporation, Inc. *Genryu,* 2nd ed. (Tokyo, Japan: Sony Inc.).

20. Ibid., 207.

21. John Nathan, *Sony: The Private Life* (New York: Houghton-Mifflin. 1999), 152.

22. Richard Gershon and Tsutomu Kanayama, "The Sony Corporation: A Case Study in Transnational Media Management," *The International Journal on Media Management.* 4, no. 2 (2002): 44–56.

23. Nathan, *Sony: The Private Life,* 143.

24. Gershon and Kanayama, "The Sony Corporation: A Case Study in Transnational Media Management."

25. Louise Krasniewicz, *Walt Disney: A Biography* (Santa Barbara, CA: Greenwood, 2010).

26. Ron Grover, *The Disney Touch* (Homewood, IL: Irwin, 1991).

27. Krasniewicz, *Walt Disney: A Biography.*

28. Gershon, *Media, Telecommunications and Business Strategy.*

29. The Imagineers, *Walt Disney Imagineering.*

30. Adam Lashinsky, *The Decade of Steve. The Legacy of Steve Jobs 1955–2011* (New York: Fortune Books, 2011).

31. Jeffrey Young and William Simon, *iCon: Steve Jobs* (New York: John Wiley & Sons, 2005).

32. Ibid.

33. Shane Mittan, "Apple Inc., A Case Study Analysis," (paper presentation, International Telecommunications Education and Research Association (ITERA) Conference, Louisville, KY. April, 2010).

34. Michael Scott was the first CEO of Apple Computer from 1977 to 1981. On February 25, 1981, the day known as Black Wednesday, Scott fired 40 Apple employees personally, including half of the Apple II team, in a belief that they were redundant. He was then demoted to vice chair, and Mike Markkula replaced him as CEO.

35. "Yes, Microsoft Did Change the World More Than Apple," *Business Insider,* September 8, 2011, http://www.businessinsider.com/yes-microsoft-did-change-the-world-more-than-apple-2011–9

36. John Bell, "Aug. 6, 1997, Apple Rescued by Microsoft," Wired, July 8, 2009, http://www.wired.com/2009/08/dayintech_0806/

37. Adam Lashinsky, *Inside Apple* (New York: Business Plus, 2012).

38. Walter Isaacson, *Steve Jobs* (New York: Simon & Schuster, 2011), 98.

39. Steve Jobs, "Keynote Address," Macworld Convention, San Francisco, CA. June 9, 2007, http://www.engadget.com/2007/01/09/live-from-macworld-2007-steve-jobs-keynote/

40. Isaacson, *Steve Jobs.*

41. Lashinsky, *Inside Apple.*

42. Amanda Walker, "Smartphones and Public Spaces," Scenario Journal (Fall 2012), http://scenariojournal.com/lu-smart-phones/

CHAPTER 4

Business Process Innovation

Almost all quality improvement comes via simplification of design, manufacturing . . . layout, processes and procedures.

—Tom Peters

Our business is about technology, yes. But it's also about operations and customer relationships.

—Michael Dell, Dell Inc.

Introduction

Today, innovation is about much more than developing new products. It is about reinventing business processes and building entirely new markets to meet untapped customer needs. A business process implies a strong emphasis on how work gets done within an organization. A business process can touch on a number of different organizational parts, including product manufacturing, inventory management, R&D, customer service, marketing, and distribution. A well-constructed business process renders two important consequences. First, it is transformative; that is, a successful business process creates internal and external efficiencies that provide added value to the organization. Second, it sets into motion a host of imitators who see the inherent value in applying the same business process to their own organizations.[1]

Author's Note: The information contained in this chapter is based on a previous chapter that was part of an edited works collection: Richard Gershon. "Business Process Innovation and the Intelligent Network." In *Managing Media Economy, Media Content, and Technology in the Age of Digital Convergence*, edited by Z. Vukanovic and P. Faustino, 59–85. Lisbon, Portugal: Media XXI/ Formal Press, 2011.

As an example, HBO's use of satellite communication transformed the delivery of television programmers to cable operators, thus demonstrating the efficiency and economies of scale factors associated with satellite/cable networking. Other cable programmers, including ESPN (1979), CNN (1980), and MTV (1981) would soon follow suit, adopting the same long-haul television distribution process. Similarly, Amazon.com experimented and developed many of the EC online shopping order forms and techniques that have since been adopted by numerous other EC merchants. Such companies set the benchmark for others to follow. Table 4.1 provides a comparison of six media and telecommunications companies that are industry leaders in the use of business process innovation. Each of the said companies has rendered a host of imitators in the way they have developed their business processes.

This chapter will look at the relationship between intelligent networking and business process innovation. Special attention will be given to Dell Inc., Walt Disney Company (specifically, Walt Disney World) and Netflix Inc. Each company represents a different kind of business process innovation. The first kind of business

Table 4.1 Six Media and Telecommunications Companies: The Transformative Impact of Business Process Innovation	
Home Box Office (HBO)	In 1975, HBO helped advance the principle of satellite and cable networking by using satellite communication to advance long-haul television distribution.
Dell	Dell computers developed a highly successful business process in the area of PC manufacturing, utilizing just-in-time manufacturing (JITM) techniques, global inventory management, as well as direct-to-home sales capability.
Walt Disney Company	Disney championed the belief that customer service is a business process as evidenced in how it manages large numbers of people at its theme parks (i.e., guest flow and transportation).
Pixar Studios	Pixar developed a first-of-its-kind computer-generated animation graphics utilizing a specialized digital animation rendering technique in contrast to traditional cartoon animation. Examples include *Toy Story, Finding Nemo, Monsters Inc., The Incredibles, Cars,* and so on.
Apple	The combination of the Apple iPod and iTunes media store created the first sustainable music downloading business model of its kind.
Netflix	Having developed a highly efficient warehouse inventory management system, Netflix has become the world's largest online DVD rental service offering subscribers flat-rate rental by mail as well as online video streaming.

process examines a supply chain management (SCM) system network where the emphasis is on global inventory management and just-in-time manufacturing. The second example looks at customer service as a business process. The third kind looks at the power of the Internet to create a virtual business enterprise. Each of these examples shares the common goal of improving the customer experience as well as organizational performance.

Business Process: Theoretical Traditions

Business process innovation involves creating entirely new systems and methods for improving organizational performance. The study of business process and organizational performance has a long history dating back to Frederick Winslow Taylor and his original time and motion studies.[2] Throughout the latter half of the 20th century, there has evolved a number of theoretical traditions that are central to any discussion involving business process innovation, including total quality management (TQM), Six Sigma, and reengineering. What each of the theoretical traditions share in common is an exacting focus on finding new ways to improve quality and organizational performance.

Total Quality Management

TQM is a philosophy where business is committed to improving product quality and customer satisfaction at every level of the organization. TQM has been described as "a comprehensive and structured approach to organizational management that seeks to improve the quality of products and services through ongoing refinements in response to continuous feedback."[3] The principles of TQM can be traced to the work of Americans W. Edwards Deming and Joseph Juran, who served as business consultants to a number of Japanese companies in the years following World War II. TQM adheres to an operating philosophy of delivering the best possible products and services to the end consumer. There is a strong emphasis on quality control. Workers operating on the shop floor are a key essential in assuring product quality. Accordingly, they should be given responsibility and authority for making decisions that can affect product quality output.[4] A second important principle is that everyone both inside and outside the organization should be considered customers. TQM emphasizes the importance of continuous improvement as the basis for producing long-term results.

Six Sigma

Six Sigma is a business process that enables companies to achieve greater efficiency by streamlining operations, improving quality, and eliminating defects in all aspects of the company's manufacturing operations. Six Sigma is a highly disciplined process that helps a business focus on developing and delivering near-perfect products and services. The concept of Six Sigma originated with the work of Bill Smith at Motorola Corporation, who in 1986 began to develop a set of process improvement strategies known as Six Sigma.[5] The goal of Six Sigma is to systematically improve processes by eliminating defects. A *defect* is defined as a failure to deliver what the customer wants. Six Sigma was later adopted by General Electric (GE) in the early 1990s. There are three critical elements when considering the principles of Six Sigma. They include the customer, the process, and the employee. The customer represents the first critical element. The customer should be able to expect a high-quality product, on-time delivery, competitive prices, reliability, and excellent follow-up and support. The second element of Six Sigma is that manufacturing and business processes can be measured, analyzed, and controlled. There should be a continuous effort to reduce variations (or defects) in process outputs.[6] The third element of Six Sigma training and thinking is to empower managers and employees to make decisions on the shop floor. Quality is the responsibility of every employee.

Reengineering

Reengineering is an organizational change concept that has been written about by a number of management scholars. In 1993, Hammer and Champy (1993) popularized the term to the general public when they published *Reengineering the Corporation: A Manifesto for Business Revolution.*[7] Since then, the term *reengineering* is often used to describe situations where a company decides to reorganize or downsize its business operations. The decision to reengineer often comes at a time when a company is faced with major competitive threats or recognizes that its operations are costly and inefficient. Another term for reengineering is *business process redesign*. Business process redesign means starting over. It represents a fundamental rethinking of business processes to bring about dramatic improvements in organizational performance. Such improvements can be measured in a variety of ways, including reduced manufacturing costs, greater speed and efficiency, more personalized customer service, and so forth.[8] Reengineering presupposes the ability to organize around key business processes rather than defined organizational hierarchies, departments, or assembly lines.

Business Process and Organizational Performance

Business process innovation focuses on creating new and adaptive systems for improving organizational performance. Davenport and Short (1990) define a business process as "a set of logically related tasks performed to achieve a defined business outcome."[9] In their view, an effective business process cuts across organizational boundaries in support of both internal and external customers. For manufacturing companies, business process innovation can include things such as integrating new production methods to help advance product quality, engaging in just-in-time manufacturing techniques, or developing an enterprise resource management network that provides both the manufacturer and customer with timely, up-to-date information. For cable television programmers, business process

innovation is about finding the best technology and software combination to provide high-quality digital television programming and other enhanced services to
the end consumer for the least cost. Technology alone is rarely the key to unlocking
economic value. Companies create real value when they combine technology with
new ways of doing business.[10] In sum, people make the difference.

Lean Process Improvement

Business process innovation involves creating systems and methods for improving organizational performance. One technique for identifying a business process
within an organization is based on a set of principles known as lean process
improvement. The goal is to offer the customer a level of value that exceeds the cost
of the activities, thereby resulting in improved organizational performance. Lean
process improvement looks at ways to improve organizational performance by
focusing on business processes. All business enterprises consist of both primary
and secondary processes. They are the series of steps that must be carried out to
create value for customers. The goal is to maximize customer value while minimiz-
ing waste. A lean organization understands customer value. There are four goals of
lean process improvement.[11]

Improve Quality. Quality is the ability of one's product or service to meet or exceed
your customer requirements. Everyone within the organization from senior management to the worker on the floor has a responsibility to improve product and service quality. Continuous improvement means that the organization benefits from a
shared sense of responsibility to regularly improve products and business processes.

Eliminate Waste. Waste is the activities that take up time, resources, and space but
do not add value to a product or service. There are multiple contributing factors
that contribute to waste, including product defects, waiting for parts or suppliers,
overproduction (i.e., producing too much of something), transportation failures or
breakdowns, and the underutilization of people.

Reduce Lead Time. Lead time is the total time it takes to complete a series of tasks
within a process. Accurate forecasting goes a long way in determining the time it
will take to produce and distribute a product to the end consumer.

Reduce Total Cost. Total costs are the direct and indirect costs associated with the
production of a product or service. How much money does the organization spend
in terms of its sales staff (i.e., customer expense account, food, lodging, etc.)?

Lean process improvement utilizes the principle of value stream mapping as a
way to identify and chart the flow of information processes across an organization's
entire supply chain from supplier to the end user. A *value stream* is all the actions,
both added and taken away, that are required to bring a product to market. Lean
systems are customer driven. Products and services should be created and delivered
in the right amounts to the right location at the right cost.

Supply Chain Management

SCM is a complex business model that takes into consideration the entire set of linking steps necessary to produce and deliver a product to the end consumer. A *supply chain* consists of all parties involved, directly or indirectly, in fulfilling a customer request. The supply chain not only includes the manufacturer and suppliers but also transporters, warehouses, retailers, and customers themselves.[12] SCM has two distinct and equally important parts: 1) Philosophy and 2) Methodology. SCM philosophy is grounded in the belief that everyone involved in the supply chain is both a supplier and customer and requires access to timely, up-to-date information. The goal is to optimize exchange efficiency and meet the needs for both suppliers and customers. SCM methodology has to do with the specifics of strategy implementation. Information is key. At issue is the ability to share timely information across the entire supply chain system. A well-designed SCM system gives automated intelligence to an extended network of suppliers, manufacturers, distributors, as well as a host of other trading partners.[13] A supply chain is connected by transportation and storage activities and coordinated through planning and networked information activities.

Enterprise Resource Planning

A supply chain is connected by transportation and storage activities and coordinated through planning and networked information activities. Central to any discussion of SCM and intelligent networking is the principle of enterprise resource planning (ERP), which attempts to integrate all departments and functions across an entire company onto a single computer system using a common database and a shared set of reporting tools. Dredden and Bergdolt (2007) define *ERP* as "information systems that integrate processes in an organization using a common database and shared reporting tools."[14]

There is a tendency among large (sometimes older) organizations to compartmentalize information. In the past, it was not uncommon to find several divisions within an organization having their own separate databases. The information was often duplicated and seldom shared among departments. This was especially true for such organizations as General Motors, Eastman Kodak, and the National Security Agency, to name only a few. The duplication of effort was both costly and inefficient. Today, the emphasis is on the sharing of information resources across divisional lines, thus promoting greater efficiency in product planning, manufacturing, marketing, and distribution. This is at the heart of ERP, which allows various players within an organization to be a part of a larger network of shared information. ERP attempts to integrate all departments and functions across an entire company onto a single computer system using a common database and a shared set of reporting tools.[15] The goal of an ERP system is to replace stand-alone programs such as accounting, manufacturing, human resources, warehousing, and transportation and replace them with a single, unified software program.[16] This is lean process improvement in its most essential form.

Dell Inc.

Dell Inc. was established by Michael Dell in 1984 and has grown to become one of the world's preeminent manufacturers of desktop and laptop computers. What is interesting about the Dell story is not so much the hardware itself but rather the innovative business processes that the company put into place from a manufacturing and delivery standpoint. Dell builds computers to customer order and specification using just-in-time manufacturing techniques. The company has built its reputation on direct sales delivery to the end consumer combined with strong customer support. Dell's business model is simple in concept but very difficult to execute in practice.[17] It is premised on a highly sophisticated SCM system.

Michael Dell started out as a premed student at the University of Texas. Dell soon became fascinated by computers and created a small niche in the assembly and sale of PCs and PC components out of his dormitory room. Dell bought excess supplies at cost from IBM dealers, which allowed him to resell the components at 10 to 15 percent below the regular retail price. He then began to assemble and sell PC clones by purchasing retailers' surplus stock at cost and then upgrading the units with video cards, hard disks, and memory. Dell then sold the newly assembled IBM clones at 40 percent below the cost of an IBM PC. By April 1984, with sales reaching $80,000 a month, Dell dropped out of the university and formed a company called PCs Limited. The ability to sell directly to the end user at a discounted price proved to be a winning formula, and by the end of 1986, sales had reached $33 million. PCs Limited was renamed Dell Computers in 1987, and the company soon opened its first set of international offices.

From 1990 to 1993, Dell experimented with traditional retail distribution in hopes of faster growth, but soon realized that bricks-and-mortar stores were less profitable, and refocused his efforts on direct sales. By 1996, Internet sales had taken off, and the company realized that computer-savvy shoppers preferred the convenience of custom ordering what they wanted directly from Dell and having it delivered to their door. During this time, Dell had become master innovators involving three important business processes. The first process was customization using a just-in-time manufacturing capability. Dell built computers to customer order and specification, thereby eliminating excess inventory and the need for storage. The second important process was direct-to-consumer sales delivery, thus avoiding costly investment in retail store infrastructure. It was a process model that other computer manufacturers would later adopt. The third business process is global inventory management, which enabled Dell to transnationalize the manufacturing process.[18]

Just-in-Time Manufacturing

Most large-scale companies have access to excellent hardware and software capabilities that enable them to operate in an international business environment. The distinguishing factor often centers on speed and turnaround time. Just-in-time manufacturing (JITM) is a production model that allows a company to meet customer orders by producing goods and services on demand. The purpose of JITM is to avoid waste associated with overproduction and excess inventory. JITM is designed to meet a customer order in the least amount of time. To accomplish this, JITM relies on the use of SCM and ERP systems for the purpose of tracking customer orders.[19] They are designed to interface with Universal Product Codes (i.e., bar codes) or Radio Frequency Identification (RFID) tags, which enable Dell to track the status of a product throughout the entire manufacturing and delivery cycle. This can include reacting to customer needs (i.e., answering customer inquiries about production status, delivery dates, etc.) In sum, a well-designed JITM capability is designed to integrate both internal and external processes of the organization.

Global Inventory Management

Telecommunications has collapsed the time and distance factors that once separated nations, people, and business organizations. Communication is instantaneous. Faster product cycles and the ability to train and produce worldwide production teams have transnationalized the manufacturing process. It is the ability to apply time-based competitive strategies at the international level that enables companies like Dell to manage inventories across borders.[20] We call this global inventory management.

Today, Dell Inc. is one of the largest PC manufacturers in the world. The company has an international workforce of more than 108,000 employees located in 34 countries and three major regions of the world, including the Americas, Europe, and the Middle East/Asia Pacific. Dell's selection of geographic locations and production facilities has largely been driven by it foreign direct investment strategy, including the perceived profitability of the market and growth potential. Each of the three regional hub sites has its own headquarters and set of assembly plants. Dell's international market presence and JITM capability requires a global network of suppliers and contract manufacturers to support each production facility. Instead of producing all the necessary components itself, Dell contracts with other manufacturers to produce subassembly parts, such as circuit boards, monitors, and so on. Dell, for its part, maintains control over the final assembly portion, paying particular attention to customized feature elements.[21] Dell's global inventory management system requires an efficient method of communication to meet customer demands and ensure a ready supply of parts on hand to support various kinds of configuration requests. Over time, Dell has built a complex, global inventory management system that tracks information among suppliers, distributors, and other key component players involved in product manufacturing and support.

During its early years of operation, Dell's approach to computer manufacturing involved a standardized assembly line process, whereby a single individual would install a single component and the partly assembled PC was sent on to the next station. Starting in 1997, Dell undertook a major process redesign known as *cell manufacturing* by which a team of workers would work together to assemble an entire PC at a workstation or cell.[22] This technique has resulted in a steep decline in assembly time and increased productivity per square foot of assembly space. Cell manufacturing has allowed the company to achieve greater efficiencies in terms of quality, cycle time, and delivery cost. According to Michael Dell, "We will innovate and adapt our supply chain model to help drive differentiated product design, manufacturing and distribution models."[23] In recent years, Dell has experienced some decline in sales due in large measure to a leveling off and maturity of the PC market.

Walt Disney Company:
Disney World Park and Resort

Customer Service Is a Process

Successful product design often requires a well-considered business and logistics process. The design and operation of both Disneyland and Disney World presuppose a deep appreciation for the fact that customer service is a process. The Walt Disney Company employs one of the most sophisticated employee training programs in the world. To ensure that employees at all levels are guided by a common sense of purpose, founder Walt Disney established a formal training program that has come to be known as Disney University Training. It begins with an appreciation for the fact that appearance is everything. Disney employees are referred to as cast members. Training includes everything from the way in which Disney employees interact with the public to the clothes they wear. In creating the right appearance, cast members are taught to be polite. They are taught to understand that park attendees are to be treated as guests.[24] The issue of employee training becomes all the more important when one considers Disney's multiple worldwide facilities.

In creating the original Disneyland, Disney knew that delivering an enjoyable experience was dependent on developing a set of processes that ensured a successful visit each and every time. From professional staff in costume to clean restrooms, there is a strong attention to detail. Nowhere is this more evident than in managing people, lines, and transportation at the company's various parks.

Guest Flow

Managing the thousands of daily visitors both traveling to and from Disney World requires a deep understanding of logistics and transport. There is a distinct science in managing large numbers of people when they have to wait in line for an upcoming ride or attraction. Standing in line and wait time are the biggest customer complaints that visitors have when attending Disney World. Part of the task is in finding ways to entertain (sometimes distract) guests while they wait in line.[25] Planners refer to it as the *psychology of the queue.* The sight of a long line can be discouraging. To offset that, planners create barriers and distractions that make it difficult for people to see the full extent of the line. Most of the longer lines feature videos, interactive games, and animatronic characters to entertain park attendees. Beneath Cinderella Castle at Disney World is an operational command center that oversees logistics, including problems associated with long line waits. Disney's operations staff monitor large screens that depict various attractions using different colors to represent wait-time gradations.[26] Sometimes the solution is technical (i.e., order more conveyance vehicles at select rides and attractions). Other times, the decision is made to have Disney characters and other entertainers fill in where lines are extra long. Another way to address the problem is to maximize so-called off-peak times for guests and visitors. Disney provides a one-hour early start time for guests staying at Disney resorts. In 1999, Disney introduced the FastPass, which is a virtual queuing system that lets park visitors return to a ride at a scheduled time when there is a shorter line. The FastPass+ system now works off a special app that provides scheduling information to one's smartphone. Disney also sells special VIP tours (at a significantly higher price) that provide more customized visits and eliminate wait times for all rides and attractions.

Transportation Management

Disney combines creativity with practical function when it comes to moving people from one location to another. Walt Disney World uses a variety of transportation vehicles, including buses, watercraft vehicles, a monorail system, and trams. This becomes important when one considers that an estimated 53,000 people visit Disney World each day. The creativity part comes in the form of watercraft (ferries and boats) and a monorail system that provide unique ways to access park attractions. The Disney bus system provides the most direct transportation from hotels to all of the major park locations. Disney utilizes trams to take guests from the park entrances to the exterior visitor parking lots. At the end of the day, guests should not leave the park only to find that they have difficulty locating their cars. Consider it the epilogue to the Disney experience. Each parking lot area has its own identifier. In addition, tram drivers keep a simple list of what rows they work each morning, which is distributed to team members at the end of the day. This allows guests to simply mark the time they arrived, and the late afternoon and evening drivers will know what location each guest parked in. Transportation and the managing of large numbers of people is a key essential when it comes to planning major sporting events in terms of time, efficiency, and security. It is not surprising that the Disney Institute provides regular training for prospective planners of large-scale, international sporting events including the Olympics and World Cup soccer.

Netflix

Netflix is an online, subscription-based DVD rental service. Netflix was founded by Reed Hastings in 1997. The story goes that Hastings found an overdue rental copy of *Apollo 13* in his closet and was forced to pay $40 in late fees. The business that emerged from Hastings's frustration was a rental company that uses a combination of the Internet and the U.S. Postal Service (USPS) to deliver DVDs to subscribers directly. Netflix was founded during the emergent days of EC, when companies like

Amazon.com and Dell Computers were starting to gain prominence. Netflix offers the public a cost-effective and easy-to-use EC system by which consumers can rent and return films.

Understanding the External Competitive Environment

Netflix was conceived at a time when the home video industry was largely dominated by two major home video retail chains, Blockbuster Video and Hollywood Video, as well as a number of smaller retail outlets. Customers rented movies, primarily on VHS cassettes, from a retail location for a specified time period and paid a $3 to $4 fee for each movie rented. Companies like Blockbuster fully recognized that renting a movie is largely an impulse decision. Having access to the latest movies was a high priority for most would-be renters. Market research at the time showed that new releases represented more than 70 percent of total rentals.[27]

The challenge for Hastings was whether he wanted to duplicate the traditional bricks-and-mortar approach used by companies such as Blockbuster. The alternative was to utilize the power of the Internet for placing video rental orders and providing online customer service. Early on, Netflix focused their efforts on early-technology adopters who had recently purchased DVD players. In contrast, most video rental store outlets were still using VHS cassette tapes. According to Reed Hastings, "We were targeting people who just bought DVD players."[28]

Netflix and Business Process Innovation

Netflix offers its customers a great value proposition, namely, unlimited DVDs for a fixed monthly price. In practical terms, the average consumer may only receive two to five DVDs in a week's time given the particular service plan as well as the subscriber's personal viewing habits. The general perception is that Netflix provides greater value to the consumer when compared to traditional video rental stores, which charge by the individual DVD rental unit. Netflix offers consumers greater convenience in the form of "no late fees." The subscriber is free to hold on to a specific video as long as he/she wants.[29]

Netflix is a master of business process innovation and has engaged in a number of strategies that has enabled the company to be successful. First, Netflix has developed a highly sophisticated SCM system that enables the company to offer subscribers both good selection as well as a fast turnaround time. Early on, Netflix made the decision to partner with the USPS to deliver DVDs to its online subscriber base. DVDs are small and light, enabling inexpensive delivery, including the highly recognizable red envelope, which has become synonymous with the Netflix brand.

Second, Netflix has harnessed the power of the Internet to create a virtual store. The company maintains a set of centers that serve as hub sites for DVD collection, packaging, and redistribution. Netflix presorts all outgoing DVD mail deliveries by zip code, thus cutting down sorting time by the USPS.[30]

Third, a big part of Netflix's success is the direct result of personalized marketing, which involves knowing more about the particular interests and viewing habits of one's customers. Netflix fully utilizes a proprietary software recommendation system. The software recommendation system makes suggestions of other films that the consumer might like based on past selections and a brief evaluation that the subscriber is asked to fill out. The proprietary software recommendation system has the added benefit of stimulating demand for lesser-known movies and taking the pressure off recently released feature films, where demand sometimes outstrips availability.[31] The focus on lesser-known films is in keeping with Anderson's (2006) "long tail" principle.[32] The term describes the niche strategy of businesses such as Netflix or Amazon.com, which sell a large number of unique items in relatively small quantities. Through the power of intelligent networking, such companies are able to sell a small number of hard-to-find items to a large number of customers. This stands in marked contrast to the blockbuster (or major hit) approach used by filmmakers and book publishers.

Fourth, Netflix has steadily adapted to changing technology by offering a Watch Instantly feature, which enables streaming of near-DVD-quality movies and recorded television shows (at additional cost) instantly to subscribers equipped with a computer and high-speed Internet connectivity. What is interesting to note is that the video streaming of movies is delivering in real time and in greater numbers what cable television has failed to achieve in terms of its highly touted video-on-demand system capability. Services such as Netflix, Hulu, and HBO-Go are now referred to as over-the-top services that enable cable subscribers to effectively cut the cord and depend exclusively on their broadband connection for the delivery of video services. The Watch Instantly feature is steadily being positioned to eventually replace the traditional delivery of DVDs by mail.

The main strategic challenge for Netflix is product inventory. In its formative years, Netflix had a contract with all of the major U.S. studios as well as select international studios for the rights to use their movie inventory as part of their program service. That is changing as more and more movie studios are electing to video stream their own television and film programs. Critics point to the low number of titles available for streaming. The decrease in program inventory is forcing Netflix to develop more original programming such as *House of Cards* and other made-for-television series. Netflix, for its part, now considers itself more of a television channel than a library of film product. In practical terms, Netflix is becoming more like HBO, and HBO is becoming more like Netflix. That said, Netflix's long-term prospects remain positive. Hastings has said on several occasions that Netflix's purpose is not to provide DVDs via the mail but rather to allow for the best home video viewing for its customers. The real issue is exchange efficiencies. In looking to the future, video streaming will become more and more the main delivery engine in terms of how Netflix plans to distribute its television and film service.

Discussion

Sometimes the beauty of a great innovation lies in the process. Business process innovation is about creating added value for both the organization and its customers. Innovation, without value creation, is simply a technology-driven effort that may provide incremental improvements to the organization but does not address the larger question of how to make the customer experience better. Value creation can translate in many different ways and formats. Dell's direct-to-home retail sales strategy was greatly aided by its JITM capability and global inventory management system. Disney's knowledge of guest flow and transportation management greatly aids the visitor experience at Disney World. Disney recognizes that customer relations is a process. Netflix has harnessed the power of the Internet to create a virtual organization. Netflix adapted some of the best features of the HBO business model and combined it with some unique distribution efficiencies developed through its partnership with the USPS. Netflix took micromarketing to a whole new level with the development of its proprietary recommendation software. Each of the said companies proved to be major innovators by creating internal business efficiencies while improving the customer experience. See Table 4.2.

Table 4.2 Comparison of Business Process Innovation and Application			
	Dell Computers	*Walt Disney Company*	*Netflix*
Major Business Areas Supported	The manufacture of desktop and laptop computers	Creating an optimum entertainment experience for guests visiting Walt Disney World theme parks	The delivery of premium television and film program services
Planning Goals	To support an extended SCM system and help advance ERP	Developing new rides and attractions; finding ways to improve guest flow (waiting in line) and transportation to and from the major park attractions	Develop cost-effective delivery of television and film programming to subscribers via the Internet, including both HDTV and video streaming capability
Functionality and Benefits	Optimize information flow throughout the extended supply chain, thus enabling global in-ventory management and JITM capability	Ensure a "magical" experience for visiting guests through the combination of entertainment and strong customer service	Provide a fast and efficient EC model that enables subscribers to access premium television and film via the Internet
Relationship With Customers	Provide timely infor-mation on production status and make possible direct-to-home delivery of computer equipment	Reinforce the Disney brand at all levels of the visitor experience to the various parks, rides, and attractions	No late fees; is fast and convenient; utilizes a proprietary recommendation software system

Forward-thinking companies routinely look for ways to improve organizational performance. Process innovators are obsessive problem solvers. There is a constant focus on finding new ways to improve quality and optimize performance. Strong, innovative companies succeed by creating a culture where everyone has a role to play in making the organization better. As Netflix CEO Reed Hastings points out, "We call Netflix's corporate culture the *freedom and responsibility culture.* We want responsible people who are self-motivating and self-disciplined, and we reward them with freedom . . . At Netflix, we think you have to build a sense of responsibility where people care about the enterprise. Hard work, like long hours at the office, doesn't matter as much to us. We care about great work."[33]

Endnotes

1. Richard A. Gershon, "Business Process Innovation and the Intelligent Network," in *Managing Media Economy, Media Content, and Technology in the Age of Digital Convergence,* eds. Z. Vukanovic and P. Faustino (Lisbon, Portugal: Media XXI/Formal Press, 2011), 59–85.
2. Frederick Winslow Taylor was an American mechanical engineer who sought to improve industrial efficiency. He is regarded as the father of scientific management. See Frederick Winslow Taylor, *The Principles of Scientific Management* (New York: Harper & Brothers, 1911).
3. "Total Quality Management," *TechTarget.com,* http://searchcio.techtarget.com/definition/Total-Quality-Management
4. W. Edwards Deming, *Out of Crisis,* (Cambridge, MA: Cambridge University Press, 1982).
5. Richard Gershon, *Media, Telecommunications and Business Strategy,* 2nd ed. (New York: Routledge, 2013), 342–343.
6. Peter Pande and Larry Holpp, *What is Six Sigma?* (New York: McGraw-Hill, 2002).
7. Michael Hammer and James Champy, *Reengineering the Corporation: A Manifesto for Business Revolution* (New York: Harper Business, 1993), 31.
8. Ibid.
9. T. Davenport and J. Short, "The New Industrial Engineering: Information Technology and Business Process Redesign," *Sloan Management Review* (Summer 1990): 11–27.
10. Richard Gershon, "Intelligent Networking And Business Process Innovation," in *Handbook of Research on Telecommunications Planning and Management,* ed. I. Lee (Hershey, PA: IGI Global, 2009), 459–471.
11. Ibid.
12. Sunil Chopral and Peter Meindl, *Supply Chain Management,* 2nd ed. (Upper Saddle River, NJ: Pearson Prentice-Hall, 2004).
13. S. Zheng, D. Yen, and J. M. Tarn, "The New Spectrum of the Cross-enterprise Solution: The Integration of Supply Chain Management and Enterprise Resource Planning Systems," *The Journal of Computer Information Systems* 41, no. 2 (2000): 84–93.
14. G. Dredden and J. Bergdolt, "Enterprise Resource Planning," *Air Force Journal of Logistics* 31, no. 2 (2007): 48–52.
15. J. M. Tarn, M. Razi, D. Yen, and Z. Xu, "Linking ERP and SCM Systems," *International Journal of Manufacturing Technology & Management* 4, no. 5 (2002): 420–439.
16. J. M. Tarn, D. Yen, and M. Beumont, "Exploring the Rationales for ERP and SCM Integration," *Industrial Management & Data Systems* 102, no. 1 (2002): 26–34.

17. Michael Dell, *Direct From Dell* (New York: Harper Business, 1999).

18. Gershon, "Business Process Innovation and the Intelligent Network."

19. A. Thompson and A. Strickland, *Strategic Management,* 11th ed. (New York: McGraw-Hill, 1999). See also "Case Study Series: Dell Computer Corporation," http://www.mhhe.com/business/management/thompson/11e/case/dell.html

20. G. Fields, "Innovation, Time and Territory: Space and the Business Organization of Dell Computer," *Economic Geography* 82, no. 2 (2006): 119–147.

21. Gershon, *Media, Telecommunications and Business Strategy,* 305–307.

22. Thompson and Strickland, *Strategic Management;* "Dell Computer Corporation."

23. William Hoffman, "Dell's Logistics Restart," *Traffic World,* Feb. 26, 2007, 1.

24. Theodore Kinni, *Be Our Guest: Perfecting the Art of Customer Service* (Burbank, CA: Disney Institute Book, Disney Enterprises Inc., 2001), 60.

25. Ibid., 145.

26. "Disney Tackles Major Theme Park Problem: Lines," *New York Times,* December 28, 2010, http://www.nytimes.com/2010/12/28/business/media/28disney.html?_r=0'

27. E-Business Strategies, *Netflix: Transforming the DVD Rental Business* (Alpharetta, GA: E-Business Strategies Inc., October 2002), 1–10.

28. W. Shih, S. Kaufman, and D. Spinola, "Netflix," in *Harvard Business School Case Study Series* (9–607–138) (Cambridge, MA: Harvard Business School, 2007), 1–15.

29. Gershon, "Business Process Innovation and the Intelligent Network."

30. Shih, Kaufman, and Spinola, "Netflix."

31. Gershon, "Business Process Innovation and the Intelligent Network," 77–79.

32. Chris Anderson, *The Long Tail: Why the Future of Business is Selling Less of More* (New York: Hyperion, 2006).

33. Reed Hastings, "How to Set Your Employees Free," *Bloomberg BusinessWeek,* April 12, 2012, http://www.bloomberg.com/bw/articles/2012-04-12/how-to-set-your-employees-free-reed-hastings

CHAPTER 5

Business and Innovation Failure

The Challenges of Reinvention

Large corporations welcome innovation and individualism in the same way that dinosaurs welcomed large meteors.

—Scott Adams, Dilbert

Introduction

This chapter looks at modern media, information technology (IT), and the problems associated with preserving market leadership. We begin by asking the question: What is business failure? At first glance, business failure is typically associated with bankruptcy or poor financial performance. But at a deeper level, business failure is also about the proverbial "fall from grace." A company that once dominated an industry no longer finds itself the market leader.[1] Worse still, the very same company is faced with the public perception that it has lost all relevancy in an otherwise highly competitive business and technology environment.

Author's Note: The information contained in this chapter is based on two previous chapters that were part of two edited works collections: Richard Gershon. "Innovation Failure: A Case Study Analysis of Eastman Kodak and Blockbuster Video." In *Media Management and Economics Research in a Transmedia Environment,* edited by A. Albarran, 46–68 (New York: Routledge, 2013); Richard Gershon. "The Sony Corporation: Market Leadership, Innovation Failure and the Challenges of Business Reinvention." In *Handbook in East Asia Entrepreneurship,* edited by Fu Lai Yu and Ho-Don Yan, 225–239 (London, UK: Routledge, 2014).

Business and Innovation Failure

Business failure refers to a company that is no longer able to continue its operations. The company is no longer able to generate sufficient revenue to offset its expenses. The consequences are very real both symbolically as well as financially. The company's fall from grace is best illustrated by a dramatic downturn in the company's stock value.[2] But more importantly, it means the discontinuation of a once-successful product line and the loss of jobs for thousands of employees who were once part of the company's name and business mission.

In this chapter, we consider five reasons that help to explain why companies experience business failure. They include: 1) Tyranny of success, 2) Organizational culture, 3) Executive leadership failures, 4) Risk-averse culture, and 5) Disruptive technology. A major argument is that the warning signs of a troubled business often exist for long periods of time before they combine with enabling conditions to produce a significant business failure.[3] Special attention is given to the Eastman Kodak Company and Blockbuster Video, who knew they were at risk of failing well in advance of their eventual decline. This chapter also considers the problem of business reinvention. Specifically, we consider the following question: Why do good companies fail to remain innovative over time? A major argument is that even highly successful companies are susceptible to business failure. The Sony Corporation provides a good illustration of a company once known for being a worldwide leader in innovation and the challenges associated with preserving market leadership. Sony is the tale of a once-proud company that traded on its name and reputation rather than face the realities of a highly competitive global marketplace.

The Tyranny of Success

Past success can sometimes make an organization very complacent; that is, they lose the sense of urgency to create new opportunities.[4] Collins (2001) makes the point unequivocally when he writes that "good is the enemy of great."[5] Companies, like people, can become easily satisfied with organizational routines. They become preoccupied with fine-tuning and making slight adjustments to an existing product line rather than preparing for the future. They are engaged in what MIT's Negroponte (1995) describes as the problem of "incrementalism." Says Negroponte, "Incrementalism is innovation's worst enemy."[6] The history of business is filled with examples of past companies where senior management failed to plan or react quickly enough to sudden changes in the marketplace. Such companies do not anticipate a time when a substitute product (or changing market conditions) might come along and dramatically alter the playing field.

BlackBerry. Research in Motion (RIM), makers of the BlackBerry smartphone, grew to become one of the world's most valuable tech companies. The Black-Berry became the requisite accessory of business executives, government officials,

(Continued)

(Continued)

and sports celebrities who were on their phones daily checking e-mail, browsing the web, and texting nonstop. The 2007 introduction of the Apple iPhone with its touchscreen display, iOS mobile operating system, and clean aesthetic lines rapidly usurped BlackBerry's onetime dominant position. Samsung added to the problem with the launch of its Galaxy smartphone two years later. Once a fast-moving innovator that kept well ahead of the competition, RIM grew into a stumbling corporation, blinded by its own success.[7] RIM was slow to respond and repeatedly missed the mark with consumers.

When RIM made public in December 2011 that a new line of BlackBerry phones would not appear until the end of 2012, that announcement provoked both shock and surprise among its many users. At a time when BlackBerry was experiencing a significant drop in market share, the company could ill afford further delays in manufacturing given the growing success of its chief rivals. Analysts were skeptical about the company's explanation that the delay stemmed from its decision to wait for a new, improved microprocessor. Those delays made it impossible for RIM to begin selling its new Z10 smartphone in early 2012, as was originally planned.[8]

The reaction was swift and sharp. The stock fell to an eight-year low following the announcement. One reason for concern, analysts said, was that no amount of advertising could help increase the sale of BlackBerrys given that public confidence in the company was starting to quickly erode.[9] The eventual launch of the Z10 was only modestly successful. By then, the company was in catch-up mode with the ever more popular Apple iPhone and Samsung Galaxy. Their time as a mobile communication luminary was over. Management had failed to appreciate RIM's competitive environment, most notably, RIM's declining market presence and dramatically reduced share price. RIM has become a reactionary company trying to compete in a fast-paced ever changing industry.[10]

Organizational Culture

Organizational culture (or corporate culture) refers to the collection of beliefs, values, and expectations shared by an organization's members and transmitted from one generation of employees to another.[11] Organizations (even large ones) are human constructions. They are made and transformed by individuals. Culture is embedded and transmitted through both implicit and explicit messages such as formal statements, organizational philosophy, adherence to management orthodoxies, deliberate role modeling, and behavioral displays by senior management.[12]

But what happens when organizational culture stands in the way of innovation? What happens when being tied to the past (and past practices) interferes with a company's ability to move forward? The combination of past success coupled with an unbending adherence to management orthodoxy can seriously undermine a company's ability to step out of itself and plan for the future. Suddenly, creative thinking and the ability to float new ideas gets caught up in a stifling bureaucracy. Sometimes what passes for management wisdom and experience is inflexibility masquerading as absolute truth.[13]

AT&T. The breakup of AT&T in 1984 was a watershed event in the history and development of telecommunications in the United States. The AT&T divestiture, and the subsequent competition that followed, ushered in a whole new era in telecommunication products and services for business and residential users, including: 1) Customer-owned telephone sets, 2) Choice of long distance carriers, 3) Cellular telephony, and 4) the Internet, to name only a few. Throughout most of its hundred-year history, AT&T never had to concern itself with the effects of competition in the marketplace and things such as marketing its services to the public. AT&T controlled 80 percent of the U.S. local telephone market and virtually all of its long distance operation. Theirs was a guaranteed market.

Following the divestiture agreement, one of the company's most pressing issues was how to address the organization's own internal culture. The management at AT&T understood the external challenges. The problem was how to overcome the company's institutionalized bureaucracy dating back to the days of Alexander Graham Bell. The culture was sometimes irreverently referred to as "carpet land." As journalist Leslie Cauley (2005) writes,

> Literally a century in the making, the culture was so omnipresent that it even had its own nickname: the Machine. At AT&T's operational headquarters in Basking Ridge, New Jersey, meetings could ramble on for weeks or even months. It was not uncommon for AT&T execs to have meetings to talk about meetings. The Machine steadfastly resisted change, and embraced those who did the same.[14]

Starting in the decade of the 1990s, AT&T was faced with competitive challenges on a number of fronts, including competitive services from the Regional Bell Operating Companies (RBOCs), Verizon, and SBC as well as the rapid rise of cellular telephony. Long distance telephony was fast becoming a commodity and was no longer a sustainable business. Talented employees who attempted to test the boundary waters of AT&T's organizational culture were met with well-worn corporate phrases such as "That's not the AT&T way." It would only be a matter of time before AT&T would be sold off in pieces to the highest bidder. In January 2005, Southwestern Bell Communications (SBC), the second-largest RBOC in the United States agreed to acquire AT&T business and residential services for more than $16.9 billion. The proposed deal seemingly marked the final chapter in the 120-year history of AT&T, the first great American company of the information age and the original model for telecommunications companies worldwide. The phoenix would indeed rise from the ashes. In 2006, SBC would rename itself the new AT&T.

Executive Leadership Failures

Leadership is a process that involves influence and the art of directing people within an organization to achieve a clearly defined set of goals and outcomes. Successful leaders know what they want to accomplish in terms of organizational outcomes. The challenge for a company occurs when the executive leader loses perspective on his/her own role within the organization. In time, the executive leader becomes bigger than the company itself. They become an example of what Collins (2001) describes as the "celebrity leader."[15] Such individuals feel that by virtue of their position, intelligence, or compensation, they are in charge of every key decision that is made on behalf of the business enterprise. Sometimes it works. But sometimes it does not because the people who are responsible for executing strategy have a better understanding of what's happening on the ground. Fellow managers and board members are less likely to challenge the strategic vision of a charismatic leader out of respect for the CEO's past success or by not wanting to appear contrary. Over time, the celebrity leader tends to become more isolated from others and makes unilateral decisions without seeking input from the company's senior management team. The celebrity leader becomes more concerned with his/her own ideas and reputation rather than securing the company's future.[16]

AOL-Time Warner Merger. On January 10, 2000, America Online (AOL), the largest Internet service provider in the United States, announced that it would purchase Time Warner Inc. for $162 billion. What was particularly unique about the deal was that AOL, with one-fifth of the revenue and 15 percent of the workforce of Time Warner, was planning to purchase the largest transnational media corporation (TNMC) in the world. Such was the nature of Internet economics at the time that allowed Wall Street to assign a monetary value to AOL well in excess of its actual value. The proposed venture between AOL and Time Warner was touted as the marriage of old media and new media. In principle, an AOL-Time Warner combination would provide AOL with broadband distribution capability to Time Warner's 13 million cable households. AOL-Time Warner cable subscribers would have faster Internet service as well as access to a wide variety of interactive and Internet software products.[17]

The AOL-Time Warner merger may well be remembered as one of the worst mergers in U.S. corporate history. The first signs of trouble occurred in the aftermath of the dot-com crash beginning in March 2000. AOL, like most other Internet stocks, took an immediate hit. AOL's ad sales experienced a free fall, and subscriber rates flattened out. By 2001, AOL-Time Warner stock was down 70 percent.[18] AOL found itself financially weaker than it was a year earlier because of rising debt and a falling share price, which left it without the financial means to pursue future deals. The once hoped-for synergies did not materialize, leaving the company with an unwieldy structure and bitter corporate infighting. The real disrupter, of course, was the development of the cable modem, which allowed users direct access to the Internet.

For Time Warner CEO Gerald Levin, pursuing the AOL merger was intended to be his final legacy. It should be understood that Levin had a long history of strategic deal making. Levin was the leading force behind HBO's commitment to use satellite communication and the same person who helped engineer Time Inc.'s merger with Warner Communication. In retrospect, CEO Levin was a victim of empire building, that is, a love of deal making and a singular willingness to decide what deals, products, and strategies were best for his company, his shareholders, and the public at large. As Lieberman (2002) notes, "He frequently made those decisions alone, without opening himself up to questions or critics."[19] The cable modem would make the need for AOL much less important.

In the end, Gerald Levin bet the future of Time Warner on the so-called marriage of old media and new media, leaving employees, investors, and consumers questioning his judgment as well as having to sort through the unintended consequences of that action. In January 2003, AOL-Time Warner reported a $99 billion loss from the previous year, making it the highest recorded loss in U.S. corporate history. Perhaps the most symbolic aspect of AOL-Time Warner as a failed business strategy was the decision in September 2003 by the company's board of directors to change the name AOL-Time Warner back to the original Time Warner Inc. In subsequent years, AOL would prove to be a troubling asset, never fulfilling its once-heralded promise.[20] In January 2010, Gerald Levin acknowledged his past mistakes. "I was the CEO. I was in charge. I'm really very sorry about the pain and suffering and loss that was caused. . . . I take responsibility."[21]

Risk-averse Culture

Successful businesses with an established customer base find it hard to change. There is a clear pattern of success that translates into customers, clients, predictable revenue, and public awareness for the work that has been accomplished to date. The adage "why mess with a winning formula" slowly becomes the corporate norm. There are no guarantees of success when it comes to new project ventures. The difficulty, of course, is that playing it safe presents its own unique hazards. Even well-managed companies can suddenly find themselves outflanked by changing market conditions and advancing new technologies. At the same time, forward-thinking companies recognize the need to develop new business opportunities.

RadioShack. *RadioShack* is a set of U.S. electronics stores founded in 1921 by two London-born brothers, Theodore and Milton Deutschmann. The brothers set up shop in Boston, and their audience and appeal was ham radio enthusiasts. They chose the name *RadioShack,* a colloquial reference to a small section of a ship that houses onboard radio equipment. By 1962, the company had become a leading distributor of electronics equipment in the northeast United States. The next year, Texas-based Charles Tandy, who ran a chain of leather stores, bought the company for about $300,000. He moved the company to Fort Worth, Texas. Over the next four decades, RadioShack carved out a unique niche in retailing by appealing to hobbyists and consumers wanting to purchase low-cost, easy-to-find electronics parts. RadioShack stores tended to be small, managed by a knowledgeable staff, and were found everywhere throughout the United States.[22]

RadioShack grew from 100 stores in 1966 to well over 7,000 in 2006. They could be found in such countries as Australia, Belgium, Canada, China, France,

(Continued)

(Continued)

Malaysia, Mexico, and the UK. A typical RadioShack location housed a variety of equipment including batteries, coaxial cables, cordless soldering irons, portable CD players, small stereo speakers, and the like. In time, RadioShack would be the go-to place for gadgets including CB radios during the 1970s. The company designed and manufactured the TRS-80 computer; one of the first prototype PCs ever built. RadioShack also became the place where computer enthusiasts modified their own computer.

During the decade of the 1990s, RadioShack began to sell cell phones and serve as a retail distributor for some of the emerging cell phone carriers. RadioShack's early success with wireless phones didn't last. If ever there was a company that fell victim to changing market conditions: RadioShack. In time, all the major cell phone carriers began to operate their own retail locations. The cell phone (and later smartphone technology) would eventually have a downward cascading effect on other parts of RadioShack's business, including answering machines, GPS, camcorders, and so forth. Rather than staking a claim in either computers and/or cell phones, RadioShack sold its cell phone manufacturing business and phased out its computer business in 1993. The field of consumer electronics retail sales was also changing. RadioShack faced stiff competition by several major box store retailers for the time, including Best Buy, Circuit City, Office Depot, and Staples, which carried similar types of electronic parts equipment.[23] And from a consumer's perspective, the stores for many years appeared outdated and expensive.

Last, RadioShack fell victim to the devastating effects of EC. Companies like Amazon.com and dedicated computer companies such as Dell, Apple, and HP made RadioShack's brick-and-mortar approach both expensive and redundant. RadioShack could have been at the center of the communications revolution.

Disruptive Technology

A disruptive technology is the quintessential game changer. *Disruptive technologies*, by their very definition, set into motion a whole host of intended and unintended consequences on the marketplace. One of the accompanying rules of creative destruction is that once a technology or service has been introduced, there is no going backward. Authors Collins and Porras (1994) make the argument that highly successful companies are those that are willing to experiment and not rest on their past success. Over time, tastes, preference, and technology change. Innovative companies keep abreast of such changes, anticipate them, and make the necessary adjustments in strategy and new product development.[24] The question may be asked: If strategic adjustment and innovation are such basic elements, why then don't more companies succeed at it? Researcher Clayton Christensen (1997) makes the argument that even the best managed companies are susceptible to innovation failure.[25] In fact, past success can sometimes become the very root cause of innovation failure going forward. Ironically, the decisions that lead to failure are made by executives who work for companies widely regarded as the best in their field.

The Innovator's Dilemma

Christensen (1997) posits what he calls the "innovator's dilemma," namely, that a company's very strengths (i.e., successful product line and realizing consistent profits) now become barriers to change and the agents of a company's potential decline.[26] Successful companies are highly committed to serving their existing customers and are often unable to take apart a thriving business in favor of advancing unfamiliar and unproven new technology. In contrast, advancing new technologies and services requires expensive retooling and whose ultimate success is hard to predict. Such companies lose because they fail to invest in new product development and/or because they fail to notice small, niche players who enter the market and are prepared to offer customers alternative solutions at better value. The anticipated profit margins in developing a future market niche can be hard to justify given the high cost of entry, not to mention the possible destabilization of an otherwise highly successful business. Therein lies the innovator's dilemma.

The Innovator's Dilemma and Product Life Cycle

Product life cycle theory was first proposed by Raymond Vernon (1966) and explains the evolution of a product's development from the point of its introduction into the marketplace to its final stages of decline. The theory of product life cycle has evolved over the years and has come to include a series of four stages, including: 1) Introduction, 2) Growth, 3) Maturity, and 4) Decline.[27] After a product or service is launched, it goes through the various stages of a life cycle and reaches a natural decline point. Part of the innovator's dilemma is to know when in the course of the product life cycle to innovate. (See Figure 5.1.) The decision to innovate represents a strategic choice to discontinue (or phase out) a mature product in favor of an untested one. The decision to innovate has to occur well before the product hits its decline phase to allow sufficient time for development. This means that the critical decision occurs during the very time when the product is mature and realizing its

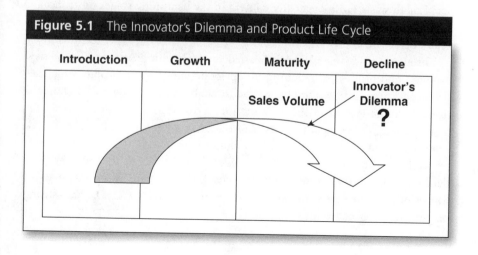

Figure 5.1 The Innovator's Dilemma and Product Life Cycle

highest profits. The downside risk is that the manufacturer may get it wrong and thereby destabilize an otherwise highly successful product line.[28]

The history of media and telecommunications is replete with examples of companies faced with the innovator's dilemma. It is worth noting that many companies that are highly regarded as innovative can momentarily lose their innovative edge only to rebound at a later time (i.e., IBM, Disney, Apple, Nintendo, etc.). In sum, few companies are able to remain consistently innovative across time.

The Eastman Kodak Company

The Eastman Kodak Company was a pioneering company in the field of photography. The company was founded by George Eastman in 1889 and is headquartered in Rochester, New York. Kodak is best known for a wide range of photographic and imaging equipment. Throughout most of the 20th century, Kodak was singularly the most important company in the production and sale of film equipment. The company's visibility and dominance was evidenced by the phrase "Kodak moment," which became a popular way to describe a personal event worthy of being recorded for posterity.[29] On January 19, 2012, the 131-year-old company filed for bankruptcy. It was several years in the making, but Kodak steadily faltered beneath the wave of advancing digital media technology.[30]

The Start of Kodak

Founded in 1880 by George Eastman, Kodak became one of America's most recognized brand names, helping to establish the market for film and instamatic cameras, which the company dominated for the better part of the 20th century. Eastman did not invent photography. He did, however, make it accessible to the public at large. As Genzlinger (2000) points out, "Before Eastman, photography was like portrait painting. Subjects would sit prim and still while a photographer wielding a bulky camera, glass plates and assorted chemicals caught the moment."[31] Eastman's work led to the creation of the Kodak camera. The Kodak was a fairly expensive camera in the beginning stages of its design. It would eventually give way to the Brownie family camera designed by Kodak's Frank Brownell.

Throughout the years, Kodak has led the way with an abundance of new products and processes, including the introduction of Kodachrome, which set the stage for color photographs. Kodachrome became the color film standard throughout the 1950s and 1960s. In the 1960s, Kodak also introduced the instamatic camera. The company achieved $1 billion in sales in 1962. By 1976, Kodak captured the majority of the U.S. film and camera market (90 and 85 percent, respectively). Kodak's photofinishing process quickly became the industry standard for quality.[32] As a result, a major focus of the company was on its massive film-making plant. Traditionally, most of the company's CEOs had strong manufacturing backgrounds.

The External Challenges: Rivalry With Fujifilm

Starting in the 1970s, Kodak was faced with a number of foreign competitors, most notably, Fujifilm of Japan, which undercut Kodak's prices. In the beginning, Kodak did not take the competitive threat seriously. That complacency proved costly when the company passed on the opportunity to become the official film sponsor of the 1984 Summer Olympics in Los Angeles, California. That decision gave Fuji high visibility, sponsorship rights, and a permanent foothold in the U.S. film market. Soon thereafter, Fuji opened up a film plant in the United States, cut prices, and aggressively marketed its film product. Fuji increased its U.S. market share by more than 20 percent by the late 1990s. At the same time, Kodak was unsuccessful in penetrating the Japanese market, then considered the second-largest market for film and paper. Kodak's financial results for fiscal year 1997 showed that corporate revenues dropped more than 10 percent from $15.9 billion to $14.3 billion, including a simultaneous drop in market share. Kodak was rightly criticized for being slow to react and for underestimating its rivals.[33]

Kodak was also at odds with its chief camera rival, the Polaroid Corporation. In October 1990, Kodak found itself on the losing end of the largest patent infringement case of its kind. The company was forced to pay Polaroid $909.4 million for infringing on seven of Polaroid's instant photography patents. That decision forced Kodak out of the instant photography business.[34]

The Shift to Digital Cameras

As early as 1981, Kodak recognized that a shift toward digital camera technology was underway. That year, Sony Corporation announced the launch of a new digital camera called Mavica. Kodak had some prior experience with digital cameras, having developed one of the early prototype designs in 1975. Digital photography has many advantages over traditional film. Digital photos are convenient and allow the user to see the results instantly. Digital photos don't require the costs associated with film and development time. Digital cameras enable the user to take multiple shots at no additional cost. They can be stored on a variety of digital devices, including PCs, smartphones, and tablets as well as being uploaded onto the Internet. In sum, the transition to digital media is not just about a single product but rather about significant changes to communication display and storage processes.[35]

Throughout the decade of the 1980s, Kodak introduced more than 50 products that were tied to digital photography and the storage of images. Yet the company was unable to successfully commercialize them. At the same time, Kodak was fully committed to traditional film technology and processing. By the 1990s, the onset of digital photography started to erode the demand for conventional film and processing, thereby putting a squeeze on Kodak's business. Digital photography proved to be the ultimate disruptive technology. It was only a matter of time before traditional film processing would become obsolete.

Executive Leadership Challenges

Between 1983 and 1993, Kodak underwent seven organizational restructurings. In 1993, Kay Whitmore (a Kodak insider) stepped down as CEO and was succeeded by George Fisher. Fisher was recruited from Motorola, where he had successfully revitalized that company. As Kodak's newly appointed CEO, Fisher began steering the company to embrace a digital future. Fisher clearly recognized that the organizational culture at Kodak had to change. The importance of digital media and communication had to be understood and embraced at all levels of the organization. The challenge, however, would prove formidable. While Kodak recognized the importance of digital media to its future, company executives could not imagine a world without traditional film.[36] Specifically, they wanted to engage the process in its own way while staying within the confines of its Rochester, New York, headquarters. This was ultimately a recipe for failure. The creativity demands for producing digital media are so vastly different than traditional photography. Kodak's leadership was not prepared to impose the kind of disruptive changes on the organization that would have been required.[37]

Kodak eventually settled on a combination strategy, whereby they created a separate digital and applied imaging division while still preserving its core capabilities in traditional film. By 1993, Kodak had spent $5 billion to research and develop digital cameras and imaging equipment. While Kodak had the right intentions, the company's middle management resisted the move toward digital photography. At issue were the high costs associated with developing new production facilities as well as a genuine concern that such changes might result in a loss of jobs. In the meantime, Kodak continued to miss critical target dates and experienced multiple setbacks in R&D.

Business Reinvention

The year 2001 proved to be an important cutover point. The company experienced a significant drop in film sales. CEO Daniel Carp (Fisher's successor) continued the process of moving the company into digital cameras. They began by introducing the EasyShare family of digital cameras. By 2005, Kodak became the number one digital camera manufacturer in the United States, with sales having risen 40 percent to $5.7 billion. Their success was short-lived. Despite an impressive start, Kodak's digital camera line became quickly copied by a host of Asian competitors that could produce equivalent cameras at lower cost. Digital cameras soon proved to be a low-profit margin item. To stay competitive, Kodak found itself losing money on every digital camera sold.[38]

Consumer electronics companies like Sony, Panasonic, and Canon could afford to be patient and lose money on select line items because they had hundreds of other products to offset potential losses. This was not so for Kodak, which had a limited product line. The final coup de grace came with the onset of cell phones equipped with cameras. In one sense, the cell phone camera represents the dumbing down of picture taking as the quality is not as good as a camera. That said, a younger generation of users are willing to sacrifice picture quality for convenience. Today, cameras have become a standard feature on all smartphone devices.

Adjusting to Market Realities and Bankruptcy

By 2011, Kodak's financial reserves had reached a critical stage. The company had $5.1 billion in assets and nearly $6.8 billion in debts. Its biggest group of unsecured creditors was bondholders represented by the Bank of New York Mellon, who were owed $658 million. Kodak filed for Chapter 11 protection in January 2012. The company closed thirteen manufacturing plants and 130 processing labs while reducing their workforce by 47,000 employees.[39] In a final effort to stabilize their finances, Kodak hired asset management firm Lazard Ltd. to sell 1,100 of its digital imaging patents. This proved too little too late. Kodak failed to generate enough potential interest, driven in part by fears of the company's deteriorating financial health. In the end, George Fisher was unable to transform Kodak into a high-tech growth company. Fisher's belief in the future of digital communication lacked urgency and did not permeate all levels of the organization. Nor were his successors Daniel Carp (2000–2005) and Antonio Pérez (2005–2012) any more successful. The price of Kodak shares decreased from around $25 in 2005 to less than $1 by September 30, 2011. It was emblematic of the fall of a once-great American company.[40]

Blockbuster

Blockbuster Inc. is an American-based DVD and video game rental service. Blockbuster was founded by David Cook, who used his experience with managing large database networks as the foundation for Blockbuster's retail distribution model. At its peak in 2009, Blockbuster had an estimated 7,100 retail stores in the United States with additional locations in seventeen countries worldwide. Blockbuster employed more than 60,000 employees in the United States and worldwide. The company is headquartered in McKinney, Texas. The Blockbuster business model would eventually prove unsustainable given the Internet and the rise of EC video rental services like Netflix. Blockbuster would sustain significant revenue losses in later years. The company filed for bankruptcy just shy of its twenty-fifth anniversary on September 22, 2010.[41] In April 2011, Blockbuster was acquired by satellite television service provider Dish Network at an auction price of $233 million and the assumption of $87 million in liabilities and other obligations.

The Start of Blockbuster Video

The first Blockbuster store opened October 1985 in Dallas, Texas. Shortly thereafter, company founder David Cook opened several additional stores and later built a $6 million warehouse in Garland, Texas, that could service them all. The key to Blockbuster's early success was the convenience and ease of renting film entertainment for consumer use. Another important factor to Blockbuster's early success was their timely access to recently released feature films combined with films on VHS geared to the neighborhood demographics of its local retail outlets. In 1987, Waste Management President Wayne Huizenga and his business partner John Melk paid Cook $18 million for a controlling interest in the new, upstart company. Together, they used the lessons from their experience with Waste Management to build Blockbuster into a global enterprise. Huizenga took the company public in 1989 and aggressively transformed it from a $7 million business with nineteen stores to a $4 billion global enterprise with more than 3,700 stores in eleven countries.[42]

Viacom Acquires Blockbuster Video

Despite Blockbuster's success, Huizenga felt that it was only a matter of time before technology advancements would directly challenge Blockbuster's brick-and-mortar approach. Blockbuster was the right technology for the time. It was a twenty-year interim technology that provided a practical solution in meeting the needs for home television viewing. As early as 1994, Wayne Huizenga understood the limitations of Blockbuster's business model and strategy. He sold the company to Viacom. His concerns were shared by any number of observers throughout the industry. On the immediate horizon was cable television and its promise of video-on-demand service. Less obvious was the future of EC and the disruptive technologies made possible by the Internet. One of those disruptive technologies would take the form of a unique business process innovation and a company called Netflix.

Netflix. Netflix is an online, subscription-based DVD rental service. Netflix was founded by Reed Hastings in 1997 during the emergent days of EC when companies like Amazon and Dell Computers were starting to gain prominence.[43] Netflix offers its customers a great value proposition, namely, two to three DVDs per week (depending on the service plan) for a fixed monthly price. In practical terms, Netflix provides greater value to the consumer when compared to a traditional video rental store, which charges by the individual DVD rental unit. Second, Netflix utilizes the power of the Internet to promote a proprietary software recommendation system (see Chapter 4). A common complaint with Blockbuster was the experience of renting an unfamiliar movie and being dissatisfied with the viewing experience later on. The Netflix software recommendation system, on the other hand, makes suggestions of other films that the consumer might like based on past selections and a brief evaluation that the subscriber is asked to fill out. Netflix proved to be the ultimate game changer by transforming the DVD rental business through the use of business process innovation and its EC technology platform.[44]

Blockbuster Fails to React

Blockbuster had more than sufficient time to react to the competition and revise its business model. As early as 2001, Blockbuster was in a position to strategically reposition itself. The company could have possibly acquired Netflix or modified its strategy by duplicating many of the same EC efficiencies that Netflix's business model had already demonstrated. Alternatively, it could have opened kiosks (i.e., similar to RedBox) and begun closing stores. This would have reduced capital costs and improved convenience.[45]

Instead, Blockbuster chose to ignore the competitive threat posed by Netflix. They were doing quite well for the moment and didn't want to destabilize an otherwise successful business enterprise (i.e., the innovator's dilemma). In practical terms, Netflix was allowed to go unchallenged for six years before Blockbuster launched their own EC service in 2004. By then, Netflix had brand recognition, 3 million customers, and a strong business momentum.[46] In a bid to slow the competition, Blockbuster introduced a flat monthly fee and later eliminated late fees as well. Subscriptions did increase but not enough to offset the $300 million loss the company absorbed by eliminating late fees. The combined strategy wound up costing the company an estimated $400 million.[47] Critics point to the fact that Blockbuster CEO John Antioco should have taken the Netflix threat more seriously and acted sooner. Blockbuster's business complacency coupled with a failure to appreciate the power of EC would prove costly in securing the company's long-term future.

Blockbuster's Executive Leadership and Activist Board

In 2004, Viacom (which still owned 80 percent of the company) chose to sell its stake in Blockbuster and took a $1.3 billion charge to reflect the declining value of the business. Later that same year, a second major change occurred that affected the company's organizational dynamics when activist investor Carl Icahn bought nearly $10 million shares of Blockbuster stock. Shortly thereafter, Icahn began to publicly criticize Antioco by giving interviews to the press and writing letters to shareholders. He was critical of Antioco for spending too much money on developing its online business as well as his decision to eliminate late fees. Icahn proceeded to launch a proxy fight.

For Antioco and his management team, a set of contentious directors meant having to constantly justify and explain each business decision. To the public, Blockbuster's evolving business strategy seemed disjointed, evidenced by an inconsistent policy involving late fees. The problem was made worse by the fact that Antioco and the company's board of directors were at serious odds with one another. Icahn routinely battled with Antioco about how to revive the company. Antioco wanted to keep the company independent, while Icahn wanted to sell it to a private equity firm.[48]

In December 2006, the situation came to a head over executive compensation. The board decided to significantly reduce Antioco's bonus compensation. Antioco chose to negotiate a severance deal with Blockbuster rather than accept the reduced bonus amount. Set against the backdrop of some highly intense corporate infighting, the board approved the hiring of Jim Keyes, who was the former head of 7-Eleven. He had a difficult assignment that included quelling the unrest at Blockbuster while trying to develop a strategy for the future. Unfortunately, the hiring of Jim Keyes was too little too late. By now, it was clear to everyone that Blockbuster was a company in trouble. In the end, Blockbuster video failed because it was unable to adapt to the technical realities of EC.[49] It was too slow in reacting to the competitive challenges posed by Netflix and Redbox. This, in combination with a highly contentious board of directors, proved to be a toxic mixture. By January 2014, all of Blockbuster's remaining stores were closed.

The Sony Corporation

The Challenges of Business Reinvention

The Sony Corporation is a leading TNMC in the production and sale of consumer electronics, music, film entertainment, and video game technology. Throughout its more than sixty-year history, the Sony name has been synonymous with great innovation. Words like *Walkman, compact disk,* and *Playstation* have become part of the global lexicon of terms to describe consumer electronics. Such products were truly innovative from a planning and design standpoint. They have contributed to a profound change in consumer lifestyle.[50] Starting in 2002, Sony saw the beginning of a decade-long decline in major product development. In time, the company found itself less willing to experiment and engage in new product innovation, something that was once a signature feature of the Sony name and brand. Between 2008 and 2011, Sony experienced four straight years of revenue decline.[51] Sony's decline was the result of a number of self-inflicted wounds. What went wrong is a story of missed business opportunities, repeated failures to take necessary risks, and disastrous corporate infighting. This inability to develop timely, innovative products has made Sony's day-to-day business environment punishingly difficult. Today, Sony is being challenged on a number of technology fronts by a host of international rivals that include South Korea's Samsung and LG as well as America's Apple and Microsoft, to name only a few.

Executive Leadership Failures

Some of Sony's current business challenges can be traced back to the leadership of Nobuyuki Idei, who introduced an altogether new management philosophy. Under Idei's tenure, Sony underwent a corporate reorganization that was built on what the company called its five pillars of operation. This included: 1) Electronics, 2) Entertainment, 3) Financial services, 4) Game, and 5) Internet services. The objective was to transfer day-to-day management responsibility from Sony's Tokyo headquarters to the company's foreign operations. The organizational model was described as "integrated/decentralized management."[52] At the time, Sony officials believed that to be more globally competitive, the company had to promote greater responsibility and autonomy in the field. The Sony manager was expected to rely less on corporate headquarters and display more individual initiative. In time, the integrated/decentralized management approach would set into motion a number of unintended consequences. One such consequence was that individual companies became increasingly more risk averse. They came to rely on dependable products that could be tapped for quick, reliable profits. Instead of planning for the next generation in product design, there was a strong tendency toward legacy products (i.e., products with a proven track record).

One of Sony's long-standing problems is the fact that senior management (past and present) has had trouble wielding authority over the company's many subsidiaries and divisions. The integrated and decentralized management approach made it difficult for CEO Idei and his senior administrative staff to interfere with individual company decisions, especially when they were making money. As an example, Sony's audio and video divisions were highly profitable during the beginning years of the 21st century. Both divisions felt no pressing need to develop digital technology.[53] The TV business began responding only after it began suffering huge losses in 2003. Suddenly, the company found itself in catch-up mode rather than being the industry leader that it should have been. A related problem has to do with the effective collaboration and sharing of information among divisions and departments. Executives complain privately of recalcitrant managers who refuse to share information or work with other divisions. Sony's top management, both publicly and privately, acknowledges that Sony remains dominated by proud, territorial engineers who often shun cooperation. The Japanese refer to it as *tatewari*. For many such engineers, ceding intellectual territory and cost cutting are the enemies of creativity.

Streamlining Business Operations

Nobuyuki Idei also made the controversial decision to streamline and downsize the company. A number of Sony executives and engineers were given early retirement options. There was a substantial brain drain of veteran and middle-aged engineers and technicians. Several played critical roles in helping to advance Sony's past success. Many found employment elsewhere, specifically South Korea, working for companies that would one day become some of Sony's most challenging competitors. As one observer wryly noted, "Korea and Taiwan immediately welcomed the exiting Sony techies with open arms. It was better than industrial espionage—Samsung could openly buy the technology that Sony had developed simply by rehiring their best and brightest."[54]

The loss of intellectual capital combined with low-cost foreign production have taken a major financial toll. In April 2005, Sony appointed Welch-born Howard Stringer, then president of Sony Corporation of America, to the position of chairman and CEO. It was a first for Sony given the fact that Stringer was not Japanese born or spoke the language for that matter. At his first news conference, Stringer made it known that he would "accelerate cross-company collaboration, thereby revitalizing the company and promoting creativity." Despite his best effort, Stringer was unable to tear down many of the existing business fiefdoms at Sony. In February 2012, Stringer was replaced by Kazuo Hirai, head of consumer products. Hirai's most immediate task is the need for better cooperation among the company's various operating divisions for the purpose of harnessing natural synergies and creating a more unified information and entertainment experience for the user.

Risk-averse Culture

The loss of many of Sony's top engineers in 2000 and 2001 left behind a younger group of engineers and technicians who were more risk averse and less willing to experiment. Sony was engaged in a default strategy, whereby instead of playing to win, it was trying not to lose.[55] Consider, for example, the impact that the Apple iPod had on the Sony Walkman portable music player. As noted earlier, the Walkman created an entirely new market for portable music systems. By combining the features of mobility and privacy, the Walkman contributed to a major change in consumer lifestyle. But even a company as respected as Sony was not invulnerable to the problems associated with disruptive technology. As illegal music downloads exploded in popularity in the late 1990s, Sony, like the rest of the music industry, was unable or unwilling to adapt to the changing technology environment. With its catalog of music and foundation in electronics, Sony had the tools to create a version of the iPod long before Apple introduced it in 2001. Yet Sony was not prepared to move quickly enough and adjust strategy to preserve market leadership in the area of portable music. Instead, Sony's audio division was fully committed to its own proprietary (now defunct) MiniDisc technology. Even when the threat of MP3 design was clear and obvious, Sony responded with an improved version of MiniDisc players that ultimately failed in the end.[56]

In 2004, the Apple iPod in combination with the iTunes music store transformed the music industry by creating the first sustainable music downloading business model of its kind. By the time Sony's music and hardware divisions were forced to cooperate, that effort proved too little too late. Sony's Connect online store (the company's answer to the Apple iTunes music store) was discontinued after three years. During the next five years, Sony lost an estimated 65 percent of the portable music market.

Despite having been a pioneer in television set design (including Sony's early prototype work in high-definition TV), the world's population was now buying LCD plasma TVs from South Korea-based Samsung and LG. They proved to be less expensive and well designed, and the difference in quality was not significant. Samsung surpassed Sony in terms of market capitalization. Samsung became a master of business process innovation. They fully embraced the principles of fast and efficient low-cost television manufacturing.[57] One by one, every major product category where Sony was once dominant—from portable music players (i.e., Sony Walkman) to music recording devices (the CD) to video game systems (i.e., Sony Playstation)—has felt the punishing effects of disruptive, changing technology as well as unrelenting competitive challengers.

Discussion

The warning signs of a troubled business often exist for long periods of time before they reach a crisis stage and result in climactic business failure. Collins (2009) refers to this as "the silent creep of impending doom."[58] The business failures at both Kodak and Blockbuster share one thing in common. Each failed to recognize the early warning signs of advancing technological change.

Kodak

Kodak was paralyzed by an organizational culture that was highly resistant to change. While Kodak had the right intentions, the company was not prepared to make the costly changes needed to fully embrace the business of digital media and IT. As Lucas and Goh (2009) point out that when a business is confronted with a highly disruptive technology, senior management has to be a catalyst for change at all levels of the organization.[59] Although Kodak recognized the external threats, the company's organizational culture prevented them from moving forward. Kanter (2012) suggests that Kodak was very Rochester centric and never really developed an innovation presence in other parts of the world that were creating leading-edge media technologies. Instead, Kodak adhered to a kind of old-line manufacturing mentality.[60] They were in the film business plain and simple. It was, after all, what made them profitable in the past.

Blockbuster

In retrospect, it seems clear that the practice of driving to a store to rent a movie was a business process destined to fail as the Internet became more of a factor in the world of EC. For years, business analysts and professional observers have recognized that Blockbuster was a flawed business model that would be difficult to sustain in the wake of advancing technology. As early as 1994, Wayne Huizenga understood the limitations of a brick-and-mortar approach when he sold Blockbuster to Viacom Inc. Ten year later, Viacom CEO Sumner Redstone came to same conclusion when he sold his 80 percent stake in the company as well. Both Huizenga and Redstone operated at a time when the conventional wisdom and smart money was on cable television and its highly touted video-on-demand service. Despite many attempts, video-on-demand television has never realized its full potential.[61] It too failed. The Internet, however, is an entirely different story. For Blockbuster, disruption came in the form of an EC company called Netflix. The situation at Blockbuster was further complicated because of failures in executive leadership coupled with a highly contentious board of directors. The standoff between CEO John Antioco and the company's board resulted in business strategy gridlock and a public loss of confidence in the company's future.

Sony

From the Sony Trinitron TV set to the Playstation video game system, Sony possessed an astonishing ability to meet the next technical challenge: a brighter TV set with increased resolution, a more versatile CD player with better sound capability, an integrated camcorder, and the list goes on. Sony could do it better and faster than any of its nearest competitors. All this changed with the rapid rise of Apple and Samsung at the start of the 21st century. Apple took a page out of Sony's playbook by redefining the principle of mobility in a whole new way, allowing listeners to customize their music playlists and to place an entire collection of songs onto a simple device that could fit into one's coat pocket.

Apple let music lovers browse and download a song or album in a fraction of the time it had previously taken to record music onto a Sony Walkman tape or CD. Sony missed the MP3 revolution and was caught flat-footed. It was adhering to an old industrial model where the emphasis was on stand-alone products sold in great volume.[62]

Sony was challenged in the area of television manufacturing as well. Samsung proved to be the organizational master in fast and efficient (almost military-like) production. Samsung focused on becoming a superior manufacturer. The company learned how to manage and work through the highly volatile world of commoditized products. In contrast, Sony's organization steadily became more bureaucratic over time, and its business units tended to operate as independent silos, which made strategic planning and resource allocation very inefficient. Sony's current challenges are the result of past organizational failures to make everyone accountable to the larger Sony mission.

The Lessons of Business History

The lessons of business history have taught us that there is no such thing as a static market. This is especially true in the field of media and telecommunications where today's tech superstar can quickly become yesterday's news, supplanted by the next communication start-up with a good idea; think AOL, AT&T long distance telephone service, BlackBerry, and RadioShack, to name only a few. The resulting effects of creative destruction can be significant, including the failure to preserve market leadership, the discontinuation of a once highly successful product, and ultimately business failure itself. Both Eastman Kodak and Blockbuster were highly successful companies that once dominated their respective areas of specialty. Their previous strengths and one-time success ultimately laid the groundwork for their eventual decline. Each was susceptible to the innovator's dilemma. Both companies knew they were in trouble but were unable to make the necessary adjustments in business strategy to prevent business failure. In the end, the requirements for change proved too formidable an obstacle.[63]

Sony's present situation is very different from the other two companies. In contrast to Kodak and Blockbuster, Sony is not reliant on a single product, technology, or service category—quite the opposite. Sony is a highly diverse media company whose product categories include consumer electronics, music, film, and insurance. The best companies find ways to reinvent themselves despite serious setbacks. Sony is well positioned to do the same. In looking to the future, Sony will need to sharpen its focus by being excellent at a few things. The company will have to cultivate a new management approach, whereby all departments (and senior executives) are answerable to the larger corporate mission. CEO Kazuo Hirai wants to rationalize the electronic divisions and unify the company under his "One Sony" plan. The one thread that ties all of it together is television. Despite previous losses, Sony remains fully committed to the future of television and video. Sony, like many at-risk companies before them, will eventually make their way forward.[64]

Endnotes

1. Richard Gershon, "Innovation Failure: A Case Study Analysis of Eastman Kodak and Blockbuster Video," in *Media Management and Economics Research in a Transmedia Environment,* ed. A. Albarran (New York: Routledge, 2013), 46–68.

2. Richard Gershon, "The Sony Corporation: Market Leadership, Innovation Failure and the Challenges of Business Reinvention," in *Handbook in East Asia Entrepreneurship,* eds. Fu Lai Yu and Ho-Don Yan (London, UK: Routledge, 2014), 225–239.

3. Jim Collins, *How the Mighty Fall* (New York: Harper Collins, 2009).

4. Michael Tushman and Charles O'Reilly, *Winning Through Innovation* (Boston, MA: Harvard Business School Press, 1997).

5. Jim Collins, *Good to Great* (New York: Harper Collins, 2001), 16.

6. Nicholas Negroponte, "Incrementalism is Innovation's Worst Enemy," *Wired,* April 1995, 188.

7. "Inside the Fall of BlackBerry: How the Smartphone Inventor Failed to Adapt," *The Globe and Mail,* last modified November 6, 2013, http://www.theglobeandmail.com/report-on-business/the-inside-story-of-why-blackberry-is-failing/article14563602/?page=all

8. "A Boggle of BlackBerrys," *New York Times,* last modified December 16, 2011, http://www.nytimes.com/2011/12/17/technology/rim-stock-hits-eight-year-low.html

9. Chris Martin, "BlackBerry's 5 Bad Calls That Doom the Company," *TechHive,* last modified August 17, 2013, http://www.techhive.com/article/2046890/blackberrys-5-bad-calls-that-doom-the-company.html

10. Juliette Garside, "Shareholders Put Pressure on BlackBerry Chiefs to Sell Up," *The Guardian,* last modified October 12, 2011, http://www.theguardian.com/technology/2011/oct/12/blackberry-chiefs-under-pressure

11. E. Schein, "The Role of the Founder in Creating Organizational Culture," *Organizational Dynamics* 11 (1983): 13–28.

12. J. Pilotta, T. Widman, and S. Jasko, "Meaning and Action in the Organizational Setting: An Interpretive Approach," in *Communication Yearbook 12* (New York: Sage, 1988), 310–334.

13. Gary Hamel, "The What, Why and How of Management Innovation," *Harvard Business Review* (February 2006): 72–87.

14. Leslie Cauley, *End of the Line: The Rise and Fall of AT&T* (New York: Free Press, 2005), 116–117.

15. Collins, *Good to Great.*

16. Richard Gershon, *Media, Telecommunications and Business Strategy,* 2nd ed. (New York: Routledge, 2013).

17. Richard Gershon and Abubakar Alhassan, "AOL Time Warner & WorldCom: Corporate Governance and the Diffusion of Authority" (presentation, Sixth World Media Economics Conference, Montreal, Canada, May 2004).

18. "AOL, You've Got Misery," *Business Week,* Apr. 8, 2002, 58–59.

19. D. Lieberman, "For Better or Worse, Levin Traveled a Rock Road," *USA Today,* May 20, 2002, 2B.

20. Richard Gershon, "The Deregulation Paradox: Whatever Happened to Media Business Accountability?" (presentation, special conference on *Value Oriented Media Management. Decision-making between Profit and Responsibility,* Catholic University, Eichstätt, Germany, November 2012).

21. "Gerald Levin Apologizes for AOL-Time Warner Merger," *The Hollywood Reporter,* Jan. 4, 2010, http://www.hollywoodreporter.com/news/gerald-levin-apologizes-aol-tw-19082

22. Joshua Brustein, "Inside RadioShack's Collapse," *Bloomberg Businessweek,* Feb. 15, 2015, 54–59.

23. Steven Solomon, "A History of Misses for RadioShack," *New York Times,* Sept. 16, 2014, http://dealbook.nytimes.com/2014/09/16/for-radioshack-a-history-of-misses/?_r=0

24. Jim Collins and Jerry Porras, *Built to Last* (New York: Harper Collins, 1994).

25. Clayton Christensen, *The Innovator's Dilemma* (Boston, MA: Harvard Business School Press, 1997).

26. Ibid.

27. Raymond Vernon, "International Investment and International Trade in the Product Cycle," *Quarterly Journal of Economics* 80, no. 2 (1966): 190–207.

28. Richard Gershon, "Media Innovation: Three Strategic Approaches to Business Transformation" (presentation, Sixty-first International Communication Association [ICA] Conference, Boston, Massachusetts, May 29, 2011).

29. Richard Gershon, "Eastman Kodak, Blockbuster Video and Creative Destruction: The Rise and Fall of Two Great Iconic Companies" (presentation, The International Association for Media and Communication Research Conference, Dublin, Ireland, June 28, 2013).

30. M. DeLaMerced, "Eastman Kodak Files for Bankruptcy," *New York Times,* Jan. 19, 2012, http://dealbook.nytimes.com/2012/01/19/eastman-kodak-files-for-bankruptcy/?_r=0

31. N. Genzlinger, "Television Review: He Changed Photography and Transformed Society," *New York Times,* May 22, 2000, http://www.nytimes.com/2000/05/22/arts/television-review-he-changed-photography-and-transformed-society.html

32. "Kodak's Legacy," *New York Times,* Jan. 19, 2012, http://www.nytimes.com/interactive/2012/01/19/business/dealbook/dbgfx-kodaks-legacy.html?_r=0

33. T. Finnerty, *Kodak v. Fuji: The Battle for Global Market Share* (unpublished report, New York, Pace University—Lubin School of Business, 2000).

34. "Kodak's Legacy."

35. Yue-Ling Wong, *Digital Media Primer* (Upper Saddle River, NJ: Pearson Prentice-Hall, 2009).

36. Giovanni Gavetti, Rebecca Henderson, and Simona Giorgi, *Kodak and the Digital Revolution* (Cambridge, MA: Harvard Business School Press, 2005).

37. Alecia Swasy, *Changing Focus: Kodak and the Battle to Save a Great American Company* (New York: Times Business—Random House, 1997).

38. Henry Lucas and Jie Mein Goh, "Disruptive Technology: How Kodak Missed the Digital Photography Revolution," *Journal of Strategic Information Systems* 18 (2009): 46–55.

39. DeLaMerced, "Eastman Kodak Files for Bankruptcy."

40. Gershon, "Innovation Failure."

41. Richard Gershon, "Innovation Failure: A Case Study Analysis of Eastman Kodak and Blockbuster Video," *Research Symposium: Media Management and Economics Research in a Transmedia Environment* (presentation, Fifty-seventh Annual Broadcast Education Association Conference, Las Vegas, Nevada, April 2012).

42. Gail DeGeorge, *The Making of a Blockbuster: How Wayne Huizenga Built a Sports and Entertainment Empire from Trash, Grit, and Videotape* (New York: John Wiley, 1996).

43. W. Shih, S. Kaufman, and D. Spinola, "Netflix," in *Harvard Business School Case Study Series* (9–607–138) (Cambridge, MA: Harvard Business School, 2007), 1–15.

44. Gershon, "Innovation Failure."

45. M. Woloszynowicz, "Business Lessons from Blockbuster's Failure," *Web 2.0 Development and Business Lessons,* last modified September 22, 2010, http://www.w2lessons .com/2010/09/business-lessons-from-blockbusters.html

46. "How Blockbuster Failed at Failing," *Time,* Oct. 11, 2010, 38–40.

47. J. Poggi, "Blockbuster's Rise and Fall: The Long, Rewinding Road," *The Street,* last modified September 23, 2010, http://www.thestreet.com/story/10867574/1/the-rise-and-fall-of-blockbuster-the-long-rewinding-road.html

48. J. Antioco, "How I Did It? Blockbuster's Former CEO on Sparring with an Activist Shareholder," *Harvard Business Review* (April 2011): 39–44.

49. "How Blockbuster Failed at Failing."

50. Richard Gershon and Tsutomu Kanayama, "The Sony Corporation: A Case Study in Transnational Media Management," *The International Journal on Media Management* 4, no. 2 (2002): 44–56.

51. A. Hartung, "Sayonara Sony: How Industrial, MBA-style Leadership Killed a Once Great Company," *Forbes,* April 4, 2012, http://www.forbes.com/sites/adamhartung/2012/04/20/ sayonara-sony-how-industrial-mba-style-leadership-killed-once-great-company/2

52. Gershon and Kanayama, "The Sony Corporation."

53. Sea-Jin Chang, *Sony vs. Samsung: The Inside Story of the Electronics Giants' Battle for Global Supremacy* (Singapore: John Wiley & Sons, 2008), 117.

54. "How Sony Is Turning into a Ghost in Japan and around the World," *Kotaku,* last modified November 14, 2012, http://kotaku.com/5960411/how-sony-is-turning-into-a-ghost-in-japan-and-around-the-world

55. Ibid.

56. Gershon, "The Sony Corporation."

57. Chang, *Sony vs. Samsung.*

58. Collins, *How the Mighty Fall,* 1.

59. Lucas and Goh, "Disruptive Technology."

60. R. Kanter, "The Last Kodak Moment?" *The Economist,* Jan. 14, 2012, http://www.econo mist.com/node/21542796

61. Gershon, "Innovation Failure."

62. Hartung, "Sayonara Sony."

63. Gershon, "Innovation Failure."

64. Gershon, "The Sony Corporation."

CHAPTER 6

The Diffusion of Innovation Revisited

Product Launch Strategy in the Digital Age

Introduction

In 1962, communication scholar Everett Rogers wrote the first edition of his seminal work *Diffusion of Innovations*. This book is considered a classic in the field of communication and has subsequently gone through multiple editions and updates since that time. *Diffusion of innovation* is a set of theories that seeks to explain how new ideas and technologies diffuse though a specific population.[1] It further considers the rate of adoption, that is, the speed at which some members of a social system accept, reject, or delay an innovative change or practice. Anyone purporting to effect change, whether it be an educator, health-care professional, or marketing specialist needs to understand the rate of adoption process. Whereas the basic principles of diffusion of innovation have stayed the same since Rogers first introduced the concept, what's different today is the speed at which new product launches and introductions are diffused into the public sector. Terms like *diffusion, communication channels,* and *members of a social system* take on a whole new meaning when we consider them in light of today's digital media environment. Digital storytelling is the art of using electronic media and information tools to tell a story. From online newspapers to social media, digital storytelling assumes a wide range of electronic media narratives. It has greatly increased the speed at which a product, service, or idea can be diffused.

Diffusion of Innovation

Rogers (2003) defines *diffusion* as "the process by which an innovation is communicated through certain channels over time among the members of a social system."[2] Rogers's definition contains four elements that are present in the diffusion process. They include: 1) Innovation, 2) Communication channels, 3) Time, and 4) Members of a social system.

An Innovation

Rogers (1995) defines innovation as "an idea, practice or object that is perceived as new by an individual."[3] As noted earlier, there are two kinds of innovation, namely, sustaining technologies versus disruptive technologies. A sustaining technology (or incremental innovation) has to do with product improvement and performance. The goal is to improve on an existing technology or service by adding new and enhanced feature elements.[4] Incremental innovation is important because it provides steady and necessary improvements in product design while demonstrating a commitment to brand enhancement. In contrast, a disruptive (or breakthrough) technology represents an altogether different approach to an existing product design and process. It redefines the playing field by introducing to the marketplace a unique value proposition.[5]

A Communication Channel

A communication channel is the means by which messages are transmitted to an intended audience. Mass media channels like television are more effective in generating information about new product innovations, whereas interpersonal channels of communication are more effective in forming and changing attitudes and thus can directly influence the decision to adopt or reject a new idea. Today, the combination of the Internet and social media has fundamentally changed the method and speed at which information is conveyed to a social group or organization. Social media sites like Facebook, Twitter, and LinkedIn have taken on increasing importance by providing opportunities to comment on the launch of a new product or service.

Over Time

Over time refers to the length of time involved in the innovation/decision process (i.e., how quickly someone adopts the use of a new communications technology). Consider, for example, the rate of adoption between the telephone and the Internet. Following its introduction in 1876, the telephone took five decades to reach 10 percent of all U.S. households. In contrast, the Internet achieved the same penetration rate in only five years. As a general proposition, both technologies are examples of interactive communication and have allowed humankind to surpass the limits of physical space. But the rate of diffusion is markedly different given the more than 120 years that separate the two technologies. Figure 6.1 illustrates the diffusion rate, that is, the number of years it took for major media and telecommunications technologies to achieve 50 percent of all U.S. homes.[6]

Members of a Social System

In principle, *members of a social system* refer to any group of people linked together on the basis of geography, community, work setting, culture, and religion. The social system can vary in size and scope from a small rural village in South Sudan to a level-one hospital trauma center in Cleveland, Ohio. Today, of course, digital media and the power of intelligent networking have expanded the definition of social system to include virtual communities where like-minded people share common interests, whether it be political, social, religious, or professional. A Facebook users group such as the Austin (Texas) Musicians Meetup Group or the Jeep Owners of America (Louisville, Kentucky) are their own social system, albeit digital.

The Innovation/Decision Process

In his research, Rogers (1995) discusses the mental process through which an individual becomes familiar with a new technology or service and later makes the choice to adopt, reject, or delay its use. According to Rogers, there are five stages to the innovation/decision process, including: 1) Knowledge, 2) Persuasion, 3) Decision, 4) Implementation, and 5) Confirmation.[7]

Knowledge

The starting point is knowledge, whereby a person becomes aware of an innovation and related ideas as to how it functions. The source for that information can be

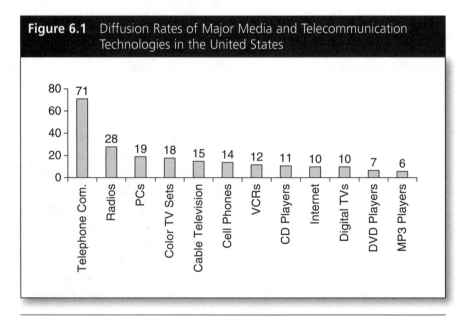

Figure 6.1 Diffusion Rates of Major Media and Telecommunication Technologies in the United States

SOURCES: Consumer Electronics Association and National Cable & Telecommunications Association.

a friend, colleague, or family member. Likewise, the source of that information can be traditional media such as television, newspapers, and magazines. Alternatively, a person's increased knowledge can be the direct result of acquiring information via the Internet, including EC sites, social media, as well as LISTSERV postings.

Persuasion

The goal of the innovator is to persuade his/her audience as to the merits of the proposed innovation. The consumer, in turn, forms a favorable or unfavorable attitude toward the innovation based on this and other sources of information. One important consideration is the importance of opinion leadership. The term *opinion leadership* dates back to the early work of Katz and Lazarsfeld (1957), who refer to opinion leaders as select individuals who wield considerable influence on those people and members who comprise a social group. The social group can be religious, political, or professional. The opinion leader is typically someone who is well respected and embodies the cultural norms and tendencies of that social group. Fast-forward to the present day, and the issue of persuasion takes on a whole new meaning when we consider the role of *digital opinion leaders,* that is, people who regularly use the power of social media, blogs, and Internet postings to affect outcomes.[8] (See Chapter 11).

Decision

Decision is about making a choice. For the user, this means making a decision whether to adopt, reject, or delay a potential product purchase. Part of what affects the decision stage is the issue of user resistance. The term *user resistance* refers to anything that may cause a person to hesitate or not go forward with the product adoption or purchasing decision. It follows that after a decision is made, one has to complete the transaction. In digital parlance, this means going online, executing the order, and completing the task. It should be noted that most EC sites give the prospective shopper the opportunity to reconsider his/her purchasing decision with automated questions such as this: Are you sure you want to complete this order?

Implementation

Implementation refers to adopting a new product and putting it into practice. This can include everything from pressing the send button on an EC transaction to allowing oneself to be inoculated as part of a health-care preventative measure.

Confirmation

After making a decision and implementing the change, people sometimes need a certain degree of reassurance that they've made the right decision. *Confirmation* refers to the process of validating one's decision. Depending on the product or service, this can include immersing oneself in the newly acquired product (i.e., taking the car out for a drive or uploading multiple apps to one's newly purchased smartphone). For others, confirmation may take the form of posting an announcement on Facebook. Confirmation also means integrating the new product or service into an ongoing routine.

Rate of Adoption

The term *rate of adoption* refers to the length of time required by someone to consider and adopt the use of a new technology or service.[9] Some users of communication and IT are technology enthusiasts. They are naturally curious and experimental and want to be among the first to adopt a new product offering. In contrast, there are others who are more cautious in their approach to the adoption of a new technology or service. The rate of adoption can be defined as the "relative speed at which members of a social system adopt an innovation."[10] It can be depicted as a standard bell curve, with innovators and early adopters at the front end and laggards (or late adopters) at the back. There are five general categories of adopters, including: 1) Innovators, 2) Early adopters, 3) Early majority, 4) Late majority, and 5) Laggards. (See Figure 6.2.)

Innovators

Innovators are technology enthusiasts. They are the first to adopt a new technology or service. Innovators represent a fairly elite set of users whether we measure them in terms of education level, income, or occupation. They have a higher degree of risk tolerance since the potential investment in the said technology or service may fail.[11] The commitment, therefore, is not trivial when it comes to things like the first generation of high-definition television sets, smartphones, or iPad computer tablets. The motivation for making such purchase decisions can be for business and research, but likewise, it can be based on genuine interest and enthusiasm for the product. And for some individuals, the decision can be a

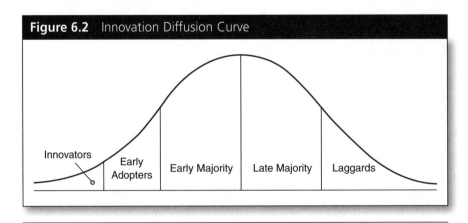

Figure 6.2   Innovation Diffusion Curve

SOURCE: Rogers, E. (1962). *Diffusion of Innovation*. New York: Free Press, p. 150.

statement about social status. Innovators tend to have greater financial resources with which to pursue their personal and professional interests.

Early Adopters

Early adopters comprise the second-fastest category of individuals who adopt an innovation. Such individuals are typically younger in age and have advanced education as well as greater financial resources. Early adopters tend to be people with high-prestige positions, including doctors, lawyers, scientists, engineers, and educators. They like having the newest technology or service when it becomes available.[12] At the same time, they tend to be more discerning in their adoption choices than innovators. Early adopters are often considered opinion leaders within the groups or organizations that they participate in. In sum, there is a positive correlation between socioeconomic status and early adoption.

Early Majority

The early majority represents a large segment of the general public. Early majority adopters are genuinely interested in acquiring the newly introduced technology or service. But the rate of adoption tends to be slower. This category of users tends to be more cautious in their approach. Price and product reliability matter.[13] Product introductions are typically priced higher when compared to the second or third generation of that same product. Early majority users recognize that with the introduction of any new product or service comes a period of adjustment where design issues or flaws may surface. The early majority prefer to wait and allow the new product or service to prove itself in the marketplace.

Late Majority

Individuals in this category tend to be more resistant to change when it comes to new technology and service. Late majority individuals will adopt an innovation well after the product introduction. They display a high degree of skepticism about the product or service. They are quite content to make do with their current technology or service. In some cases, the resistance factor is due to a lack of interest (i.e., too complicated, not needed, content with what I've got, etc.), whereas in other instances the reason can be attributed to a lack of financial resources.

Laggards

Laggards are the last to adopt an innovation. Such individuals are typically older and more resistant to change. They don't see the practical need for making the change until a friend or family member prompts them to think about making one. Late adopters are more reluctant to spend money on new technology. They tend to place a greater emphasis on the value of family and tradition.

Categorically, late adopters have less discretionary income and tend to be more resistant to change. Both late majority and laggards tend to exhibit little in the way of opinion leadership.

Product Launches and Introductions

In his book *Crossing the Chasm,* author Geoffrey Moore (2002) reconsiders Rogers' rate of adoption model by arguing that there is a chasm between the early adopters of a product (visionaries) and the early majority (the pragmatists). Moore believes that both groups operate with a different set of expectations in terms of the adoption process. The early adopters (or visionaries) represent a unique group of people who possess the insight necessary to match an emerging technology with strategic opportunity. The visionary has the right temperament and personality to engage the rest of their organization to buy into an untested project idea. As a group, visionaries are highly motivated. They want to achieve a business or product design goal that makes a difference. Technology is a means to an end, not an end unto itself. Visionaries, in most cases, are willing to take risks with what at the beginning is an unproven technology to achieve breakthrough improvements in productivity and customer service.

In contrast, the early majority (or pragmatists) shares some of the visionary's enthusiasm for new technology and what it can do. At the same time, they are driven by a strong sense of practicality. Pragmatists are less risk tolerant because they have seen enough examples of highly touted new technologies that eventually fail in the marketplace. Pragmatists are driven by a keen sense of performance and cost. They want to see an established track record before investing substantially. In identifying the differences, Moore (2002) writes:

> Visionaries are the first people in their industry segment to see the potential of new technology. Fundamentally, they see themselves as smarter than their opposite numbers in competitive companies—and, quite often, they are. Indeed, it is their ability to see things first that they want to leverage into a competitive advantage. . . . Pragmatists, on the other hand, deeply value the experience of their colleagues in other companies. When they buy, they expect extensive references, and they want a good number to come from companies in their own industry segment.[14]

There is a natural chasm (or divide) between early adopters who are willing to try new technologies and the early majority, which tends to be much more cautious. The chasm represents the time interval during which a product launch takes place. It is the time period during which the product rollout will either succeed or fail.

In Moore's view, both categories of users are essential to a successful product launch. But each group requires a different strategy and approach. Such product launches and introductions present the critical window of opportunity.[15] Moore explains that many technologies elicit strong enthusiasm in the beginning stages

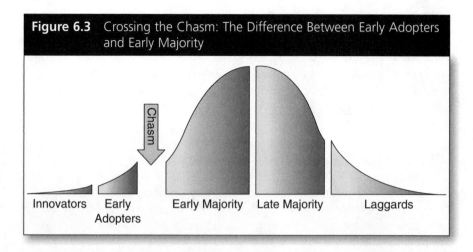

Figure 6.3   Crossing the Chasm: The Difference Between Early Adopters and Early Majority

but later fail to obtain wider adoption. There are several contributing reasons that help to explain why a product fails to gain sufficient traction in the later stages of the product diffusion process.

Why New Product Launches Sometimes Fail

New product launches often fail because of a lack of preparation. A product launch that is riddled by design flaws or failures in delivery execution will generate confusion as well as prove costly in terms of people, time, and resources. When such problems do occur, they are often linked to the project team and the individuals responsible for product development and delivery. Too often, companies are so focused on meeting delivery schedules that they postpone the difficult task of knowing how to market and sustain product delivery weeks and months after the initial launch.[16] This is especially true for global product launches, where regional teams need to be in place to ensure a successful product introduction. The success of a product launch can be undermined by shifting responsibilities throughout development and delivery process.

Managing a successful product launch requires a clear, disciplined approach to product growth. For that reason, it's important to think of the product launch as a process rather than a singular event. In the absence of a well-defined leadership structure (and coordinated effort), tasks and responsibilities such as sales, customer service, delivery, and training are not effectively aligned toward an achievable outcome.[17] A product launch failure represents a breakdown in the diffusion process. In a manner of speaking, they are unable to cross Moore's chasm. (See Figure 6.3.) The user resistance factors prove insurmountable. A product launch can fail for a number of reasons. They include: 1) Product viability, 2) Unsustainable business model, 3) Product design flaws, and 4) Timing and the vagaries of the marketplace.

Product Viability. Sometimes a product is compelling, but there is no market for it. The proposed product launch is steeped in the *Field of Dream's* belief that if you build it, they will come. A major issue in technology-driven environments is the tendency of the R&D department to drive the technology design without giving consideration to the market itself. Sometimes the solution requires an insightful senior manager who is prepared to ask the tough questions: "Who will buy this, and at what price?" A telling example can be seen when Sony Corporation was involved with the design specifications for its original CD.

> **Early Designs for the Sony CD.** Sony President Norio Ohga, a former student of music, was enamored with the possibilities of digital recording. In 1975, he designated a small group of Sony engineers to give the laser disc top priority. In the spring of 1976, the team of audio engineers proudly presented Ohga with an audio laser disc 30 centimeters wide (approximately the size of an LP record). It was capable of providing the listener with 3 hours and 20 minutes of digital sound. Ohga was not pleased. As Nathan (1999) writes, "for their pains, they received a withering lecture on the folly of engineering for its own sake and the importance of developing a business sense."[18]

A new product concept needs to be clear to the consumer in simple easy-to-understand ways. The consumer must be able to grasp the immediate benefits of acquiring the product or service. If the product requires a lot of explanation and individualized training, it will flounder in terms of consumer acceptance. In the best sense, a successful product launch clearly shows how the product/service will satisfy an unfilled need.

Unsustainable Business Model. A successful product launch requires a business model that is sustainable over time. The business logic has to be clear and maintainable. According to Osterwalder and Pigneur (2010), a business model describes the rationale of how an organization creates and delivers value to both the end consumer as well as itself.[19] Regardless of how innovative a company might be, if the resource and infrastructure demands are too costly, the product launch will falter. This was particularly true during the period known as the dotcom bubble (1997–2001) in which a number of Internet-based companies failed to live up to the promise of EC. The combination of rapidly increasing stock prices and the wide availability of venture capital created an environment in which many investors were willing to overlook unsustainable business models in favor of Internet enthusiasm and the ability to turn future profits.

> **Webvan.** In 1997, Louis Borders, a successful book retailing entrepreneur, saw an opportunity to modernize American grocery retailing. Borders believed that automated warehouses combined with computerized scheduling would provide the basis for a virtual supermarket. It was a very compelling idea for the busy, working professional. It could mean fewer weekly trips to the grocery store

and/or waiting in long lines at the checkout counter. Webvan was launched in June 1999 in the San Francisco Bay area. The company offered customers access to 24/7 online grocery shopping via the Internet. The company promised to deliver orders within a thirty-minute agreed-upon window. Webvan represented the quintessential EC company of the future.

Louis Borders was able to attract financing from a number of capital investment firms, including Benchmark Capital, Sequoia Capital, and Goldman Sachs. One important consideration in determining business model sustainability is revenue in relation to capital investment and margins. Webvan's initial capital investments were huge. The company's 300,000-square-foot distribution centers would require a highly sophisticated SCM system. To be successful, Webvan would need a large number of customers spending considerable sums of money per order, or the company would have to achieve significant distribution efficiencies. As Mullins (2003) points out, supermarket retail stores work on very thin sales margins. For starters, Webvan lacked the buying power of Wal-Mart, Kroger, and other large chains. Without the savings realized by its competitors, Webvan was unable to keep its food costs low.[20] The challenge, therefore, was whether customers would be willing to pay more for convenience. If not, then savings would have to be realized by achieving cost efficiencies in distribution. And then, of course, there were the intangibles. Would consumers trust Webvan to select and deliver fresh produce? If a certain food item was unavailable, how much would it affect the week's dinner menu?

By the end of 2000, Webvan's San Francisco customer list had grown to some 47,000 households, with fourth-quarter sales totaling $9.1 million. But customer orders averaged only $81, far less than the $103 Webvan's plans required. As noted earlier, Webvan either needed huge sales volumes or significant operating efficiencies to make its business model work. What became apparent is that the process of fulfilling customer orders was particularly expensive. In a regular supermarket setting, the customer does this work at no cost to the retailer. Webvan charged a $4.95 delivery fee for orders under $50, which later increased to $75 in November 2000, as delivery expenses exceeded budgets. In time, it became clear that cost-effective grocery delivery can only work in densely populated areas that don't require expensive and complicated distribution systems. One can achieve business sustainability if it's a matter of having a minimum-paid worker packing groceries and riding elevators in a tightly populated area. All this changes when distribution costs involve running trucks to the suburbs and paying delivery drivers $25 to $35 an hour.

By July 2001, after just two years in business, Webvan had spent most of its $1.2 billion in outside capital investment. While on the surface Webvan appeared to be a burgeoning EC company, the reality is that it was a very traditional company in terms of its cost structure. Webvan was susceptible to razor-thin product margins, high warehouse costs, and a fleet of vans and distribution costs that proved unsustainable. Webvan closed its doors on July 9, 2001.

Product Design Flaws. A product that is introduced before it's ready can create a whole host of problems for the sponsoring company. There is nothing worse to a manufacturer's reputation than to be subjected to a product recall because of a design flaw in the planning and design process. Such design flaws were either not taken into account or ignored prior to the product launch. In the case of software launches, the problem translates into having to issue multiple software upgrades and patches, thereby undermining public confidence in the company and its product offerings.

Windows Vista. In January 2007, after years of hype and anticipation, Microsoft unveiled Windows Vista to a decidedly lukewarm reception by the PC community, IT pros, and tech-savvy users alike. Instead of a revolutionary next-generation OS that was supposed to have a variety of new features, the professional business community got an underwhelming rehash with very little going for it. Vista was plagued with performance and compatibility problems from the start. Following its immediate launch, Vista proved significantly less stable than its predecessor XP operating system. Computer users experienced more hard locks, crashes, and blue screens in the first weeks of use than was the case of the XP operating system. Considering that improved stability was one of the important reasons for creating Vista, users were understandably upset. According to an internal Microsoft memo (later made public), 18 percent of all Vista crashes reported during the months immediately following its launch were due to unstable graphics card drivers. A second problem had to do with performance speed. Today's computer user is very mindful of the time it takes to process a file or connect to the Internet. Such routine tasks are measured in seconds. Imagine what happens when that same task takes two to three times as long to occur. The Windows Vista operating system was seen as anything but an improvement in performance.[21] In time, six different versions of Vista would be offered to the public plus multiple service packs. A third problem had to do with compatibility issues. Getting Vista to work with various application software and peripheral devices such as printers and scanners became a major problem for users. Additionally, if the user needed to connect to a virtual private network (VPN) that wasn't supported by Vista's built-in client, the user was probably stuck. Officials at Microsoft have conceded that the company failed in terms of the product launch. Microsoft rushed the Vista product launch before it was ready. There was poor coordination of information and missed deadlines between senior level software designers, marketers, and original equipment manufacturers (OEMs). The Vista launch failure resulted in a loss of public confidence in Microsoft's flagship products.

Timing and the Vagaries of the Marketplace. The ability to design and implement a strategy quickly is essential in a global, fast-paced business environment. Being first-to-market is both an opportunity and a problem. On the one hand, being first-to-market can prove to be an important strategic advantage as evidenced by the successful debut of HBO, the Apple iPhone, and Amazon.com. In each case, the said companies were able to traverse Moore's chasm and establish a sizeable lead in their respective markets before the next, nearest competitor was able to grab a foothold. On the other hand, being first-to-market is not without some risks. A company that tries to introduce a product (including a possible change in standards) before the market is ready can wind up spending a lot of time and money and ultimately fail. The history of media and telecommunication is replete with examples of companies that learned the difficulties that sometimes occur when being first-to-market. (See Table 6.1.) What each of the said companies share in common was a combination of bad timing and/or a failure to launch the said product or service correctly.

Table 6.1 Product Launch Failure and the Problems of Being First-to-Market	
• Sony Corporation	• The Betamax VCR
• Time Warner, Inc.	• The Full Service Network, enhanced cable network
• Walt Disney Company	• Euro Disney "Paris" theme park
• Apple Inc.	• The Apple Newton, personal digital assistant
• TiVo	• DVR prototype
• News Corporation Ltd.	• Myspace, social networking site

Despite one's best planning efforts, a new product launch is sometimes subject to the vagaries of the marketplace. This is the proverbial joker in the deck; "we didn't see it coming." A failure to fully understand consumer tastes, anticompetitive behavior by one's rivals, and/or the emergence of rival technology can undermine the best-laid plans.

TiVo. TiVo is a digital video recorder (DVR) that was developed by Jim Barton and Mike Ramsey and introduced to the public at the Consumer Electronics Show in 1999. TiVo provides an on-screen guide of scheduled television programs, whose features include the ability to record selected programs for later viewing. The value proposition for the consumer is the ability to record one's favorite television programs for later viewing, including the ability to skip over commercial TV ads.[22] TiVo includes a wish list function that allows users to find and record shows that match their interests by title, category, or key word. TiVo soon proved to be the quintessential disruptive technology. At issue was the fact that the traditional broadcast advertising business model was now being challenged by a technology that would enable viewers to effectively skip over commercials. TiVo and the principle of digital video recording sent shock waves throughout the industry.

What distinguished TiVo from the previous generation's VCR recording technology was that it was software based, enabling the user to simultaneously record, play back, and fast-forward television programs. The second key attribute was the program guide itself, which drove the function of the machine.[23] TiVo made a name for itself following its initial product launch by selling its devices at reduced cost while making up the difference in subscription fees. In order for TiVo to work, the company had to work in concert with multi-channel television service providers like cable television, satellite TV, and later

(Continued)

(Continued)

telephone-based IPTV systems. For a time, TiVo functioned as a stand-alone service with a steadily increasing monthly subscription fee. Over time, America's multichannel television service providers began to offer a stripped-down version of TiVo. In doing so, they effectively bypassed the need for TiVo, making the latter a redundant service. The new TiVo Premiere is an impressive-looking device with a wide assortment of compelling features. At the same time, it begs the question; why would a consumer elect to pay for TiVo when he/she can obtain the same basic recording functions from a cable operator at a reduced cost? Today, digital video recording has become a mainstream service feature offered by all multichannel television service providers, leaving TiVo unable to share in the success of the market it once helped create.[24]

Creative Destruction in the Digital Age

Change is never easy. Change is especially difficult when a new start-up company (and technology) is poised to displace a well-established business. The launch of a new product or service routinely triggers suspicion and user resistance by those immediate industries and people who are directly affected by its introduction.

User Resistance

User resistance is the lack of willingness to try a new product, technology, or service. For the product innovator, it's important to understand the reasons why various stakeholders are sometimes resistant to the introduction of a new product or service. Such reasons can include: 1) Fear of change, 2) Lack of trust, 3) Competitive threats, and 4) Wanting to stay with what's familiar. It is important to note that user resistance in one area does not necessarily translate into other areas. In other words, a person who is unlikely to use a social media service like Twitter is not necessarily resistant to using a smartphone.

Fear of Change. People often fear what they don't know how to do. This is particularly true when it comes to IT. There are numerous documented examples of workers employed by traditional manufacturers where long-standing employees are resistant to the idea of learning new IT skills that will enable them to do their jobs better. At issue is the fear of being unable to keep up. In some cases, the requirements for change may mean having to learn certain types of math and/or basic programming skills that appear to be beyond the comprehension of the user or employee. Sometimes, the simple downloading of software can prove to be a major barrier for the non-technically inclined person. The fear of making a mistake can paralyze the learning process.

Lack of Trust. This issue is particularly true when it comes to EC transactions. For some users, the entering of personal data (i.e., social security and credit card numbers) can be very challenging. Such users fear that the system will not execute the transaction correctly and that a mistake may occur. The 2013 highly publicized computer hacking of consumer credit card data at Target department stores in the United States underscores that fear. The data breach that affected Target cost the company an estimated $148 million in lost sales as well as recovery costs. For companies like Target, Home Depot, and Sony, the year's revenue loss was nothing compared to the loss in customer confidence in the company.

Competitive Threats. The actions of one's competitors can force a change in terms of one's current business strategy. At issue is the fear that the adoption of a new technology or service could adversely affect an existing industry or mean the elimination of jobs. Consider, for example, the actions of Finland-based Nokia Corporation, once recognized as the world's leading manufacturer in cell phone technology. Nokia was an early innovator in the use of 2G digital signaling systems. For years, Nokia relied on the mass market production of its cell phones. Each generation of Nokia cell phones proved incrementally better than previous versions.[25] Yet even as big and successful as Nokia is, the company was not insulated from direct competition. The success of the Apple iPhone ultimately proved to be a real game changer in terms of its smartphone design as well as its multi-touch capability. Nokia, for its part, was slow to react to the successful launch of the Apple iPhone.

Wanting to Stay With What's Familiar. People are often creatures of habit. They tend to stay with what's familiar to them. This is particularly true when it comes to IT. A typical example is the person who becomes fully comfortable with a certain type of computer and software system. They will go to extraordinary lengths to preserve the current system and not be forced to upgrade to the next-generation system. Microsoft XP, for example, was one of the company's all-time best operating systems. It was originally introduced in 2003. In 2012, Microsoft announced that they would stop supporting the XP platform by the year 2014 in favor of its Windows 7 and 8 operating systems. Despite the company's decision to phase out the XP operating platform, an estimated 27 percent of Microsoft users were still using Windows XP in 2014, making it the second-most widely adopted Microsoft operating system when compared to Windows 7, which came in at 43 percent.

The Sharing Economy

Start-up companies like Vacation Rental by Owners, Uber, and Airbnb are examples of what some observers have called the *sharing economy*. Such peer-to-peer networks allow users to harness the power and immediacy of the Internet with the goal of monetizing primary assets (i.e., cars, homes, apartments, and spare bedrooms).[26] As Stein (2015) points out, the sharing economy is made possible by the fact that while we may distrust strangers, we totally trust people. The trust factor becomes practical and real when everyday users can access the ratings and comments section found in EC services like eBay, Amazon, and Vacation Rental by Owner, to name only a few.[27] And for some, the sharing economy is more trustworthy than government or large business. It is not surprising, therefore, that start-up companies like Uber and Airbnb have become a lightning rod for criticism by challenging the well-established business models of the taxi and hotel industries, respectively. Cities throughout the world are grappling with how to handle the world of technology-enabled digital services.

Uber. Uber is a mobile transportation network company based in San Francisco, California, that connects passengers with drivers of vehicles for hire and ridesharing services. Users are equipped with a mobile app that provides real-time information of drivers for hire. Cars are reserved by sending a text message or by using a mobile app. Using the apps, customers can track their reserved car's location. Uber was founded as UberCab by Garrett Camp and Travis Kalanick in 2009. Uber mobile app service was officially launched in San Francisco in June 2010. Since then, the company has expanded to an estimated 130 cities worldwide.

Airbnb. Airbnb is a Web site for people to rent out lodging. The company has an estimated 600,000 listings in more than 34,000 cities and 190 countries. Airbnb was founded in August 2008 by Brian Chesky and Joe Gebbia in San Francisco, California. Airbnb allows users to access the company's Web site, create a profile listing, and then rent out a spare bedroom or an entire apartment. The profile includes a brief description of the lodging facility, recommendations by other users, reviews by previous guests, as well as a response rating and private messaging system. As Airbnb has become more fully established, there has been a steady shift in the reasons why people rent room space online. Initially, a large segment of Airbnb users were tourists in foreign cities who wanted a more authentic and less expensive form of lodging in a local neighborhood setting. More of today's bookings now include business travelers as well as conference attendees. Many of Airbnb guests like being within walking distance to an area's better restaurants and main attractions. An estimated 425,000 people use it every night on a worldwide basis.[28]

Digital Diffusion Meets User Resistance

Thousands of European taxi drivers have engaged in public protests against Uber in cities across the continent, including London, Paris, Berlin, and Madrid. Their complaint centers on the fact that private taxi services like Uber do not adhere to the same tests, costs, and licensing requirements that regular taxi drivers are expected to follow. In December 2014, Uber discontinued its Spanish operations following a judge's ruling that Uber violated the law by giving it an unfair advantage over taxi drivers. The scale of protests across Europe underscores the extent to which the Internet and digital lifestyle are challenging one of the world's most regulated industries. It is creative destruction in its most essential form.

Similarly, Airbnb has also come under scrutiny given the fact that room and apartment sharing services effectively bypass the need for hotel lodging. Critics of

Airbnb point to the fact that it is an unregulated industry where the host apartment may or may not be committed to the basics of the hospitality industry. They are quick to point out that so much depends on the unique situation and readiness of the host in terms of furniture, level of cleanliness, security, and so forth. There are, indeed, any number of stories that abound involving renters who find the apartment lacking in the most basic amenities, including little or no furniture, no linens and towels, and so on. The opposite problem is equally true. Sometimes, an unruly guest can cause a lot of problems for the host, but more importantly, it is the building owner who is ultimately responsible for a guest that misbehaves.

> In New York, using Airbnb is illegal in many circumstances, thanks to provisions mandating what constitutes a hotel. But more than that, New York just hates Airbnb—if it's not pressure from the powerful hotel lobby to heavily regulate and tax Airbnb usage, it's pushback from the apartment dwellers who don't want their Airbnb-hosting neighbors to give keys to the front door to complete strangers.[29]

Cities like San Francisco, New Orleans, London, Paris, and New York have specific ordinances regarding the subletting of apartments for short-term use. New York State lawmakers toughened a 1929 set of ordinances prohibiting rentals of less than 30 days in an attempt to regulate Airbnb and equivalent services. In some cases, people who rent out space on Airbnb are facing fines and possible eviction by various city planning and housing authorities. One of the direct consequences of the sharing economy is that it demonstrates disruptive technology in the best sense of the term by introducing an altogether new value proposition for the consumer. Start-up companies like Uber and Airbnb are facing user resistance on a number of fronts, including entrenched business interests as well as outmoded regulatory systems that are unable to keep up with the pace of change.[30] Such are the growing pains of two new emerging industries in today's fast-paced digital economy.

The Tipping Point

Much has been written about the profound effect of the *tipping point,* the moment at which a product innovation catches fire—spreading wildly through the population. Writer Malcolm Gladwell (2002) identifies three key factors that are central in determining whether a particular product idea will expand into wide scale popularity. Gladwell's discussion includes the: 1) Stickiness factor, 2) Law of the Few, and 3) Power of context.[31] The stickiness factor is an intangible but very important idea. Does the proposed idea elicit curiosity and fascination? Consider, for example, the idea of creating a theme park built around a magic kingdom or city of tomorrow with period architecture, design, and characters. One important feature of any great innovation is that it begins with a compelling idea. To use the colloquial, "it takes our breath away."

The Law of the Few contends that every great innovation needs a chief spokesperson and advocate. Gladwell describes such individuals as mavens, salesmen, and connectors.[32] They become the champion for the new product concept. Part of that effort involves making the right connections with various designers, marketers and outside investors who will help advance the product launch. When Steve Jobs pitched the iPhone at the 2007 Macworld exposition, he wanted to engage the audience in the iPhone's stickiness factor. Similarly, Sony's Norio Ohga had to elicit support for the CD that was considered a highly disruptive technology for its time given the entrenched interests of the music industry. In both cases, Jobs and Ohga were the salesmen and connectors for their respective product introductions.

Gladwell defines the term *context V*ery broadly, discussing the implications of how timing and circumstances are a major consideration in whether a new product idea will be successfully received. Is the public ready? Diffusion of innovation depends on the readiness and receptivity of the group, neighborhood, or community. In 1964, AT&T test-marketed a first-generation video telephone service called Picturephone. It was introduced at the 1964 New York World's Fair as well as Disneyland in California. The public was invited to place calls between special exhibits at both locations. In 1970, commercial Picturephone service debuted in downtown Pittsburgh. The company's senior leadership was fully convinced that a million Picturephone sets would be in use by 1980. It never happened. The general public was not ready to accept an otherwise highly intrusive medium of communication into the privacy of one's home. People did not want to be on display. The context for using video was not there. In contrast, today we routinely engage in international Skype and Facetime calls via our laptop computers and cell phones. Organizations regularly schedule videoconferences and webinars for the purpose of sharing information. And the posting of pictures and videos on Facebook has become a daily occurrence. In sum, context is everything. We have become a video-savvy generation of users.

Discussion

Digital storytelling is the art of using enhanced media and information tools to tell a story. The launch of a new product, service, or idea is a kind of story. Whether it's the introduction of a next-generation smartphone or the launch of an altogether new project design, the astute marketer recognizes that the first prerequisite for any product launch is to show how the product, service, or idea will make a difference. Specifically, how will the product, service, or idea improve one's life or provide a solution to a legitimate problem? The focus should be on promoting one or two product features (or issue ideas) that people really care about.

The message should be simple, clear, and compelling. Digital storytelling is greatly aided by the power of digital opinion leaders. Such power and persuasion techniques can take a number of different forms including blogs and social media postings as well as ratings and evaluation comments on EC sites. Digital opinion leaders legitimize and speed up the diffusion process. Nowhere is this more evident than when a product or an idea goes viral on the Internet.

The Tipping Point and Going Viral

Viral marketing is the Internet version of word-of-mouth communication. It involves posting a Facebook message, creating a Web site, uploading a video, or sending a Twitter message that becomes so infectious that consumers will want to pass it along to their friends. Because the content comes from a friend, the receiver is more likely to pay attention and use it to make informed purchasing decisions while passing it along to others voluntarily. Viral marketing often uses existing social networks, like Facebook, Twitter, and YouTube, as conduits.[33] What's central to this discussion is the speed at which an idea, commentary, or mobilizing effort catches fire due to the power of social media and intelligent networking.

Intended versus Unintended Consequences

The diffusion of new technology brings with it both intended as well as unintended consequences on the marketplace. From a business standpoint, the intention is rational and is in keeping with a firm's larger business mission. Product designers and business strategists are hopeful that a successful product launch will result in wholesale product adoption among intended consumers as well as increased revenues and market share. These represent the intended consequences of product diffusion.

In contrast, the unintended consequences of product diffusion represent a set of results that are wholly unexpected. Sometimes, the results are immediate and can be easily seen. Sometimes, the unintended consequences of a new product introduction are long term and take a while for the public to discern. The example often used by sociologists is the development of the automobile in the 20th century. In a matter of decades, the automobile went from being a luxury good of the wealthy elite to the preferred, everyday method of passenger travel in most developed countries. The steady diffusion of the car introduced sweeping changes in daily life. While mass-produced automobiles represented a revolution in mobility and convenience, the long-term consequences have been significant, including the development of the modern suburb, where people choose to live and work, commuting, traffic, increased roads and highways, as well as environmental impact. While acknowledging the benefits of newly introduced technology, French writer and sociologist Jacques Ellul (1964) makes the case that there is always a price to be paid by society in their adoption.[34] A good example of this can be seen with the introduction of smartphone technology. The widespread diffusion of smartphones in the early 21st century has set into motion the obvious benefits of mobile voice communication as well as the convenience of being able to access the Internet anytime and anywhere. At the same time, the public has become steadily more aware of the unanticipated consequences ranging from mobile phones going off in movie theaters and restaurants to the dangers of texting and driving. As Ellul (1962) points out, each innovation creates "pernicious effects that are inseparable from favorable effects."[35] The power of innovation still comes down to quality design and the power of a good idea. Therein lies the opportunity and challenge.

Endnotes

1. Everett Rogers, *Diffusion of Innovation* (New York: Free Press, 1962).
2. Everett Rogers, *Diffusion of Innovation,* 5th ed. (New York: Free Press, 2003), 5.
3. Ibid, p. 11.
4. Clayton Christensen, *The Innovator's Solution* (Boston, MA: Harvard Business School Press, 2003).
5. W. Chan Kim and Renée Mauborgne, *Blue Ocean Strategy* (Boston, MA: Harvard Business School Press, 2005).
6. H. Chen and K. Crowston, "Comparative Diffusion of the Telephone and the World Wide Web: An Analysis of Rates of Adoption. Proceedings of the WebNet '97," (presentation, World Conference of the WWW, Internet and Intranet, Toronto, Canada, 1997), 110–115.
7. Everett Rogers, *Diffusion of Innovation,* 4th ed. (New York: Free Press, 1995).
8. Elihu Katz, "The Two-Step Flow of Communication: An Up-to-date Report on a Hypothesis," *Public Opinion Quarterly* 21, no. 1 (1957): 61–78; Elihu Katz and Paul Lazarsfeld, *Personal Influence* (New York: Free Press, 1957).
9. Rogers, *Diffusion of Innovation,* 4th ed.
10. Everett Rogers, *Diffusion of Innovation,* 3rd ed. (New York: Free Press, 1983), 21, 23.
11. Rogers, *Diffusion of Innovation,* 5th ed., 282
12. Rogers, *Diffusion of Innovation,* 5th ed., 282–283.
13. Rogers, *Diffusion of Innovation,* 5th ed., 282–283.
14. Geoffery Moore, *Crossing the Chasm* (HarperBusiness), 41–42.
15. Moore, *Crossing the Chasm.*
16. Larry Bossidy and Ram Charran, *Execution: The Discipline of Getting Things Done* (New York: Crown Business, 2002).
17. D. Sull, R. Homkes, and C. Sull, "Why Strategy Execution Unravels," *Harvard Business Review* (March 2015): 58–66.
18. John Nathan, *Sony: The Private Life* (New York: Houghton-Mifflin, 1999), 138.
19. Alexander Osterwalder and Yves Pigneur, *Business Model Generation* (Hoboken, NJ: John Wiley & Sons, 2010), 14.
20. In the United States, margins of 2 to 3 percent are considered healthy; 1 percent is not uncommon. John Mullins, *The New Business Road Test* (New York: Pearson Education, 2003), 118–122.
21. Richard Gershon, *Media, Telecommunications and Business Strategy,* 2nd ed. (New York: Routledge, 2013), 315.
22. Mike Ramsey, "TiVo," in *Founders at Work,* ed. J. Livingston (New York: Apress, 2007), 191–204.
23. Ramsey, "TiVo."
24. S. Olster, "Why Did the iPod Win and TiVo Lose?" *CNN/Money,* last modified April 27, 2011, http://tech.fortune.cnn.com/2011/04/27/why-did-the-ipod-win-and-tivo-lose/
25. Dan Steinbock, *The Nokia Revolution* (New York: Amacom, 2001).
26. Christopher Koopman, Matthew Mitchell, and Adam Thierer, *The Sharing Economy and Consumer Protection Regulation: The Case for Policy Change* (Arlington, VA: Mercatus Center, George Mason University, 2014).
27. Joel Stein, "Baby You Can Drive My Car," *Time,* February 9, 2015, 32–40.
28. Stein, "Baby You Can Drive My Car."
29. Matt Weinberger, "Airnbnb, Uber and Problems with the Sharing Economy," Computerworld, last modified November 5, 2014, http://www.computerworld.com/article/2842913/airbnb-uber-and-problems-with-the-digital-sharing-economy.html

30. Christopher Koopman, Matthew Mitchell, and Adam Thierer, *The Sharing Economy and Consumer Protection Regulation: The Case for Policy Change.*

31. Malcolm Gladwell, *The Tipping Point* (New York: Little Brown and Company, 2000).

32. Gladwell, *The Tipping Point.*

33. Gershon, *Media, Telecommunications and Business Strategy.* 260.

34. Jacques Ellul, *The Technological Society* (New York: Alfred A. Knopf, 1964). Originally published (Paris, France: Librairie Armand Colin, 1954).

35. Jacques Ellul, "The Technological Order," *Technology and Culture* 3, no. 4 (Fall 1962): 412.

CHAPTER 7

The Intelligent Network

Information and Communication Design Principles

The original idea of the web was that it should be a collaborative space where you can communicate through sharing information.

—Tim Berners-Lee

Introduction

International business has been transformed by the power of instantaneous communication. The combination of computer and telecommunications has collapsed the time and distance factors that once separated nations, people, and business organizations. This chapter will examine the subject of intelligent networks, which provide the technology and electronic pathways that makes global communication possible for small and large organizations alike. We start with the premise that the intelligent network is not one network but a series of networks designed to enhance worldwide communication for business and residential users.[1] What gives the network its unique intelligence are the people and users of the system and the value-added contributions they bring to the system via critical gateway points.

In this chapter, we introduce the Information and Telecommunications Systems (ITS) model as a way to explain a select number of network design

---

Author's Note: The information contained in this chapter is based on a monograph: Richard Gershon, "Intelligent Networks and International Business Communication: A Systems Theory Interpretation." *Media Markets Monographs,* No. 12 (Pamplona, Spain: Universidad de Navarra Press, 2011).

principles. (See Figure 7.1.) Several examples of intelligent networking will be discussed, including telephony, cable television, and the Internet. Intelligent networks, by definition, presuppose permeable boundaries, that is, structured entry points that allow users to access and contribute to the overall system design. The same gateway points also mean opening up the system to any number of unwanted influences and outcomes. Accordingly, special attention is given to what I call the *permeability predicament*. A more detailed discussion of this will be considered later in this chapter.

In Chapters 8 and 9, we consider the human element, that is, the social/technological interaction between people, organizations, and IT network systems. Central to the discussion is that intelligent networks do not operate in a vacuum. Rather, the use of intelligent networks is part of a greater human and organizational decision-making process.[2] As Tim Berners-Lee (1999) points out, the Internet is as much a social creation as it is a technical one.[3] While several of the terms listed in the ITS model are familiar to business and communication practitioners, they nevertheless provide an essential understanding of how intelligent networks operate. In sum, the combination of these network design elements and applications provide the structural basis for today's information economy.

We begin by asking the following question. What makes an intelligent network intelligent? Specifically, what are the defining characteristics and features that comprise so-called intelligent networks? Special attention will be given to six key design principles. We will utilize the principles of systems theory as a way to look at the questions under investigation. The reason for selecting a systems theory approach is based on the assumption that intelligent networks (like human biology) do indeed function as integrated systems. Systems theory provides us with a distinct lens and labeling scheme that best accomplishes this task.

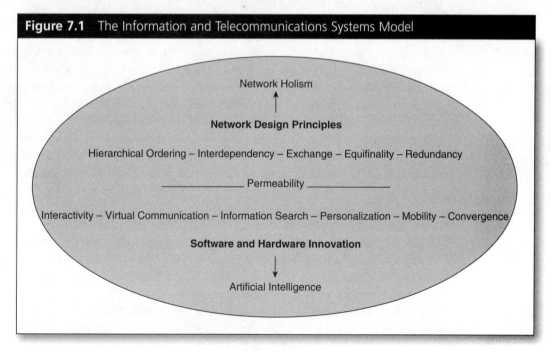

Figure 7.1 The Information and Telecommunications Systems Model

Network Holism

↑

Network Design Principles

Hierarchical Ordering – Interdependency – Exchange – Equifinality – Redundancy

——————— Permeability ———————

Interactivity – Virtual Communication – Information Search – Personalization – Mobility – Convergence

Software and Hardware Innovation

↓

Artificial Intelligence

The Intelligent Network

The origins of systems theory can be traced to the fields of biology and engineering. One of the principal founders of the systems theory approach was Ludwig von Bertalanffy, a theoretical biologist. Bertalanffy published *General Systems Theory* in 1968 in which he argued that systems theory was equally appropriate for the social sciences as it was for biology.[4] In the field of communication, systems theory was first adopted by Katz and Kahn (1966) in an influential work titled *The Social Psychology of Organizations*.[5] In this book, the authors argue that organizations function as complex open systems that involve interaction among component parts as well as interaction with the environment.

Throughout the 1970s and 1980s, a great many researchers utilized systems theory as a way of understanding the relationship between organizational behavior and communication. Systems theory took on increasing importance as a way of explaining the principles of exchange, feedback, and interdependence, concepts that are fundamental to understanding the operations of a highly complex organization. Out of the systems theory tradition developed one theoretical approach known as *network analysis*.[6] The goal of network analysis is to understand the process by which participants create and share information to reach a mutual understanding.[7] Network analysis emphasizes the importance of human and organizational relationships as it defines the nature of the communication links between people, groups, and organizations. To that end, we will adopt a select set of systems theory principles as a way to better explain the structures and substructures of intelligent networks and how they are used by business and individual users.[8]

Understanding Internal Structures and System Processes

Intelligence can be defined as the ability to reason, problem solve, think abstractly, comprehend complex ideas, and learn. Halal (1997) describes *organizational intelligence* as the "capacity of an organization to create knowledge and use it to strategically plan and adapt to its environment."[9] Intelligent networks, therefore, are the systems of communication that organize, transmit, and display information with the goal of improving organizational performance. Intelligent networks are also responsible for providing decision support and analysis. The intelligent network provides three levels of functionality as illustrated in Figure 7.2. They include: 1) Transmission, Display, and Storage; 2) Decision Support Analysis; and 3) Artificial Intelligence (AI).[10]

The first level can be described as *Transmission, Display, and Storage (TDS)*. The role of the intelligent network is to provide the proper switching and routing of information between a sender and an intended audience. This can vary in size and complexity from a simple Skype video exchange to an international videoconference involving project teams from around the world. In both cases, the goal is to transmit information to an intended audience.

The second level can be described as *Decision Support Analysis*. Here the emphasis is on providing the user with critical information for purposes of information

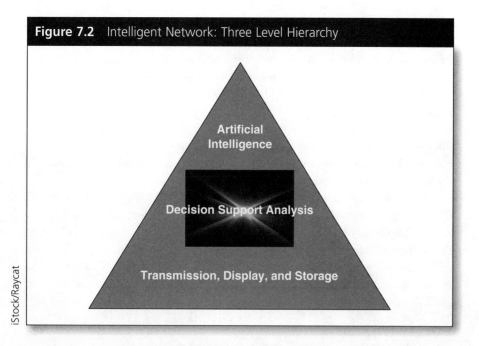

Figure 7.2   Intelligent Network: Three Level Hierarchy

Artificial
Intelligence

Decision Support Analysis

Transmission, Display, and Storage

gathering, planning, designing, and decision making. The intelligent network is responsible for providing the organization and its users immediate access to a whole host of internal and external database services that might include investigating infectious diseases (i.e., U.S. Center for Disease Control and Prevention) or pursuing a criminal investigation of a suspected international terrorist (i.e., Interpol or U.S. Department of Homeland Security).

Depending on how the information is organized and sorted, there is an abundance of information that can provide the user with critical analysis capability.[11] The third level can be described as *Artificial Intelligence* (AI). The goal of the intelligent network is to make preprogrammed decisions. The network is designed to make recommendations to the user and/or take corrective action based on established algorithms. Once again, examples can vary in size and complexity starting with a proprietary software recommendation system built by EC companies like Amazon, Netflix, and Apple. Such companies make personalized product recommendations (i.e., books, films, and music) via their EC Web sites based on past selections. At a more complex level, AI refers to pre-programmed decision making. As an example, modern aviation relies on an automated flight control management system to control the aircraft. The flight control system can control and automate all phases of a flight operation, including takeoff and ascent, flight guidance (autopilot), descent, approach, and landing.

Four Working Assumptions About Intelligent Networks

When engineers discuss the architecture of a network, they are describing how the physical parts of the network are organized, including: 1) Information

Pathways (network configurations), 2) Terminals (computers, smartphones, etc.), 3) Software (applications and protocols), and 4) Data Enhancement Equipment (modems, laser printers, Wi-Fi, etc.). First, as noted earlier, the intelligent network is not one network but a series of networks designed to enhance worldwide communication for business and individual users alike.[12] Second, what gives the network its unique intelligence are the people and users of the system and the value-added contributions they bring via critical gateway points. Today, the Internet has grown exponentially in size and complexity due to the many contributions of its users, ranging from powerful search engines to unique Web site design as well as the aggregation of content.

A third assumption is that intelligent networks do not operate in a vacuum. Rather, the use of intelligent networks are part of a greater human communication and organizational decision-making process.[13] Nowhere is this more evident than in the creation of enterprise resource planning (ERP) and just-in-time manufacturing (JITM) networks designed to aid business process as discussed in Chapter 4. And fourth, as intelligent networks grow and evolve, they often exhibit self-learning qualities in what Monge, Heiss, and Magolin (2008) describe as *network evolution*.[14] This is a crucial element in helping to explain what makes an intelligent network intelligent. More decidedly, it speaks to the importance of AI. According to the ITS model, there are six key essential parts that comprise intelligent network design. They include: 1) Hierarchical Ordering, 2) Interdependency, 3) Exchange, 4) Equifinality, 5) Redundancy, and 6) Network Holism.

Hierarchical Ordering

Today, basic telephone service includes both local and long distance telephone communication. All of the major telephone carriers offer combined local and long distance telephone service packages as well as cellular telephony and enhanced information services. The public switched telephone network (PSTN) provides the major pathways for the switching and routing of voice, data, and video traffic. The PSTN is premised on a type of hierarchical ordering scheme. The principle of hierarchical ordering suggests a prescribed set of steps that are necessary for the completion of a telephone call and/or the routing of a data transmission.[15]

In the United States, prior to the divestiture (or breakup) of AT&T in 1984, the Bell system network hierarchy utilized a Class 5 telephone switching and call-processing standard that defined the procedures for the setup, management, and completion of a call between telephone users. This earlier network hierarchy provided for five levels of switching offices, with the Class 5 office being the end office. The end office was managed by the local exchange carrier (LEC) and was responsible for providing a dial tone to the customer and served as the interface between the end user and the PSTN. Since the AT&T divestiture, advancements in switching technology have allowed many of the switching levels to be combined. The new hierarchy consists of fewer levels, consolidating many of the functions of the previous hierarchy into three layers.[16] (See Figure 7.3.)

Figure 7.3   Telephone System Hierarchy

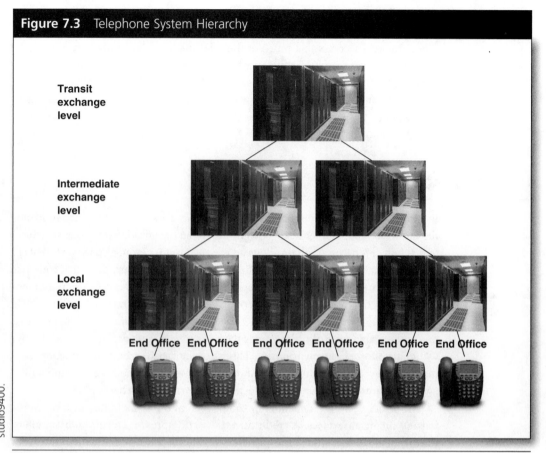

Server photo from iStock/bjdlzx. Telephone photo from iStock/studio9400.

SOURCE: Adapted from "World's Biggest Data Breaches" (2015) from InformationIsBeautiful.net.

The local exchange level or end office (EO) is responsible for providing a dial tone to the customer and serves as the interface between the end user and the PSTN. All telephone calls are initially routed through the EO. A telephone network must ensure a fast and efficient connection among a set of telephone users. This presupposes a low probability of blocking, that is, a failure to establish a connection. The network must be designed with alternative routing methods so that calls can be routed to their proper destination when parts of the network are fully utilized or have failed. When a telephone call is placed, the EO determines the best available transmission path that the call will take based on a prescribed set of routing options.[17] If the first primary route is unavailable, then the system tries to find the second best route, third best route, and so forth. The best route is the one that is most direct, hence, the principle of hierarchical ordering. The same network hierarchy must also accommodate mobile telephone and e-mail traffic as it provides the backbone (or primary transmission capability) for long-haul Internet and cellular telephone traffic.

The PSTN can be thought of as the main information highway (or network of networks). It provides the physical infrastructure that enables the switching and routing of telephone calls (wired and wireless) as well as various forms of data transmission (Internet, EC, e-mail, etc.). The PSTN is an ever-evolving network.

As author Michael Noll (1997) points out,

> . . . the real secret is that much of the super-highway is already here and has been developing and evolving over the past 100 years. It is today's network of networks comprised of the public switched telephone network, cable TV, communication satellites and packet switched networks for data communication. The public telephone network goes everywhere and is essential to business in today's information economy.[18]

Interdependency

In 1962, F. H. Allport introduced his concept of *collective structures* by which he identifies the importance of interlocking behaviors. For an organization (or group structure) to function, it is necessary that various people and groups perform certain acts that are complementary in purpose. In a functioning IT system, the many parts that comprise the system are said to be highly interdependent. A highly complex organization cannot properly function without certain internal and external departments providing active assistance to one another.[19] Weick (1979) takes up the same argument and suggests that one of the major goals of organizing is the reduction of equivocality (or uncertainty) within the information environment. This is accomplished through information sharing between organizational players as well as the use of protocols (i.e., assembly rules and procedures) that set up the parameters for information exchange.[20]

The principle of interdependency can be seen in the area of intelligent networking and financial services. A credit card transaction provides a good illustration of intelligent networking and the principle of interdependency. Let's assume for a moment that a person elects to pay for dinner using a credit card. The credit card transaction sets up a three-way, interdependent relationship among the person buying dinner, the restaurant, and the credit card company.

Interdependency and Financial Markets

Intelligent networks are at the heart of international business finance. The world's financial markets have been revolutionized by the application of computer and telecommunications to the banking and investment process. The international transfer of electronic funds is premised on strong, interdependent relationships between banks, the investment community, business and individual participants. Electronic Funds Transfer (EFT) operates as information (or the promise of actual funds) and not as physical currency. The real impact of EFT on organizations and the public is greater convenience and cost savings by not having to physically handle money during routine transactions. There are prescribed rules governing both the foreign exchange and financial credit markets.[21] EFT has permeated the world of business and personal finance in five ways. They include the following:

1. Electronic Funds Transfer (EFT)—the national and international transfer of money between banks and other financial institutions.

2. Direct Deposit—the transfer of money directly into the bank account of an organization's employees.

3. ATMs—the public use of terminals and automated teller machines, which enables the user to deposit and withdraw funds via electronic access.

4. Credit and Debit Cards—the public use of credit and debit cards as the basis of payment between users and retailers that can include restaurants, gas stations, supermarkets, department stores, etc.

5. Electronic Commerce (EC)—the purchase of goods and services via the Internet, which enables the transfer of funds from one's bank account (e.g., PayPal).

PayPal and EC. PayPal is one of the world's best-known EC payment systems. PayPal allows both business and individual users to set up their own private accounts for the purpose of purchasing goods and services online. PayPal is a trusted middleman service for online purchases. Whereas wire transfers were the standard in the 20th century, PayPal has become the preferred and convenient way to transfer money online. An estimated 153 million users have PayPal accounts. Both retail merchants and buyers entrust PayPal with their credit card and bank information given the company's strong commitment to security and privacy. PayPal and equivalent online payment systems have made EC transactions both practical and reliable.

Credit Card Transactions. Let's consider a simple credit card transaction. Assume for a moment that a person pays for dinner using a credit card. The use of credit is an information-based transaction that sets up a three-way, interdependent relationship among the person buying dinner, the restaurant and the credit card company. At the restaurant, the cashier swipes the credit card through a reader at the point of sale. The credit card terminal dials a stored telephone number via modem to the credit card company (CCC). The CCC maintains an internal database that authenticates the person and guarantees to the merchant that the said person has a sufficient line of credit to cover the cost of purchase. Specifically, the CCC authenticates the person by examining the magnetic stripe or EMV security chip on the back of the card for a valid card number, expiration date and credit card limit. Afterward, the credit card transaction requires the physical administration and processing of the credit card claim, including direct payment to the merchant and issuing a billing statement to the credit card holder. The person, in turn, must make a full (or partial payment) to the CCC, and that information must be processed accordingly. In sum, no part of a credit card transaction can take place without the interdependent relationship of the three main system parts.

Exchange

In a system, *exchange* refers to something that is 1) Coming in (input), 2) Processed (throughput), and 3) Going out (output). In a financial context, exchange refers to the transfer of goods and services between a manufacturer/distributor and the consumer.

A variation on this idea is the principle of *exchange efficiency*, which was discussed in Chapter 2, having to do with creating the optimum conditions through which a consumer can obtain a product or service. An example of exchange efficiency can be seen with companies that specialize in EC such as Amazon or the Apple iTunes music store. The speed and efficiency of producing Internet-delivered music using MP3 file-sharing software has fundamentally changed the cost structure of music recording and distribution on a worldwide basis.

Apple iTunes

On April 28, 2003, Apple launched its iTunes store with the goal of providing digital music for people to buy online and download. The iTunes music store business model fundamentally challenged some basic assumptions involving traditional music sales and retailing. The launch of iTunes redefined the principle of exchange efficiency by introducing an altogether new value proposition to the marketplace, namely, convenience, affordability, and customization. Consumers could now personalize their music playlists by simply choosing from a list of more than 200,000 songs. Individual songs using an MP3 file-sharing software could be downloaded via the Internet. Users were charged $0.99 per individual song. This alone represented a major departure from having to purchase a complete CD album containing multiple songs that the user may or may not have wanted.[22] The combination of the Apple iPod and iTunes media store created the first sustainable music EC business model of its kind. More importantly, Apple forever changed the future of music retail sales delivery.

Today, iTunes has become a lot more than an efficient way to purchase music. iTunes has evolved into an EC network that manages various types of mixed-digital media files (photos, videos, music, podcasts, etc.) between the iTunes host site and the user's PC, smartphone, and/or portable tablet. The iTunes store allows the user to purchase, organize, store, and play back various types of mixed-media files to any of the above devices. The iTunes media store is a virtual store enabling people to access music and video files anywhere in the world. MP3 music file sharing and EC have given new meaning to the term *exchange efficiency*, albeit on a global level.

Equifinality

In a highly complex system, there are a variety of pathways that allow a person or organization to achieve its goal or destination point. *Equifinality* is a system process that allows one to "reach the same final state from differing initial conditions and by a variety of paths."[23] In the years following the AT&T divestiture, several major developments altered the basic design and operation of the modern telephone network, including advancements in digital switching, improvements in modern signaling systems, and the introduction of fiber-optic technology. While the basic architecture of the PSTN remains largely circuit switched, the network is controlled digitally, thus enabling the blend of voice, data, and video signals to be sent over the same network. Over time, the digitalization of the network has evolved to a more general-purpose computing platform, including out-of-band signaling, which is the basis for packet switching and Internet data transport.

The Internet and Distributed Architecture

The beginnings of the Internet can be traced back to the early 1960s. At the peak of the Cold War, researchers in the Advanced Research Projects Agency (ARPA) of the Department of Defense built a computer network to share resources among ARPA researchers and contractors in different parts of the United States. In organizing and managing the network, ARPA took a decidedly hands-off approach, which would have some long-term effects on the evolution of the network and its use. ARPA's basic approach presupposed a distributed architecture: no single network site or person would be able to control the flow of information.[24] Equally important was the principle of open access; a person connected to any node of the network could communicate with anyone else on the network or access information from other points on the network. (See Figure 7.4.)

There are two distinctly different views on how and why the original ARPANET was designed the way it was. The first view represents the Department of Defense perspective that the ARPANET was meant to provide reliable communication in the face of a nuclear attack. This is supported by a Rand research study as well as a 1995 National Science Foundation final report. The second view represented the academic community and the specific project designers and researchers who saw the network for peaceful purposes. It should be remembered that it was the 1960s, and there was a strong antiwar sentiment as well as a general distrust of centralized authority.[25] They wanted to build a system that defied centralized control. According to historian Janet Abbate (1990), "the group that designed and built ARPA's networks was dominated by academic scientists who incorporated their own values of collegiality, decentralization of authority, and open exchange of information into the system."[26] In the final analysis, the basic design of the ARPANET (forerunner of today's Internet) represented a combination of belief systems that included both the U.S. Department of Defense (i.e., project rationale and funding) and the academic community, which provided the research and design applications.

Two of the important building blocks that made the ARPA network possible included: 1) Packet Switching and 2) the TCP/IP Communication Protocol.

Packet Switching

Packet switching represents the ability to take a digital-based message and divide it into equal-sized packets of information. The said packets are then sent individually through the network to their destination, where the entire message is reassembled after all the packets arrive. The principle of packet switching was first developed by electrical engineer Paul Baran in the early 1960s while working for the Rand Corporation. Baran believed that message delivery should be fully

Figure 7.4 Distributed Network Architecture

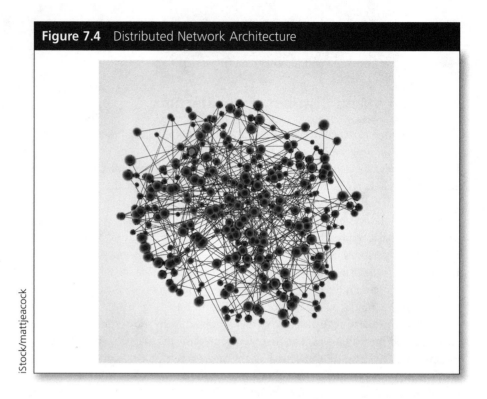

iStock/mattjeacock

distributed; that is, the network should resemble a fishnet. Each and every node should have the ability to switch and route the flow of data. Further development in packet switching technology was continued through the work of Leonard Kleinrock and Donald Davies, who did early research in the area of digital message switching.[27]

Packet switching made it possible for the ARPANET to create a reliable medium to transport data between computers. Until then, computers were connected using circuit-switched technology. In a circuit-switched network, digital data goes directly to the receiver in an orderly fashion, one after another on a single track. With packet switching, Internet routers determine a path for each packet on the fly, dynamically, ordering them to use any available route to get to its proper destination point. Upon arrival, the individual packets are reassembled by a packet assembler based on the information contained in the headers.[28] (See Figure 7.5.)

Today, packet switching dominates data networks like the Internet and is central to the principle of Voice Over Internet Protocol (VOIP) telephony. One of the important benefits of packet switching is the ability to integrate voice and data communication, which is at the heart of Internet web design, video streaming, and telephony.

TCP/IP Communication Protocol

During the beginning stages of the original Department of Defense ARPA network, the incompatibility of computers from different vendors was a major

Figure 7.5 Packet Switching Overview

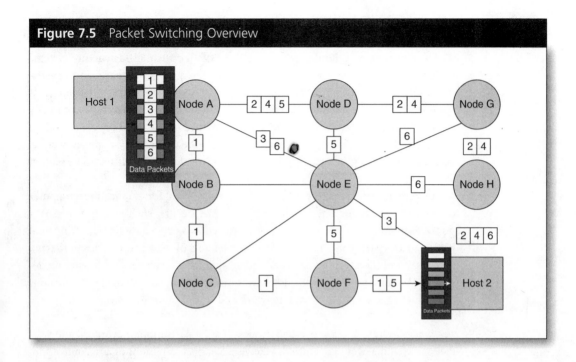

problem that limited the scope and range of what the network could do. What was needed was a common communication protocol that could cut across various platforms and vendor equipment. A protocol is to computers what language is to humans. A protocol is a set of rules that all parties understand and agree on before they can communicate with each other. To that end, a communication protocol known as the Transmission Control Protocol/Internet Protocol (TCP/IP) was adopted by ARPA (and later the Internet) for use by all interconnecting nodes.[29] TCP/IP became the major system-wide on-ramp for all users when accessing from and contributing new information content to the Internet.

Redundancy

Entropy is the second law of thermodynamics, which states that all matter has a tendency to become less and less organized, that is, to become randomly arranged. In all systems, there is a tendency for a system to pull apart or become less organized. Shannon and Weaver's (1949) seminal Mathematical Theory of Communication was responsible for seeing the fundamental parallel between information and the concept of entropy.[30] To overcome the natural entropy found in all communication networks, energy must be spent to organize matter into structured forms. In terms of information theory, entropy is associated with the amount of redundancy (or system backup) that is built into a message delivery and storage system. Building redundancy into a telecommunications network is essential given the likelihood that at some point most networks will indeed fail.

Critical Infrastructure and Disaster Recovery

The principle of redundancy is at the heart of all critical infrastructure systems including electrical power, transportation, finance, military defense, and government services. Consider what would happen if the financial record keeping at American Express was suddenly and irretrievably lost. The enormity of accurately recreating the lost data would fully destabilize the company and have a cascading effect on the world's financial markets, hence the term, *critical infrastructure*. Select examples of intelligent networking and critical infrastructure can be seen in Table 7.1.

All critical infrastructure networks require a plan for duplicating computer operations (i.e., redundancy) after a catastrophe occurs, such as a fire or earthquake. It includes routine off-site backup as well as a procedure for activating vital information systems in a new location. The lessons of 9/11 and Hurricane Katrina demonstrated the importance of redundancy and the challenges of disaster recovery. Those companies that did not have disaster recovery systems had enormous difficulty in recreating their vital network and information infrastructures.

Feedback. Feedback is a subsystem process that helps to monitor, control, and validate the system's overall operation. Likewise, feedback can monitor and control specific system components. Cybernetic theory emphasizes the role of feedback as a way to maintain the system.[31] The need for feedback is built into most forms of intelligent network design. There are different kinds of feedback, including *verification feedback,* which indicates whether the system is working properly. As an example, an EC purchase or EFT requires a method of verification feedback, whereby the sender knows that the information sent was correctly received. Another form of feedback is called *corrective feedback,* which helps to maintain the proper functioning of the system. Both data and telephone communication networks are equipped with test and measurement tools that are designed to provide immediate feedback when and if a certain part of the network goes down or is not functioning properly. In the case of an EFT, for example, the system will automatically engage in redial mode in an effort to successfully complete the transmission. Similarly, a cellular telephone switching center will switch the user to a change in frequency when and

Table 7.1   Select Examples of Intelligent Networking and Critical Infrastructure
• Banking and financial record keeping • Infectious disease and Federal Bureau of Investigation (FBI) criminal surveillance databases • Nuclear reactor and power grid operation and maintenance • Airport traffic control • University and student record keeping • Bridge, tunnel, and highway operation and maintenance • Hospitals and medical record keeping

if the cell tower's base station determines that the user is moving into a new cell zone and/or if the quality of the call is suffering.[32]

Network Holism

Taken together, the five structure elements thus described contribute to a process feature we will call *network holism;* whereby, the system becomes greater than the sum of its parts.[33] A system is greatly enhanced when the various network structures work together to make the complete network more robust. Nowhere is this more evident than in the development of cable television and the principle of broadband communication to the home.

Cable Television

A cable television system is a communication system that distributes broadcast and satellite-delivered programming by means of coaxial and/or fiber-optic cable to people's homes. A cable television system is patterned after a tree-and-branch network. The signals from the headend point (i.e., master receiving site) are distributed to population centers (or neighborhoods) on heavy-duty cable called trunk lines. (See Figure 7.6.) In the typical cable system, the drop line coming into a subscriber's home connects to an external converter box, which in turn, delivers the signals to the user's television set. At the same time, a cable television system is capable of delivering voice and data traffic upstream, that is, from the user's television box to the cable headend point.

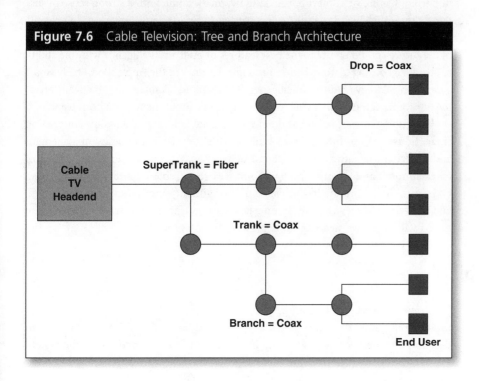

Figure 7.6   Cable Television: Tree and Branch Architecture

Drop = Coax

Cable TV Headend

SuperTrank = Fiber

Trank = Coax

Branch = Coax

End User

Cable television has redefined the nature of television programming. First, it has greatly expanded the number of television viewing options by increasing channel capacity. Second, cable television helped facilitate the principle of *narrowcasting;* that is, programming designed for specialized audiences. Examples might include: ESPN (sports), the Disney Channel (family entertainment), and the Food Network (cooking and cuisine), to name only a few. The value to the audience is greater program selection based on individual tastes and interests. The value to the advertiser is an audience composition that is more closely aligned with the featured programming and its corresponding advertising. Third, cable television and its telephone service counterpart are the two principle players engaged in the delivery of broadband communication services to the home. The term *broadband communication* refers to any system designed to deliver multichannel television and enhanced information services to the home. Today's cable television network system exhibits the qualities of network holism. As we look to the future, the cable industry will undergo a major redefinition as to its core business. While television entertainment will continue to be the main engine that drives cable television forward, the very nature of cable services will undergo a profound change.[34]

Broadband Delivery and Smart Houses

The importance of smart houses speaks to the future of digital lifestyle in its most essential form. A smart house is a residential dwelling that uses highly advanced automatic systems for lighting, temperature control, information and entertainment services, security, window and door operations, and many other functions. One important feature of a smart house design is that it's built with a strong sense of sustainability, efficient with little or no waste. A smart house appears "intelligent" because a variety of sensors monitor the daily activities of house use.[35] Smart houses of the future should combine the best features of built-in intelligence with the ability to adapt. According to Tony Fadell, principle designer of the Apple iPod, "truly smart gadgets should have built-in intelligence. They should be able to automatically adapt to your wants and needs, so you don't have to think about them if you don't want to."[36]

The importance of broadband delivery is central to any discussion concerning smart houses of the future. From multichannel television to energy management and security, the future of broadband delivery will come to include a variety of entertainment and information based services. (See Table 7.2 and Figure 7.7.)

In a multichannel digital universe, the origins of entertainment, information, and utility-based services will become less distinguishable. The future of electronic media will give new meaning to the term *television programming.*

Permeability

Intelligent networks, by definition, presuppose permeable boundaries, that is, structured entry points that allow users to access and contribute to the overall system design. Permeability means allowing information to flow in and out of the system

Table 7.2   Smart House Features

1. Multichannel Television Entertainment

- Basic and Premium Services
- High-definition Television
- Video on Demand
- Digital Video Recording

2. High-Speed Internet Access

- Electronic Commerce
- Video Streaming
- Music File Sharing and Delivery
- Electronic Banking
- Education and Training
- Research
- Online Gaming

3. Telephony

- Voice Communication
- Video Telephone Service
- Video Cameras/Monitors Surveillance

4. Energy Management

- Monitor Individual Appliance Use
- Track Overall Gas and Electric Use

5. Heating, Ventilation, and Air-Conditioning

- Temperature Control
- Monitor Energy Use

6. Medical Monitoring

- Monitoring Patient Care
- First Alert Response for Elderly Residents

7. House Management and Security

- Video Monitoring and Security
- Remote Monitoring of Utility Services and Infrastructure via One's Computer Tablet

Figure 7.7   The Future of Smart House Design

Energy Monitoring
Automated lighting system
Monitor individual appliance use
Track overall gas and electric use

Cable Telephony
Voice communication
Video telephone service

Multichannel Television Entertainment
Basic and premium services
High definition television
Video on demand
A la carte program selection

High Speed Internet Access
E-mail
Electronic commerce
Music downloads
Television/film video
streaming Electronic banking
Education, Training, and
research Online gaming

Security and Health
Video cameras/surveillance
Monitoring patient care
First alert response/crisis

iStock/RLWPhotos

or organization. The level of permeability varies according to the openness of the system.[37] The biological equivalent would be the human body's ability to interface with the external environment (e.g., breathing, eating, and learning). The intelligent network must adhere to an internal logic (i.e., system protocols) while having the capacity to grow and develop.

The Permeability Predicament

Today, the Internet has rapidly grown in size and complexity due to the many contributions of its users, ranging from powerful search engines to unique Web site design and the aggregation of content. In sum, the Internet is made better by the users of the system and the contributions they make via critical gateway points. The principle of permeability is central to this discussion since the Internet must allow easy access points for its users (e.g., PCs, smartphones, and computer tablets). At the same time, permeability also means opening up the system to any number of unwanted influences and outcomes. I call this the *permeability predicament*.[38] From a systems theory perspective, the biological equivalent is the human body's susceptibility to various kinds of colds and viruses. It is not by accident that computer professionals use the word *virus* to describe a software system that has become infected. What are some of the unwanted influences that affect network design and critical infrastructure? Such examples might include financial fraud, privacy loss, and network security threats. Let's consider the latter.

Network Security Threats. Critical infrastructure such as electrical power, banking and finance, transportation, and government services run on information networks. A network security threat is generally understood to mean unlawful attacks against an intelligent network and the information contained in such networks. Such attacks are directed against critical infrastructure resulting in the destabilization of a network and/or violence against persons and property.[39] The goal is to intimidate an organization in furtherance of a political, military, or social objective. Clark (2010) coins the term *cyberwarriors* to describe a new class of military actions taken by a country to penetrate another nation's computer networks for the purpose of intelligence gathering and/or causing severe disruption.[40] One use of cyber war is to make a conventional attack easier by disabling an enemy's defenses. In general, there are four broad categories of security threats to a network:

- Unstructured Threats—These threats primarily consist of random hackers using various tools such as password crackers, credit card number generators, and malicious telephone and e-mail scripts to access a user's account or obtain proprietary information.
- Structured Threats—These threats are more closely associated with industrial or government espionage. Such efforts are more deliberate in design and planning. The goal is to access proprietary information.
- Internal Threats—These threats are typically initiated from a disgruntled employee. The internal threat poses a serious problem to an organization given that the employee may have direct access to sensitive information.

- Denial of Service Threats—The goal is to disrupt or destabilize a proprietary network as part of a personal, political, and/or social cause.[41]

IT system hacking has become a major problem for businesses and organizations around the world. Since 2010, there have been several major data breaches that have affected both large and small organizations alike. The social and financial cost to both business and individual users is enormous. Consider, for example, that a major corporation like Target or Home Depot risks damage to reputation, including customer confidence in the company as well as its IT security capability. For other companies, the problem translates into lost productivity and operation time. The data breach that affected Target cost the company an estimated $148 million in lost sales as well as recovery costs. Table 7.3 provides a brief illustration of some of the more high-profile data breaches including the company or organization and the number of records stolen.

Table 7.3   Major International Data Breaches

Business/Organization	Number of Stolen Records
Adobe	152,000,000
Cardsystems Solutions	40,000,000
eBay	145,000,000
Heartland Pay Processor	130,000,000
Home Depot	56,000,000
JP Morgan Chase	76,000,000
Sony Playstation	77,000,000
Target	70,000,000
TJ Max	94,000,000
U.S. Military	76,000,000

SOURCE: Adapted from "World's Biggest Data Breaches" (2015) from Information is Beautiful. net.[42]

Discussion

We began this chapter by asking this question: What makes an intelligent network intelligent? The ITS model was introduced as a way to explain both the internal structures and processes of intelligent networking. There are what I call four working assumptions about intelligent networks. First, the intelligent network is not one network but a series of networks designed to enhance worldwide communication for business and individual users alike. Second, what gives the intelligent network its unique intelligence are the people and users of the system and the value-added contributions they bring to the system via critical gateway points. As noted earlier, the Internet has become the network of networks. It has grown in size and complexity due to the many contributions of its users, ranging from powerful search engines to unique Web site design and the aggregation of content. A third assumption is that intelligent networks do not operate in a vacuum. Rather, the use of intelligent networks is part of a greater human communication and organizational decision-making process. From JITM networks to global inventory management systems, the goal is to improve organizational efficiency. Fourth, intelligent networks exhibit self-learning features in what can be described as network evolution. We can see this in a variety of settings and applications, including EC (Netflix, iTunes, and Amazon.com) as well as AI and human/computer interface design.

Intelligent networks, by definition, presuppose permeable boundaries, that is, structured entry points that allow users to access and contribute to the overall system design. The principle of permeability is central to this discussion as the Internet must allow easy on-ramps for its users (e.g., PCs, smartphones, computer tablets, etc.). At the same time, permeability also means opening up the system to any number of unwanted influences and outcomes; hence the term the *permeability predicament*. From a systems theory perspective, the biological equivalent is the human body's susceptibility to various kinds of colds and viruses. In computer parlance terms, this can include things such as financial fraud, privacy loss, and network security threats, to name only a few.

The term *computer virus* (or virus) is commonly used to describe an unwanted network security threat that adversely affects the proper running of a computer system. A computer virus can be defined as a program or piece of executable code that has the ability to replicate itself. The code or list of instructions attaches itself to a sent e-mail or an access point on a social networking site. It then spreads as files are copied and sent from person to person. The computer virus has the ability to hide in the system undetected for days or months until the right set of conditions are set into place. The right conditions can be a certain date or opening up a select e-mail file at which time the virus is activated. The essential element of any computer virus is the Trojan or trapdoor. In computer parlance, a Trojan appears to be one thing but does something else. It feigns a kind of ruse, thereby allowing the unauthorized user a backdoor entrance into the system. Afterward, the Trojan can seize, change, or eliminate the user's data altogether.[43]

The success of the infamous 2000 Love Bug virus, for example, depended on Microsoft's Outlook e-mail program, which acted as the carrier, and five lines of embedded code that created an e-mail message with the subject line "I LOVE YOU." Once opened, the worm attached itself to every name in the victim's e-mail address book. When the user saw the subject tagline, "I LOVE YOU," curiosity got the better part of reason, and the victim paid a high price for carelessly downloading the attachment. The Love Bug virus is an example of cyberterrorism that struck more than 45 million computers worldwide and caused an estimated $10 billion worth of damages.[44] In 2006, a computer virus known as Storm Worm was unleashed on the general public. The concept behind the virus was that it would fool victims into downloading the application through fake links to news stories. As an example, just prior to the 2008 Olympic Games in China, a Storm Worm virus appeared in the form of e-mail subject lines that read: "China's most deadly earthquake." The Storm Worm is a Trojan that turns a victim's computer into zombies or bots. Such computers become vulnerable to remote control by the person behind the attack.[45] In the final analysis, the kind of computer virus may say as much about the author as it does about the virus itself.

> As a form of writing, the computer virus is elaborate, inscrutable, and abstract. Like their close cousins the graffiti artists, virus writers want above all else for their names to be known.[46]

Intelligent networks have to create open and accessible on-ramps that are available to all users regardless of intention and purpose. The problem is made worse by the fact that nearly 78 percent of all employees do not follow the security policies set forth by their employers. Worldwide business suffered nearly 43 million known security incidents in 2014. That equates to nearly 117,000 attacks daily![47] Therein lies the permeability predicament. With opportunity comes the chance that such vulnerabilities will be exploited. The goal of the hacker or cyberwarrior is to exploit those vulnerabilities. New computer viruses appear daily on both simple and complex systems alike. It has become an inescapable fact of life in the digital age.

Endnotes

1. Eli Noam, *Interconnecting the Network of Networks* (Cambridge, MA: MIT Press, 2001); Richard Gershon, "The Transnational Media Corporation and the Economics of Global Competition," in *Global Communication*, ed. Yahya R. Kamalipour (Belmont, CA: Wadsworth, 2002), 51–73.
2. Peter Monge and Noshir Contractor, *Theories of Communication Networks* (New York: Oxford Press, 2003).
3. Tim Berners Lee, *Weaving the Web* (New York: Harper Collins, 1999).
4. Lundwig V. Bertalanffy, *General Systems Theory* (New York: George Braziller, 1968).
5. Daniel Katz and Robert Kahn, *The Social Psychology of Organizations* (New York: Wiley, 1966).
6. Peter Monge and Eric Eisenberg, "Emergent Communication Networks," in *Handbook of Organizational Communication*, eds. F. Jablin, L. Putnam, K. Roberts, and C. O'Reilly (Norwood, NJ: Ablex, 1987), 304–342.
7. E. Rogers and D. L. Kincaid, *Communication Networks: Toward a New Paradigm for Research* (New York: The Free Press, 1981).
8. Monge and Contractor, *Theories of Communication Networks*, 30.
9. William Halal, "Organizational Intelligence: What It Is and How Managers Can Use It," *Strategy and Business* 9, no. 4 (1997): 67.
10. Richard Gershon, "Intelligent Networks and International Business Communication: A Systems Theory Interpretation," *Media Markets Monographs*, No. 12 (Pamplona, Spain: Universidad de Navarra Press, 2011).
11. Richard Gershon, *Media, Telecommunications and Business Strategy*, 2nd ed. (New York: Routledge, 2013).

12. Gershon, "Intelligent Networks"; see also: Eli Noam, *Interconnecting the Network of Networks* (Cambridge, MA: MIT Press, 2001).
13. Monge and Contractor, *Theories of Communication Networks.*
14. P. Monge, B. Heiss, and D. Magolin, "Communication Network Evolution in Organizational Communities," *Communication Theory* 18, no. 4 (2008): 449–477.
15. Gershon, *Media, Telecommunications and Business Strategy.*
16. After the divestiture of AT&T (1984), the Bell system's geographical service areas were redrawn according to a U.S. Justice Department designation called Local Access Transport Areas (LATAs). The local exchange carriers (LECs) were forced to provide long distance carriers with equal access, that is, an interface into the telephone network. Long distance is accomplished through a point-of-presence (POP) entry point.
17. Steven Jones, Ron Kovac, and Frank Groom, *Introduction to Communication Technologies,* 2nd ed. (New York: CRC Press, 2009).
18. A. M. Noll, *Highway of Dreams: A Critical View along the Information Superhighway* (Mahwah, NJ: Lawrence Erlbaum & Associates, 1997), 167.
19. F. H. Allport, "A Structuronomic Conception of Behavior: Individual and Collective," *Journal of Abnormal and Social Psychology* 64 (1962): 3–30.
20. Karl Weick, *The Social Psychology of Organizing* (Reading, MA: Addison-Wesley, 1979).
21. The Society for Worldwide Interbank Financial Telecommunication (SWIFT) is a member-owned cooperative located in 208 countries through which banks, security institutions, and corporate customers conduct the exchange of financial messages and data on a daily basis. SWIFT provides proprietary communications platform, products, and services that allow their customers to connect and exchange financial information securely and reliably.
22. Jeffrey Young and William Simon, *iCon: Steve Jobs* (New York: John Wiley & Sons, 2005).
23. Daniel Katz and Robert Kahn, "Organizations and the Systems Concept," in *The Social Psychology of Organizations,* 2nd ed. (New York: Wiley, 1978), 30.
24. Walter Isaacson, *The Innovators* (New York: Simon & Schuster, 2014), 249–251.
25. Isaacson, *The Innovators.*
26. Janet Abbate, *Inventing the Internet* (Cambridge, MA: MIT Press, 1999), 180.
27. Gershon, *Media, Telecommunications and Business Strategy.*
28. Ibid.
29. Jones, Kovac, and Groom, *Introduction to Communication Technologies.*
30. Claude Shannon and Warren Weaver, *The Mathematical Theory of Communication* (Urbana, IL: University of Illinois Press, 1949).
31. Norbert Weiner, *The Human Side of Human Beings: Cybernetics and Society* (Garden City, NY: Doubleday, 1954).
32. A cellular telephone switching center will switch the user to a change in frequency when and if the base transceiver station determines that the quality of the call is suffering. The base station (cell tower) monitors the calls in progress and can sense the signal strength of the mobile units in their own areas (and in the overlap areas of adjoining cells). The results are sent on to the Mobile Telephone Switching Office, which determines when the telephone call should be handed off upon entering a new cell site.
33. Monge and Contractor, *Theories of Communication Networks.*
34. Rouzbeh Yassini, *Planet Broadband* (Indianapolis, IN: Cisco Press, 2004), 4.
35. Jackie Craven, "What Is a Smart Home?" About Home, http://architecture.about.com/od/buildyourhous1/g/smarthouse.htm
36. Matt Vella, "Nest CEO Tony Fadell on the Future of the Smart Home," *Time,* June 26, 2014, 56.

37. Gershon, "Intelligent Networks."
38. Gershon, "Intelligent Networks."
39. Mark Clayton, "The New Cyber Arms Race." *Christian Science Monitor,* March 7, 2011, 27–33.
40. Richard Clark, *Cyber War* (New York: Harper-Collins, 2010).
41. R. Ducharme, "IT Security" (presentation, Fourth Annual WMU-HCoB IT Forum, Kalamazoo, MI, March 25, 2005).
42. "World's Biggest Data Breaches," Information Is Beautiful, last modified February 5, 2015, http://www.informationisbeautiful.net/visualizations/worlds-biggest-data-breaches-hacks/
43. Péter Ször, *The Art of Computer Virus Research and Defense* (Upper Saddle River, NJ: Addison-Wesley, 2005).
44. Julian Dibbell, "Lost Love: The Computer Virus Is an Ode to Our Digital Disaffection," *Harpers* (August 2001): 46–47.
45. Jonathan Strickland, "10 Worst Computer Viruses of all Time," *How Stuff Works,* http://computer.howstuffworks.com/worst-computer-viruses.htm#page=10
46. Dibbell, "Lost Love," 46–47.
47. AT&T, "What Every CEO Needs to Know about Cybersecurity," *AT&T Business Report,* last modified October, 2, 2015, http://www.business.att.com/content/src/csi/decodingtheadversary.pdf

CHAPTER 8

Digital Media and Innovation I

Interactivity, Virtual Communication, and Information Search

Introduction

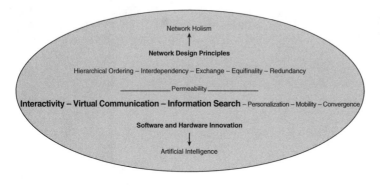

Today, the Internet has become steadily woven into all aspects of work and leisure. It has grown in size and complexity due to the many contributions of its users, including powerful search engines, unique Web site design, aggregation of content, EC, and social media, to name only a few. The Internet has transformed the world's business and social environments. In this chapter, I use the term *digital lifestyle* as a way to describe how various kinds of media and IT are used to enhance the way we live. From smartphones to smart houses, today's media users have come to expect certain things from the computer and communication devices they use.

Digital Media

Digital media represents the artistic convergence of various kinds of hardware and software design elements to create entirely new forms of communication expression.

Digital media has transformed the way we communicate and access information.[1] Booking a flight and vacation on Booking.com or Expedia is a very different value proposition than working with a travel agent. Purchasing a set of songs on iTunes or Pandora is an altogether different shopping experience than walking into a music store. And streaming a movie via Netflix on a high-definition television (HDTV) set or a computer tablet has given new meaning to the term *video on demand* (VOD). Digital media in the 21st century requires a special appreciation for speed, mobility, and convenience. Today's Internet user expects to access the web—anytime, anywhere. Location should never be an obstacle.

Digital Storytelling

Digital media has proved to be a major game changer when it comes to visual presentation. Digital storytelling is the art of using enhanced media and information tools to tell a story. From online newspapers to a highly engaging Web site display, digital storytelling assumes a wide range of electronic media narratives that might include text, still and moving imagery, and enhanced sound effects as well as being nonlinear and interactive. Such stories no longer conform to the conventions of traditional storytelling.[2] The personal diary has given way to public demonstrations of one's ideas and opinions using the power of the Internet and social media. Nowhere is this more evident than in social media sites like Facebook and Twitter. The once iconic photograph album has become more decidedly multipurpose in approach with digital imprints now available on one's phone, computer tablet, or Facebook account.

In the next two chapters, we will explore the second half of the ITS model by focusing on seven signature features. They include: 1) Interactivity, 2) Virtual communication, 3) Information search, 4) Personalization, 5) Mobility, 6) Convergence, and 7) Artificial intelligence (AI). (See Table 8.1.) Accordingly, we consider both the social and technological consequences of digital media and intelligent networks on people and organizations. One problem in measuring the technological consequences of innovation is untangling cause-and-effect relationships. As Rogers (1995)[3] points out, once a primary innovation has been fully diffused into a system, there is no going backward. Basic patterns of social and organizational behavior are forever changed.

Principals of Digital Communication and Binary Logic

Historically, older forms of communication and information technology, including radio and television broadcasting, vinyl records, and VHS tapes are considered analog forms of communication. An *analog signal* (or analogy) is a representation of something else. It is a continuous signal that can be physically measured. One of the major problems associated with analog systems of communication are their susceptibility to unwanted noise. Consider, for example, that a traditional telephone

Table 8.1   Digital Lifestyle: Signature Features

Digital Media Features	Applications and Examples
Interactivity	• Human–Computer Interface Design • Video on Demand (VOD) o Netflix, YouTube, HBO Go • Cloud Computing

Virtual Communication	• Private Virtual Networks
	• Global Virtual Teams
	  o Videoconferencing, Skype, Facetime
	• Social Media
	  o Facebook, Twitter, Linked-In

Information Search	• Querying the Internet
	• Content Service Providers
	  o Google, Yahoo
	  o Wikipedia, Trip Advisor
	  o Web MD, Vacation Rental by Owners

Personalization	• Digital Video Recording
	  o Cable, IPTV, DBS
	• Personalized Music Playlist
	  o iTunes, Pandora, Rhapsody
	• Personalized Web Site
	  o Facebook, LinkedIn page

Mobility	• Laptop Computers
	• Smartphones
	  o Google Calendar, Yahoo Weather
	• Global Positioning Services (GPS)
	  o Google Maps and Navigation

Convergence	• Digital Photography • Filmmaking and Special Effects • High-Definition Television (HDTV)
Artificial Intelligence	• Personalized Recommendation Software • Robotics • Virtual Reality

performs the function of translating one's voice into an electrical signal and transmitting it via a long distance network of switches, routers, and amplifiers. Each time the signal is re-amplified, there is the potential to introduce unwanted noise into the transmission. The same problem occurs with recording formats as well. When using an analog tape recorder, the signal is taken straight from the microphone and laid onto tape. If one wants to make a tape of a tape, each successive generation suffers a degradation in quality. Whereas, in an all-digital link, the signal is an exact replication of the original, thus eliminating any unwanted noise factors. The cut-and-paste function on a computer provides a simple illustration. If one types the word *innovation* and copies it, the quality and accuracy of the paste function is the same whether it's the first repeat or the one hundredth. This is the reason why a copy of a CD is as good as the original.

All forms of digital communication are based on the principle of binary logic, which presumes that a signaling system is essentially in one of two states: open or closed. Binary logic uses the numbers 1 and 0 arranged in different sequences to exchange information. The numbers 1 and 0 are called bits from the word *binary digit*, which is the lowest possible unit of information that can be transferred or handled.[4] A byte is an eight-bit train; that is, one byte equals eight bits. A digital signal is made up of pulses of discrete duration, that is, a stream of bits that are either on or off. Digital signals are sent as a sequence of pulses of fixed width and amplitude. (See Figure 8.1.)

Pulse Code Modulation. Traditional analog technologies and devices are incompatible with digital signaling and communication. Consequently, the situation requires a conversion process, whereby the analog signal is converted into a digital format. Consider, for example, the task of converting a Bruce Springsteen music album recorded in the 1970s into a CD. Pulse code modulation (PCM) is a conversion process, whereby the analog signal is sampled and converted into binary format, that is, a sequence of 1s and 0s.[5] The conversion process requires two steps: 1) Sampling and 2) Quantizing (companding). (See Figure 8.2.)

The first step in the conversion process involves sampling the analog signal at regular time intervals. The goal is to accurately reflect the original signal. The higher the level of sampling per second, the more accurate the reflection of the original signal. *Sampling rate* refers to the number of times the analog signal is sampled per second.[6] The sampling rate must be at least twice the highest frequency component of the analog source to faithfully reproduce the signal when it is converted into digital form. The second step in the process involves quantizing the sampled pulse, that is, forcing it to occupy a discrete set of 1 and 0 values.[7] The information is now fully digitized. Once the information has been converted to digital format, distribution and storage costs have been significantly lowered. There is an inherent economy of

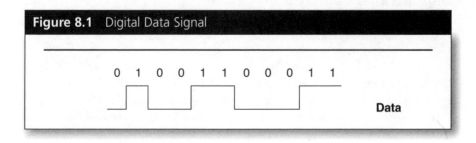

Figure 8.1   Digital Data Signal

0 1 0 0 1 1 0 0 0 1 1

Data

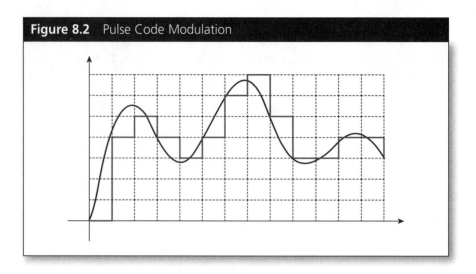

Figure 8.2 Pulse Code Modulation

scale. A CD is much less expensive to produce when compared to vinyl records. An MP3 music file can be transmitted and stored electronically for a fraction of the cost when compared to the production and delivery of a CD.

More Efficient Use of Bandwidth

The electromagnetic spectrum is a fixed and limited resource. Yet all wireless services, including television, smartphones, and satellites (to name only a few) depend on available spectrum. The critical challenge for broadcasters, cable television operators, and Internet service providers is how to optimize and make more efficient use of the electromagnetic spectrum. The term *bandwidth* refers to channel width or information carrying capacity. As an example, FM radio requires 200 KHz. of bandwidth to provide an acceptable signal to a potential radio listener. In contrast, a typical TV signal requires 4 MHz. of bandwidth. By the time one adds in sound (vestigial sideband) and a little buffer space, a TV signal requires 6 MHz. of bandwidth. The implementation of HDTV requires about two times as much information carrying capacity than was originally needed with analog TV. The solution, therefore, is to create a system that compresses existing bandwidth space allocations more efficiently.

Digital Video Compression

Digital video compression (DVC) refers to digitizing and compressing video pictures so that they may be processed, stored, and distributed with greater flexibility and ease. DVC refers to the technical ability to reduce the size of video signals so that they can be more efficiently transmitted and stored. Digital TV relies on a compression and encoding scheme known as Motion Picture Experts Group 4 (MPEG-4) to fit its high-resolution images into a lesser amount of bandwidth space. MPEG-4 reduces the amount of data to about 20 percent of the original amount.[8] MPEG-4 is the industry standard for Internet video streaming as well as satellite television broadcasts.[9]

DVC operates on the premise that some of the data present before compression is not essential for achieving good picture quality. Video compression operates off a grid system using square-shaped groups of neighboring pixels (often called *macroblocks*). These pixel groups are compared from one frame to the next, and the video codec sends only the differences within those blocks.[10] The term *lossy* is used to describe those situations where there is a high degree of redundant information within the video display. DVC works well in those situations where there is limited or no motion. The court surface, during a televised basketball game, for example, can be repeated with very little transmitted data. DVC is fully utilized by diverse technologies such as: 1) Cable television, 2) Direct broadcast satellite (DBS) television, 3) Internet video streaming, and 4) Video games.

MP3

MP3 is a patented digital audio encoding format that utilizes compression technology. MP3 is designed to greatly reduce the amount of data required to represent the audio recording while still providing a faithful reproduction of the original recording. The German company Fraunhofer-Gesellshaft is credited with being the principal developer of MP3 software technology. The lead technology designer was Karl-Heinz Brandenburg, who was a specialist in mathematics and had been researching methods for compressing music since 1977.[11] The speed and efficiency of producing Internet-delivered music using MP3 file-sharing software was a major game changer by transforming the cost structure of music recording and distribution on a worldwide basis. The combination of the Apple iPod and iTunes would eventually create the first sustainable music downloading business model of its kind.[12] It is a business model that has been replicated by others including Pandora, Spotify, and Rhapsody.

Interactivity

The principle of interactivity suggests the ability to engage in two-way communication. Interactivity can include a whole host of digital media activities ranging from interactive television to video games to virtual reality simulations. The principle of interactive communication in its earliest form can be traced back to the beginning use of touch-tone telephony that replaced rotary dial telephones in the 1970s. Touch-tone telephony utilized a concept known as *dual-tone multi frequency,* whereby each button on the telephone handset consists of two frequencies. Touch-tone provides the basis for interactive capability with a host telephone system or computer. The goal of touch-tone was to give businesses and other organizations the ability to create a menu structure of services that the user could access by pushing select number keys.

Cable Television and Interactive Communication

A good example of interactive communication can be seen in the early developments of cable television and the ability of the user to engage in pay-per-view (PPV) television and home shopping. A cable television system is capable of not only transmitting audio, video, and data signals from the headend point to the subscriber's home but can likewise send those same signals in a reverse direction. Early supporters of interactive television realized that two-way capability would allow a cable system to offer its customers a wide variety of enhanced information services.[13] The first generation of two-way interactive cable television involved home shopping channels (i.e., Home Shopping Network, QVC, etc.) that relied on hybrid networks, that is, cable television from headend source to home and telephone communication from home to the program source.[14] During the decades of the 1980s and 1990s, the second generation of interactive cable television evolved with the development of PPV television. PPV involves charging the user by the program rather than by the program channel. PPV has taken several years (and many failed attempts) to develop and has proved to be modestly successful in the delivery of special event programs (sports and concerts) as well as adult entertainment.

Video on Demand. VOD represents the third generation of PPV services and enables the cable television viewer to access feature films and concerts on request. VOD allows the user to choose programming from a large selection of titles and program categories that are hosted on a remote server. Starting in the 1990s, VOD was being touted as cable television's answer to the emerging success of the videotape and later DVD rental industry. While cable television was able to promote select forms of VOD programming, most notably, professional boxing matches, music concerts, and adult entertainment, VOD did not live up to its promise.

Digital Video Recorders and Video Streaming. Today, cable television has become much more than a conveyor of television entertainment. Cable television has become the all-essential broadband link into people's homes, thus enabling a fourth generation of interactive capability that relies on digital video recording technology as well as video streaming via the Internet. The emergence of the digital video recorder (DVR) in the late 1990s and early 21st century gave the television viewer increased control in terms of time shifting, that is, the ability to watch programs when it was convenient to the user. The DVR provides an on-screen guide of scheduled television programs, whose features include the ability to record selected programs for later viewing. One of the important features for the consumer is the ability to record one's favorite television programs for later viewing, including the ability to skip over commercial TV ads.[15]

In the 21st century, VOD is reasserting itself in an altogether unexpected way. The major game changer emerged in the form of Netflix, which in 2004 demonstrated the possibility of streaming movies via a broadband connection directly to the end user's digital television set. Video streaming involves sending information and entertainment content via the Internet in a digitally compressed format. The programming is displayed on the host television set or computer screen in real time. Netflix would be a catalyst for change, opening up the door for other video services, including Hulu, YouTube, and HBO Go. Advancements in HDTV and Dolby stereo sound have made video-streamed programming a much more attractive value proposition for the consumer.

Over-the-Top Video Services. Also important to the discussion is the future of over-the-top (OTT) video services, that is, television programming that can be video streamed via the Internet to various kinds of portable devices like laptop computers, computer tablets, and smartphones. Instead of subscribing to cable or Internet Protocol TV, the consumer elects to use the Internet as the main delivery system for his/her television viewing experience.[16] This is interactivity in its most essential form. The user is interacting with the television service provider by expressing clear preferences for select forms of television programming as well as viewing platform. More and more subscribers are engaged in what is known as *cordcutting*, whereby, the subscriber cancels one's basic cable television subscription and elects instead to use one's Internet feed for the purpose watching television. Such interactions have given new meaning to the term *video on demand*.

Human/Computer Interface Design

Today, interactive communication is the starting point for all discussions concerning how users interact with the various media and communication devices they use. Much of the research on interactivity concerns how users interact with various communication devices, including computers, smartphones, and video game systems. One group of scholars view interactivity as a function of the medium itself. This is particularly true when it comes to the development of things such as smartphones and video game systems. Here the emphasis is on hardware and software devices. Steuer (1992), for one, argues that the interactivity of mediated communication depends on three main characteristics: *speed* (i.e., how quickly a device responds to a user's commands), *range* (i.e., the level of control permitted by the device), and *mapping* (i.e., the degree of correspondence between a user's actions to control the device and how it responds to those actions).[17]

In contrast, a second group of scholars look at interactivity from the vantage point of the communication process itself. Interactivity resides in the perceptions and experiences of those who directly participate in the actual communication. This perspective is more closely associated with computer-mediated communication. According to McMillan (2002) interactivity occurs at varying levels and degrees of engagement, ranging from social networking sites to video game participation.[18] Here the emphasis is on the communication of ideas, information, and shared meaning among communicants.

Interactivity and Knowledge Transfer. Interactivity has to do with the knowledge transfer between a person and machine or between a person and a larger set of community users. To fully appreciate the breadth and scope of this idea, one needs to have an appreciation for the early work in human/computer interface design. In 1963, Douglas Engelbart of the Stanford Research Center pioneered the development of the computer mouse, which was later advanced by the Xerox Corporation in the 1970s. The computer mouse functions as a pointing device that detects and highlights text and visual displays on a two-dimensional screen. The computer mouse frees the user to a large extent from using a keyboard. It was a simple but masterful form of ergonomic design that greatly improved the way in which people interfaced with computers.[19]

Engelbart's research and design contribution demonstrated a systems theory perspective using the principles of coevolution as it might apply to the use of technology. In biological terms, each party in a coevolutionary relationship exerts synergistic pressure on the other, thereby affecting each other's evolution. The classic example is bees and the flowers they pollinate. Both have coevolved so that each has become dependent on the other for survival. Engelbart reasoned that the state of knowledge and information display is only as good as the available technology to manage it. He thus set out to create an interface design that would be faster and more efficient in terms of manipulating information on a screen.

Graphic User Interface (GUI). The development of the GUI icons by Xerox Corporation and later Apple in the 1980s further advanced the cause of human–computer interface design. A GUI offers graphical icons and visual indicators as opposed to text-based interfaces and/or typed command labels to fully represent the information and program selections available to a user. GUI has become a standard feature on all Apple, Microsoft, and Linux-based operating systems. Touch-screen technology came along in the 1980s and was used in a variety of automated banking and tourist attractions, including ATM machines and information kiosks. Today, touch-screen capability has become a standard feature found in various kinds of digital appliances, including laptop computers, mobile smartphones, computer tablets, and global positioning navigation systems (GPS).

Speech Recognition. The next and evolving generation of interface software involves speech recognition systems evidenced by the work being done in the military and health-care fields. Speech recognition software allows the user to dictate into a computer or handheld recorder, thus enabling an electronic text version of the spoken words to appear on the users' screen. Each successive generation requires less formatting of the software (i.e., identifying specialized words). Also, the software adapts to the user by keying in on select words and phrases and storing them in its internal memory. A variation on speech recognition systems are voice command systems using Bluetooth technology in cars.[20] Bluetooth represents an industry standard for personal wireless communication devices, referred to as personal area networks. Bluetooth provides a way to connect and exchange information between Bluetooth-compatible devices such as laptop computers, smartphones, and music sound systems using unlicensed short-range radio frequencies (i.e., typically 1–100 meters). Bluetooth simplifies the discovery and setup of services between devices. The voice command system can set up and execute a hands-free cellular telephone call as well as call up music and traffic reports from the vehicle's radio, DVD, or iPod control system.

Cloud Computing

The expression "putting something on the cloud" refers to the idea of storing information and data on a remote host site. Cloud computing provides both storage as well as the delivery of information services over a virtual platform using the networking capability of the Internet. Cloud computing represents an altogether different form of interactive communication. Users are able to access such services on demand. In general, the public is most familiar with public cloud services. Public cloud computing involves making available information and entertainment services to the general public by a third-party vendor. The services are hosted by the vendor and are offered free of charge or on a pay-as-you-go basis. Examples include: Google, Gmail, Calendar, Apple iTunes, Amazon.com web services, Facebook, and Pandora. The third-party vendor is responsible for managing the entire service. The end user has little control over where the data is stored and whether or not it can be available at any given time.

Private Cloud Services or community clouds operate within the firewall or boundaries of an organization. Private clouds are managed internally by an organization and are therefore responsible for organizing and securing all information. As a result, the organization will typically make a major financial commitment in software and hardware capability as well as utilizing in-house expertise to manage information flow throughout the entire transnational organization. Examples might include the international banking and airline industries. In general, there are three types of cloud computing service models including 1) Infrastructure as a service, 2) Platform as a service, and 3) Software as a service.

Infrastructure as a Service (IaaS). This represents the most basic kind of cloud support model. IaaS refers to those kinds of facilities that provide business users with extra storage space on a remote server. The basic premise is that cloud service providers manage an organization's complete data information needs remotely and host all information via a series of virtual links. The principle advantage is cost savings by not having to manage and host one's own database system of documents and records.

Platform as a Service (PaaS). PaaS is a category of cloud computing services that provides a highly refined computing platform and set of subsystems. In this model, the user creates a set of software tools using programs and/or a library from the provider. The user also controls the software deployment and configuration settings. The cloud service provider helps to advance the network, servers, storage, and other services. Examples of PaaS might include a community based geographic information system (GIS).

Software as a Service (SaaS). This service model is used for purposes of software deployment. The cloud service provider licenses various kinds of software applications on demand to customers as needed. The end-user does not manage or control infrastructure planning as it pertains to the network, servers, operating systems, storage, or software applications. Instead, SaaS provides a cost-effective alternative from having to purchase software support outright as well as simplifying maintenance and support. In a sense, the organization is leasing the software as compared to having to purchase it outright. All updates are automatically fitted into the software as a service. SaaS has proved to be a useful approach for start-up companies with limited resources that don't want to make the large up-front investment in software.

With the growth of cloud computing comes the associated challenges of information security. Both business as well as individual users who have their information stored on a third party's server are subject to security and compliance standards of operation to ensure the protection of their information. Preserving security on the cloud is one of the major concerns by users who chose to store their data remotely. The overriding concern is the control of data: how data enters a system, where it resides, how it is managed and processed, and who can access it. One of the important compliance issues is data loss. A single point of failure or intrusion could prove catastrophic for business and individual users. To offset this possibility, cloud computing service providers build in redundancy (i.e., backup systems) to ensure safety and security.

Virtual Communication

The term *virtual communication* can be used to describe the artificial space and network linkages connecting a separate and dispersed group of users using various forms of computer and communication technology. From Skype to the international business videoconference, the common denominator with all forms of virtual communication is the ability to create a simulated environment. The communication itself can be both synchronous (real time) as well as asynchronous (different times). The selection and type of communication technology is based on how much information content the sender wishes the receiver to have. Researchers Daft and Lengel (1986) refer to this as *media richness*.[21] The difference in quality and depth varies according to the communication medium.

Virtual Private Networks

A *virtual private network* (VPN) is a computer network that uses a public telecommunications infrastructure such as the Internet to provide remote users (or departments) secure access to their organizations' networks. A VPN can range in size and scale of operation from the transnational media corporation that operates on multiple continents to a major medical hospital that must provide secure health-care information to physicians and other medical professionals located in a variety of clinics and adjoining facilities. The major requirement is the ability to provide immediate and secure information available only to the organization and its affiliate sites.[22] (See Figure 8.3.)

Figure 8.3   Virtual Private Network

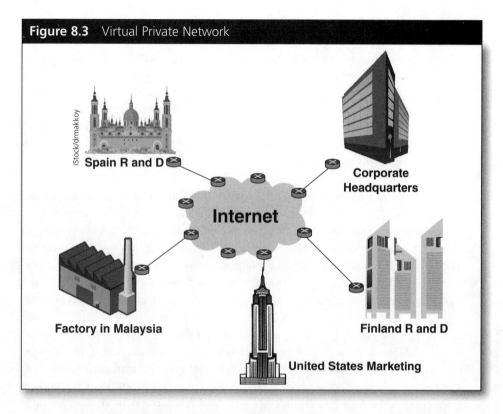

The word *virtual* can sometimes be misleading. The connections made between people and organization both within and outside an organization are quite real. As Reed (2014) reminds us:

> The seemingly placeless, ethereal world of the Web is not possible without millions of very earthbound terminals, CPUs, hundreds of thousands of miles of cords and fiber optic cables. . . . No matter how lost we may get imaginatively in cyberspace, those seemingly virtual spaces are possible only because of a massive array of material objects anchored in geographically specific places.[23]

Intelligent Networking and International Business Communication

Social and scientific terms like *knowledge economy, information society,* or *digital age* do not lend themselves to precise definition or meaning. What is beyond dispute, however, is the role of intelligent networks in helping to advance the transmission, storage, and display of media and information content within the context of international business communication. The knowledge economy involves the full integration of transnational business, nation-states, and technologies operating at high speed. It is a global economy that is being driven by free-market capitalism and the power of intelligent networking.[24] The knowledge economy stands in marked contrast to many of the basic patterns and assumptions of the Industrial age. The once highly centralized business has given way to the transnational organization that operates in multiple countries throughout the world. Instead of time and communication being highly synchronized, today's working professional lives in a digital world of asynchronous and virtual communication that allows for the international collaboration of projects regardless of time zones, geographical borders, and physical space. We have entered the era of global virtual teams where work is produced across multiple time zones and geographic spaces.[25] As Eli Noam (2001) points out, "The knowledge economy has become a society of networks. We don't talk with people; we network with them."[26]

Virtual Private Networks and the Transnational Corporation. The transnational corporation (TNC) is a nationally based company with overseas operations in two or more countries. Strategic decision making and the allocation of resources are predicated upon economic goals and efficiencies with little regard to national boundaries. The TNC has become a salient feature of our present-day global economic landscape.[27] Through a process of foreign direct investment, the TNC relies on the use of advanced IT as a way to stay globally connected. At the heart of transnational business operations is the importance of organizational control, which describes the need for a system-wide method for managing, tracking, and evaluating a TNC's domestic and foreign operations. Organizational control provides the ability to centralize decision making, thereby giving senior management the tools necessary to plan, allocate resources, and take corrective action to meet changing international conditions. The intelligent network has become the vital nervous system enabling the TNC's multiple divisions and subunits to function independently while being part of a larger communication network. As a consequence, traditional divisions and departmental hierarchies tend to be flatter, thereby permitting direct communication between and among organizational players.[28]

Global Virtual Teams. International project teams are the key to smart, flexible, and cost effective organizations. A global virtual team represents working professionals from a TNC's worldwide operations assembled together on an as-needed basis for the length of a project assignment. They are staffed by working professionals from different countries. More and more, the transnational organization uses global virtual teams as part of a larger effort to share international expertise across the entire TNC. The global virtual team offers up certain distinct advantages, including shared access to information, collaborative research and design work, reduced travel costs, and so on. Advancements in communication technology and intelligent networking have elevated the principle of teamwork to a whole new level in terms of collaborative effort.[29]

At the same time, global virtual teams bring with them a unique set of challenges. Foremost are issues pertaining to trust involving differences of culture, geographic dislocation, complex problem solving, and the effective collaboration of ideas. Specifically, how does one creatively engage a group of people that one has never physically met and trust that everyone is equal to the task?[30] The global virtual team presents a unique set of challenges in terms of blending the technical efficiencies of virtual communication with the practical needs of creating a cohesive international project group.

Skype. Skype is a free voice over IP (VOIP) service that allows users to engage in a computer-to-computer videoconference. Skype, which is an acronym for sky and peer, was created by Janus Friis (Denmark) and Niklas Zennström (Sweden) in cooperation with Ahti Heinla, Priji Kasesalu, and Jaan Tallinn (Estonia). Skype was first released to the public in August 2003. It was later acquired by Microsoft in 2011 for $8.5 billion. Telephone calls placed to other Skype subscribers are free of charge, while calls to landline telephones and mobile phones are charged via a debit-based user account system. What makes Skype unique is that its represents the first generation of real-time full-motion video telephony. Skype can be accessed not only on computers but on any video display monitor, whether it be an HDTV or a mobile phone.

Videoconferencing. One of the standard tools for the global virtual team is the videoconference. The videoconference provides an electronic meeting format using video images and audio sound. People are typically linked together at two or more locations via an Internet connection, telephone switch, or satellite. A two-way videoconference is the quintessential example of virtual communication. The videoconference permits the exchange of information, data, and/or drawings between two or more people at separate locations. The organizational videoconference has become a standard feature of transnational communication and serves as an alternative to face-to-face meetings. This can include both point-to-multipoint videoconferences using structured conference meeting rooms as well as Internet-based conferencing.

Videoconferencing offers transnational corporations (TNCs) some distinct advantages, including 1) Information exchange, 2) Increased productivity, 3) Cost savings, and 4) Employee training. First and foremost, the TNC videoconference is about information exchange. This gives the large-scale organization a level of productivity and efficiency that would otherwise be unavailable. The TNC videoconference can link together marketing and engineering teams and, thereby, eliminate the need for travel, hotel, and lodging expenses associated with travel. It also contributes to increased productivity as key management people are in the office and not in transit. Videoconferencing companies like Cisco and Polycom have tried to simplify the conferencing process by introducing easy meeting setups as well as making the design of the conferencing rooms (including table shape, wall colors, and backdrop) look as though all participating members are seated in the same room. This stands in marked contrast to older videoconferencing systems that required dedicated and expensive room-based facilities that were difficult to set up.[31]

Alternatively, an Internet-based videoconference can provide a low-cost way to electronically link members of the TNC. Today, nearly all desktop, laptop, and tablet computers are equipped with a webcam and microphone. Software applications like Skype, FaceTime, and Go to Meeting make international project meetings and consultations a fairly routine exercise. In addition, a prearranged webinar can provide transnational employees with a timely method for obtaining educational training and information updates. Typically, the webinar is scheduled ahead of time and involves an information specialist as well as written materials as part of a larger information package. Videoconferencing, both simple and complex, gives greater impetus for the TNCs to operate globally and makes practical the ability to exchange information. Today's business professional is no longer constrained by issues pertaining to time and geographical location. Videoconferencing and webinars make real-time business communication possible, enabling business professionals to have the ability to remain productive without the need for extensive travel.

Virtual Communities

One of the more compelling aspects of virtual communication has to do with the various kinds of online relationships that are formed as a result of using the Internet and the different forms of computer-mediated communication. One important consideration is *social presence theory,* which describes the degree to which a medium is perceived as conveying the presence of the communicating participants.[32] The social presence of the communicating participants depends on a variety of factors, including the full range of verbal and nonverbal cues as well as the technology and modality. Computer-mediated communication, and specifically the Internet, has proved to be a fertile ground for those scholars interested in exploring the importance of information exchange and shared meaning.[33] The term *homophily* is used to describe communication networks based on a similarity of interests (i.e., occupation, personal interests, and political causes).

The Internet, for one, brings together people who share a common interest. A number of writers refer to such networks as *virtual communities.*[34] Nowhere is the principle of virtual communities more evident than in social networking sites like Facebook, Twitter, and LinkedIn.[35] Social networking allows individuals to present themselves and maintain connections with others. As friends and acquaintances join Facebook or Twitter, they become part of a larger social grid that matters to the individual. It creates value to the individual by adding to one's social capital.[36] Because that person's friends are connected to other friends on the network, there is the opportunity to virtually expand one's circle of friends and acquaintances.[37] Each new person and extended link adds value and dynamism to the overall network (i.e., network evolution).

Twitter. Twitter is an online social networking service that enables users to send and read short 140-character text messages, called *tweets.* Twitter provides an immediate electronic gateway for the millions of registered users who wish to comment or express a viewpoint. Registered users can read and post tweets, but unregistered users can only read them. Twitter enables people to exercise a basic human impulse, the ability to communicate with large numbers of people at a time.[38] Twitter is the brainchild of Jack Dorsey, who as a kid growing up in St. Louis was fascinated with dispatch routing systems, that is, short and punctuated emergency communication used by police, fire, and rescue as well as commercial enterprises such as taxis.

Dorsey first came up with the idea that became Twitter while attending New York University. His experience using instant messaging prompted him to wonder whether it was possible to combine the immediacy of instant messaging with the mobility of an online dispatching system. He later approached Odeo business partners Biz Stone, Evan Williams, and Noah Glass with his idea. At a daylong brainstorming session, Dorsey introduced the idea of an individual using a Short Message Service (SMS) to communicate with a small group of users. The name *Twitter* reflects chirps from a bird, that is, short bursts of information. Twitter was launched in July 2006 and became its own company in April 2007. Since then, the service has achieved worldwide popularity. Twitter is one of the Internet's ten most widely visited sites. As Levinson (2013) points out, Twitter gives the user a powerful electronic platform by which to "inform, amuse or outrage" other Twitter users.[39]

As a social network, Twitter revolves around the principle of followers. On Twitter, the pound sign (or hash) turns any word or group of words that directly follow it into a searchable link. The hashtag allows the user to organize content and track discussion topics based on those key words. Clicking on that link enables the user to comment. Similarly, the @ sign followed by the user name is used for replying to other users. When the user chooses to follow another Twitter user, that user's tweets appear in reverse chronological order on the user's main Twitter page. If the user follows twelve people, he/she will see a mix of tweets scrolling down the page: music recommendations, political commentary, football results, and so on. A word, phrase, or topic that is tagged at a greater rate than other tags is said to be a *trending topic*. Trending topics become popular either through a deliberate effort by users and/or because a major event breaks into the public conversation space. Twitter provides users with an immediate and accessible platform, albeit 140 characters, with which to comment about topical events and people. This is made easier by the fact that Twitter works well with mobile phones.

Twitter's popularity and general use tends to spike during prominent events whether it's a World Cup Soccer match, a political or entertainment scandal, or comments on the death of a public figure. Twitter has increasingly become an accepted form of communication used in business and professional settings. The Twitter platform has been adopted by a number of major health organizations, including the World Health Organization (WHO), the Center for Disease Control (CDC), and the National Institute for Health (NIH). Twitter provides a unique platform to convey health messages as well as medical alerts using the power of social media.[40]

Information Search

Searching for information represents the most essential reason why someone uses the Internet, namely, to gather information about topics and issues that are important to the user. A search engine is a software tool that helps the user perform key word searches and locate specific information available on the Internet. The search engine in combination with hypertext linking provides structure and makes the Internet more accessible to navigate. Search engines come vary in size and scope, starting with general information search engines like Google, Yahoo, Bing, and Ask. Different countries of the world have an equivalent version Google, such as Google India or Google Brazil, that accommodate differing search queries by language and more specialized information and news focus. Alternatively, some countries of the world have their own general search engine equivalents such as Baidu.com and Qq.com, which are the two leading search engines in China and rank in the top 10 most frequently visited Web sites worldwide according to Alexa Internet Inc.

Less understood by the general public, however, is the importance of specialized search engine Web sites like WebMD (health care), Trip Advisor (travel), and Kelley Blue Book (automobile comparison shopping) that offer the user a more dedicated focus. The specialized search engine is responsible for organizing information resources that are distinct to a particular discipline or area of specialization. The specialized search engine is uniquely positioned to assist the individual who has more defined information needs. Typically, a search engine works by sending out a spider to fetch as many documents as possible within a defined set of research parameters and databases. This is followed by a software program called an indexer, which reads these documents and creates an index based on the words contained in each document. The search engine uses a proprietary algorithm to create a set of listings that corresponds to the user's query. WebMD, for example, advertises itself as the number one search engine site for obtaining information about health issues. The WebMD Website, available at http://www.webmd.com/ provides useful medical news and information about a variety of health issues as well as information related to finding doctors, hospitals, and specialized treatment centers. Specialized Web sites such as Web MD, Trip Advisor, and Kelley Blue Book are very attractive to advertisers. They speak to the importance of narrowcasting, albeit for the Internet.

Planning and Design Considerations

The basic reason for creating a specialized search engine is simple. By becoming a major gatekeeper of people's online experience, Internet search companies hope to build a set of loyal users who will rely on them not only for trusted information but to buy goods and services as well. Many of today's better-known search engines (e.g., Google and Yahoo) are considered multilevel Internet companies. They have positioned themselves as full-service information sites with links to a variety of information, entertainment, and adjoining services. For a company like Google, Internet search is the foundation to a whole host of value-added services such as YouTube, Google Maps, Google Translate, Google Scholar, and so on. Similarly, Yahoo has created its own full-service ecosystem as well, including news, weather, finance, food, and Flickr.

Two important features found in all search engine sites are the aggregation of content and personalization. The primary responsibility of a search engine is to collate data from a variety of information sources around the world. This is accomplished through international alliances and distribution relationships. The search engine is responsible for the organization and arranging of information, thus making it possible for key word and context-based search information. A successfully designed search engine should contain the best features of an encyclopedia, phone directory, and newsletter. The aggregation of content enables the user to comparison shop. The user should be able to locate and compare professional service providers both locally and nationally. Search engine software permits registered users to receive personalized information in the form of specialized content (e.g., daily news briefings, weather and stock reports, newly released articles, commentaries, etc.). In sum, the key to building a successful search engine is to make it an essential part of the user's Internet experience.

Power Applications (or Apps)

Central to any discussion pertaining to digital lifestyle is having an appreciation for the importance of software applications (or apps). An app is a specialized software program that can be downloaded to various kinds of mobile devices, including smartphones, computer tablets, and equivalent devices. The app allows the user to engage in different kinds of activities for purposes of information searches, utility (calendar, weather, airline reservation, etc.), and entertainment (music, video games, etc.)

User Generated Content

The Internet has proved to be the great equalizer by affording its users the opportunity to generate some of the most important and robust content found on the web. The term *user generated content* (UGC) refers to the idea that the content found on many of today's most widely used Web sites is created by the very consumers who use it. UGC can include a variety of online content such as postings, blogs, videos, customer reviews, discussion forums, photographs, and so forth.[41] As an example, Facebook, YouTube, and Wikipedia are made possible by their many users who input information, photos, or video about themselves or contribute as volunteer specialists about a topic for which they possess an expertise. Clemencia Rodriquez (2010) refers to this as citizen media.[42] UGC is made possible by a number of technological, social, and economic drivers.[43] The combination of high-speed Internet access coupled with various input devices (i.e., laptop computers, smartphones, and tablets) makes the creation and uploading of information ever more accessible. Both social media and EC Web sites strongly encourage its users to input information as well as to comment and react to other postings. Some of the more notable UGC Web sites can be seen in Table 8.2.

Widely Used Apps

It is beyond the scope of this book to consider the tens of thousands of apps that have become part of today's digital media environment. But it may prove helpful to focus our attention on a few select apps that have proved to be real innovators in the

Table 8.2   Notable Examples of User Generated Content
1. Facebook
2. Wikipedia
3. YouTube
4. Trip Advisor
5. Twitter
6. Vacation Rental by Owner
7. LinkedIn
8. Craigslist
9. Blogger
10. Tumblr
11. Angie's List

field of media and communication. One of the ways to gauge the relative success of an app is to look at its national and international ranking as part of the listing service developed by Alexa Internet Inc., which is a California-based subsidiary of Amazon.com. Alexa tracks the browsing behavior of an estimated 30 million Web sites worldwide. The information is stored and analyzed, forming the basis for the company's global ranking system of Internet Web sites. Table 8.3 provides a listing of the top ten Internet Web sites worldwide according to Alexa. Each of the said Web sites has its own equivalent mobile app version. It is interesting to note that most of the examples shown are a combination of information search as well as UGC.

Table 8.3 The Ten Most Widely Used Global Internet Web Sites	
1. Google.com	Google is the world's preeminent Internet search engine. The launch of its key word search advertising program in 2001 provided the basic business model that would propel Google forward as a major communications company.
2. Facebook.com	Facebook is the world's preeminent social networking site. Facebook reaches an estimated 1.4 billion users worldwide.
3. YouTube.com	The site is the best known video-sharing Web site. Most of the content featured on YouTube is user generated, which includes video clips, TV clips, music videos, amateur content, and so on.
4. Yahoo.com	The site is internationally recognized for its search engine, Yahoo directory, mail, news, weather, online mapping, and so on.

5. Baidu.com	Baidu is the leading Chinese-language search engine. Baidu offers multimedia content, including more than 740 million web pages, 80 million images, and 10 million multimedia files.
6. Wikipedia.org	Wikipedia is the world's largest online encyclopedia. Wikipedia's contributed articles are written by volunteers around the world, and nearly all of its articles can be edited by anyone with access to the Wikipedia Web site.
7. Twitter.com	Twitter is an online social networking service that enables users to send and read short 140-character text messages, called tweets. Users can access Twitter through smartphones and other mobile devices.
8. Qq.com	Qq.com is China's largest and most-used Internet service portal owned by Tencent, Inc. Today, Qq.com tries to provide its users with one-stop shopping in terms of information search, EC, and so on.
9. Taobao.com	Taobao Marketplace is the preeminent EC site for Chinese consumers. Shoppers choose from a wide range of products and services.
10. Amazon.com	Amazon.com is the world's preeminent EC site. Amazon has redefined online shopping for billions of people worldwide. The value proposition is exchange efficiency that includes selection, convenience, and/or low prices.

SOURCE: Adapted from information presented by Alexa.com.

Wikipedia. A wiki is a piece of server software that allows users to freely create and edit web page content using a simplified mark-up language. A wiki provides the basis for UGC as it allows the contributor to add information to a source page as well as enabling him/her to engage in an open editing process. Wikis are often used to create collaborative Web sites and to promote a sense of collective ownership of Web site information and material. The best-known example of a wiki is Wikipedia, the world's largest online, open-source encyclopedia. Wikipedia was started by Jimmy Wales and Larry Sangerand and is operated by the U.S.-based nonprofit group Wikimedia Foundation.[44] Wikipedia's contributed articles are written by an estimated 100,000 active volunteers around the world working in 270 languages. Nearly all of its articles can be edited by anyone with access to the Wikipedia Web site.

Wikipedia has taken the place of the once important encyclopedia. Wikipedia's ease of access makes it the number one starting point when the user wants to conduct a preliminary search or answer starting questions like "who is" and "what is" about a topic. Critics of Wikipedia, for example, target the Web site's biases and inaccuracies and its policy of favoring consensus over credentials in its editorial process. It should be noted that the *Encyclopedia Britannica*, arguably the best of its kind, ended its last print edition in 2010. Wikipedia raises the specter of the permeability predicament to a whole new level. As writer Andrew Keen (2007) points out,

(Continued)

(Continued)

[Wikipedia] is a press with a peculiar sort of vanity, raising up the amateur to a position of prominence exceeding that of the salaried experts who do what they do for money. Wikipedia claims to be amassing the world's largest real estate of knowledge and yet Wikipedia's readers seem to revel in its very lack of authority.[45]

TripAdvisor. TripAdvisor is a travel Web site providing directory information and consumer reviews of hotels, restaurants, and destination sites throughout the world. TripAdvisor was founded in February 2000 by Langley Steinert, Stephen Kaufer, and several others. TripAdvisor is another example of UGC. On its Web site, TripAdvisor provides its readers with a general comments sheet as well as a standardized rating system per hotel. The reviews provide the basis for an overall rank-ordered rating system of hotels within a given city. In addition, TripAdvisor provides it readers with both professional photographs (supplied by the hotel) as well as user generated photos.[46] As one writer put it, TripAdvisor "has become an indispensable part of the social fabric of the traveling process."[47] A successful rating by TripAdvisor has become an essential marketing tool for hotels wishing to court international visitors. Herein, lies the real power and appeal of TripAdvisor—the ability to provide firsthand observations and experience from those travelers who have stayed at a certain hotel now under consideration by a prospective visitor. TripAdvisor is free to users, who provide most of the content, and the Web site is supported by an advertising business model. In 2004, TripAdvisor was purchased by Interactive Corporation (IAC), parent company to Expedia. IAC spun off its travel group of businesses under the Expedia, Inc. name in August 2005. TripAdvisor has more than 125 million reviews and opinions on more than 3.7 million places to stay, places to eat, and things to do, including more than 775,000 hotels and accommodations, making it the largest travel Web site in the world.[48]

Discussion

From Skype to TripAdvisor, digital lifestyle is about taking the power of intelligent networks and information and making it work in entirely new ways. However, not all changes in the fast unfolding digital economy are for the better. Browsing in an old used book store is a thing of the past. Gone are the days of interesting and sometimes useful conversations with knowledgeable salespeople at the local music store. Both kinds of retail shops are steadily giving way to the vacuum efficiency of Amazon and EC delivery. And likewise, newspapers in the West are struggling with falling circulation and advertising revenues amid the onslaught of Internet-based news. The traditional newspaper is steadily being displaced by the computer tablet. Many readers cannot tell the difference between credible news, sensationalism, and the amateur blog. As Keen (2007) points out, in the era of blogging (and everyone is entitled to my opinion), the Internet celebrates the noble amateur over the expert.

It's sometimes easy for misinformation and rumors to proliferate on the web, where social media touts popularity rather than reliability.[49] The ever-increasing reliance on new technology has become a catalyst for change, setting into motion a number of unintended consequences. Texting and driving, cell phones going off in restaurants, and Internet cyberbullying are part of the new digital reality. There is no going backward.

Digital lifestyle also brings with it a certain measure of social and technological inequality. Social scientists refer to this as the problem of the *digital divide*. There is a gap that separates different regions of the world with respect to the availability of communication and information technology. As Eric Schmidt and Jared Cohen (2013) point out, in the digital age connectivity takes on a broader meaning than simply creating efficiencies and putting people together. Everyone will derive some benefit from connectivity but not equally.

> Soon everyone on earth will be connected. With five billion more people set to join the virtual world, the boom in digital connectivity will bring gains in productivity, health, education, quality of life and myriad other avenues in the physical world—and this will be true for everyone, from the most elite users to those at the base of the economic pyramid. But being "connected" will mean very different things to different people, largely because the problems they have to solve differ so dramatically.[50]

High Tech—High Touch

In his book, *Megatrends,* author John Naisbitt (1982) describes the challenge of trying to find the right balance between the material wonders of technology and the spiritual demands of our human nature. He refers to this as the need for "high tech—high touch."[51] Great technology and innovation can be a thing of beauty as evidenced by a well-designed Web site or a virtual reality gaming system. High-touch includes activities that keep us in touch with our basic humanity. They link us to our primary self. The effective use of technology and balanced living can be mutually supportive. The field of education is made better by having well-constructed Web sites and e-learning displays that enable classroom instructors to post a class syllabus or reading assignments, engage in online class discussion, provide special contact links for class projects, and so forth. What doesn't change is the responsibility of being a highly motivated and engaged instructor. Nothing takes the place of inspired teaching. Similarly, Facebook provides a high-tech way of sharing information with one's friends, family, and colleagues, but it remains our special obligation to tell stories that are purposeful and worth telling.

Endnotes

1. Richard Gershon, *Media, Telecommunications and Business Strategy,* 2nd ed. (New York: Routledge, 2013).
2. Joe Lambert, *Digital Storytelling: Capturing Lives, Creating Community,* 4th ed. (New York: Routledge, 2012).

3. Everett Rogers, *Diffusion of Innovation,* 4th ed. (New York: Free Press, 1995).

4. Steven Shepard, *Telecom Crash Course* (New York: McGraw-Hill, 2005).

5. P. J. Louis, *Telecommunications Internetworking* (New York: McGraw-Hill, 2000).

6. Steve Jones, Ron Kovac, and Frank Groom, *Introduction to Communications Technologies* 2nd ed. (New York: CRC Group, 2009).

7. Yue-Ling Wong, *Digital Media Primer* (Upper Saddle River, NJ: Pearson Prentice-Hall, 2009).

8. Yue-Ling Wong, *Digital Media Primer.*

9. MPEG 4 is a technical standard for the compression of audio and visual digital data. It was introduced in late 1998 and includes compression methods for Internet streaming media, CD distribution, and voice communication (telephone, videophone, and broad-cast television applications). MPEG 4 incorporates many of the features found in earlier MPEG 1 and MPEG 2 standards. MPEG 4 is designed with some degree of openness so that individual developers can decide which elements to implement.

10. "Data Compression," Princeton University, last modified 2014, http://www.princeton .edu/~achaney/tmve/wiki100k/docs/Video_compression.html

11. Karl-Heinz Brandenburg was the director of the Fraunhofer Institute for Digital Media Technology in Ilmenau, Germany. In several interviews, Brandenberg has said that the development of MP3 software technology was the work of at least a half dozen core developers and many others who made important contributions. One such person is Professor Dieter Seitzer at the University of Erlangen, whose research involved audio coding and music transfer over standard telephone lines. The inventors named on the MP3 patent are Bernhard Grill, Karl-Heinz Brandenburg, Thomas Sporer, Bernd Kurten, and Ernst Eberlein.

12. Gershon, *Media, Telecommunications and Business Strategy.*

13. Patrick Parsons and Robert Frieden, *The Cable and Satellite Television Industries* (Needham Heights, MA: Allyn & Bacon, 1998).

14. Megan Mullen, *The Rise of Cable Programming in the United States* (Austin: University of Texas Press, 2003).

15. Jessica Livingston, *Founders at Work* (New York: Apress, 2007).

16. Michael Wirth and Ron Rizutto, "Future Prospects for Cable Telecommunications in an Over-the-Top World," in *Media Management and Economics Research in a Transmedia Environment,* ed. A. Albarran (New York: Routledge, 2013), 18–45.

17. J. S. Steuer, "Defining Virtual Reality: Dimensions Determining Telepresence," *Journal of Communication* 42, no. 4 (1992): 73–93.

18. S. McMillan, "Exploring Models of Interactivity from Multiple Research Traditions: Users, Documents and Systems," in *Handbook of New Media,* eds. L. Lievrouw and S. Livingston (London, UK: Sage, 2002), 162–182.

19. In 1967, Engelbart applied for and received a patent for a wooden shell with two metal wheels (computer mouse U.S. Patent N0.3,541,541). The patent was issued in 1970. Engelbart described the patent as an "X-Y position indicator for a display system." The device was nicknamed a mouse because the tail (or connection cord) came out one end. The first integrated mouse that was shipped as a part of a computer and intended for PC use was the Xerox 8010 Start Information System in 1981.

20. Bluetooth represents an industry standard for personal wireless communication devices, referred to as *personal area networks.* Bluetooth provides a way to connect and exchange information between Bluetooth compatible devices such as PCs and laptop computers, cellular telephones, printers, and video game consoles using unlicensed short-range radio frequencies (i.e., typically 1–100 meters). Bluetooth simplifies the discovery and setup of services among devices. Many of

today's cars are equipped with Bluetooth readiness. This allows the user to receive a call on his/her cell phone while enabling the call to be played through the vehicle's speakers.

21. Richard Daft and Robert Lengel, "Information Richness: A New Approach to Managerial Behavior and Organizational Design," in *Research in Organizational Behavior*, eds. L. Cummings and B. Staw (Homewood, IL: JAI Press, 1986), 191–233.

22. Richard Gershon, "Intelligent Networks and International Business Communication: A Systems Theory Interpretation," *Media Markets Monographs*, No. 12 (Pamplona, Spain: Universidad de Navarra Press, 2011).

23. T. V. Reed, *Digitized Lives: Culture, Power and Social Change in the Internet Era* (New York: Routledge, 2014), 18.

24. Thomas Friedman, *The World Is Flat* (New York: Farrar, Straus & Giroux, 2005).

25. Gershon, "Intelligent Networks."

26. Eli Noam, *Interconnecting the Network of Networks* (Cambridge, MA: MIT Press, 2001).

27. Richard Gershon, "International Deregulation and the Rise of Transnational Media Corporations," *Journal of Media Economics* 6, no. 2 (1993), 3–22; Benjamin Compaine and Douglas Gomery, *Who Owns the Media?* 3rd ed. (Mahwah, NJ: Lawrence Erlbaum Associates, 2000); David Demers, *Global Media: Menace or Messiah* (Cresskill, NJ: Hampton Press, 1999).

28. Christopher Bartlett and Sumantra Ghoshal, *Managing Across Borders: The Transnational Solutions* (Boston, MA: Harvard Business School Press, 1998).

29. Gerardine Desanctis and Peter Monge, "Introduction to the Special Issue: Communication Processes for Virtual Organizations," *Organization Science* 10 (1999): 693–703; Jessica Lipnack and Jeffrey Stamps, *Virtual Teams: Reaching Across Space, Time and Organizations with Technology* (New York: John Wiley & Sons, 1997).

30. M. Maznevski and K. Chudoba, "Bridging Space over Time: Global Virtual Team Dynamics and Effectiveness," *Organization Science* 11, no. 5 (2000): 73–492; J. Evaristo, "The Management of Distributed Projects across Cultures," *Journal of Global Information Management* 11, no. 4 (2003): 58–70; S. Jarvenpaa, K. Knoll, and D. Leidner, "Is Anybody Out There? Antecedents of Trust in Global Teams," *Journal of Management Information Systems* 14, no. 4 (1998): 29–64.

31. David Passmore, "Videoconferencing Opportunities and Challenges," *Business Communication Review* 37, no. 2 (2007): 19–21.

32. John Short, Ederyn Williams, and Bruce Christie, *The Social Psychology of Telecommunications* (New York: John Wiley & Sons, 1976).

33. K. Ning Shen and M. Khalifa, "Exploring Multidimensional Conceptualization of Social Presence in the Context of Online Communities," *International Journal of Human-Computer Interaction* 24, no. 7 (2008): 722–748; A. Ramirez and S. Zhang, "When Online Meets Offline: The Effect of Modality Switching on Relational Communication," *Communication Monographs* 74, no. 3 (2007): 287–310.

34. M. McPherson, L. Smith-Lovin, and J. Cook, "Birds of a Feather: Homophily in Social Networks," *Annual Review of Sociology* 27 (2001): 415–444; C. Haythornwaite and B. Wellman, "Friendship and Media Use for Information Exchange in a Networked Organization," *Journal of the American Society for Information Science* 46 (1998): 1101–1114; Harold Rheingold, *The Virtual Community: Homesteading on the Electronic Frontier* (New York: Secker & Warburg, 1993).

35. Josh Bernoff and Charlene Li, "Harnessing the Power of the Oh So Special Web," *MIT Sloan Management Review* 49, no. 3 (2008): 36–42.

36. N. Ellison, C. Steinfield, and C. Lampe, "The Benefits of Facebook Friends: Social Capital and College Students' Use of Online Social Network Sites," *Journal of Computer Mediated Communication* 12, no. 4 (2007): 1143–1168.

37. Richard Stengel, "The 2010 Person of the Year," *Time,* December 27, 2010, 43.

38. Paul Ford, "What Twitter's Made Of," *Business Week,* November 17, 2013, 12–14.

39. Paul Levinson, *New New Media,* 2nd ed. (New York: Pearson, 2013).

40. J. Lee and S. Sundar, "To Tweet or to Retweet? That Is the Question for Health Professionals on Twitter," *Health Communication Research,* 28, no. 5 (2012): 509–524.

41. Paul Lester, *Digital Innovations for Mass Communications* (New York: Routledge, 2014).

42. Clemencia Rodriquez, "Citizens' Media," in *The Encyclopedia of Social Movement Media,* ed. J. Downing (Thousand Oaks, CA: Sage, 2010), 98–103.

43. N. Balasubramaniam, "User Generated Content," in *Business Aspects of the Internet of Things,* ed. F. Michahelles (Zurich, Switzerland: ETH, 2009), 28–33.

44. Levinson, *New New Media.*

45. Andrew Keen, *The Cult of the Amateur* (New York: Random House, 2007), 40.

46. Stephen Kaufer, "TripAdvisor," in *Founders at Work,* ed. J. Livingston (New York: Apress, 2007), 361–375.

47. M. Pratt, "TripAdvisor Update: Bigger and More Important Than Ever," last modified, February 20, 2014, http://www.hospitalitynet.org/news/4064118.html

48. Pratt, "TripAdvisor Update."

49. Andrew Keen, *The Cult of the Amateur* (New York: Random House, 2007).

50. Eric Schmidt and Jared Cohen, *The New Digital Age* (New York: Alfred A. Knopf, 2013), 14.

51. John Naisbitt, *Megatrends* (New York: Warner Books, 1982).

CHAPTER 9

Digital Media and Innovation II

Personalization, Mobility, Convergence, and Artificial Intelligence

> *Our technology, our machines, is part of our humanity. We created them to extend ourselves and that is what is unique about human beings.*
>
> —Ray Kurzweil

> *Computers don't create computer animation any more than a pencil creates pencil animation. What creates computer animation is the artist.*
>
> —John Lasseter, Pixar

Introduction

Today, we are witnessing the demassification of media and entertainment products made possible by the Internet and the power of intelligent networking. In his seminal book, *Technologies of Freedom*, noted author Ithiel de Sola Poole (1990) made the prescient statement that

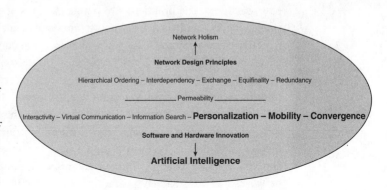

the mass media revolution is undergoing a reversal: "instead of identical messages being disseminated to millions of people, intelligent networking permits the adaptation of electronic messaging to the specialized or unique needs of individuals."[1] If that statement was true in 1990, the idea has become ever more so today.

More and more companies are tailoring their product and service offerings to meet the unique tastes of the individual. From iPods to digital video recorders, consumers now have the ability to compile, edit, and customize the media they use.[2] (See Table. 9.1.) We have entered the era of personalization.

Table 9.1 Select Examples of Digital Media and Personalization

- Cable Television and Narrowcasted Program Services
- Digital Video Recording and Personalized TV
- Customized Music Selection; iTunes, Pandora, Rhapsody
- Electronic Commerce (EC) and Personalized Marketing
- Social Networking; Personal Facebook and LinkedIn Accounts

Personalization

The Internet and Personalized Marketing

Broadcast television and large circulation newspapers are no longer seen as the primary or best means of advertising to smaller niche audiences. More and more companies are using the Internet to communicate and personalize the information exchange between an EC retailer (or advertiser) and the end consumer. Personalized marketing (or micromarketing) involves knowing more about the particular interests and buying habits of one's customers. Advanced portal software permits users to receive personalized information in the form of specialized content (i.e., daily news updates, stock reports, weather, book recommendations, etc.).[3] As an example, Amazon.com routinely sends out information updates to its customers notifying them of newly published books based on information obtained and analyzed from previous purchasing selections. Similarly, DVD rental service Netflix utilizes a proprietary recommendation software that makes suggestions of future films that the consumer might like based on past selections.[4] The proprietary recommendation software has the added benefit of stimulating demand for lesser-known movies and, thereby, taking the pressure off recently released feature films where demand sometimes outstrips availability. The focus on lesser-known films is in keeping with Anderson's (2006) "long tail" principle.[5]

Personalization reflects the principle of push-versus-pull technology, whereby traditional television is push technology (e.g., point-to-multipoint broadcasting), and the Internet is a decidedly pull technology. The importance of personalized viewing options has not been lost on traditional broadcast and cable programmers. Video services indigenous to the Internet (most notably, Netflix, YouTube, and Hulu) have become immensely popular, and the traditional television networks are now actively promoting the distribution of their programs online through a combination of network-owned and third-party-controlled Web sites. The Internet's interactive capability changes the basic relationship between the individual and media, challenging marketers to shift their emphasis from persuasion sales to relationship building.[6]

Tumblr. Tumblr is a microblogging platform and social networking Web site that allows users to post multimedia and other content to a short-form blog. Users can follow other users' blogs as well as make their blogs private. Much of the Web site's features are accessed from a dashboard interface, where the option to post content and posts of followed blogs appear. The dashboard provides a live feed of recent posts from blogs that the user follows. Users are able to comment, re-blog, and upload text posts, images, video, quotes, or links to their blog with a click of a button displayed at the top of the dashboard. Users also are able to connect their blogs to their Twitter and Facebook accounts, so whenever they make a post, it will also be sent as a tweet and a status update. Tumblr is an example of an interest graph, whereby it provides an online platform for which an individual can write about things that are of particular interest to him/her. Part of the appeal of Tumblr is that many of the posts and blogs are fairly obscure, reflecting the unique interests of the person who is commenting. An interest graph stands in marked contrast to a social graph (such as Facebook), whereby the Web site's purpose is tracking social connections among people. Tumblr was founded by David Karp and launched in February 2007. Tumblr was later acquired by Yahoo in May 2013 for a reported $1.1 billion. As Yahoo looks to reinvent itself, the Tumblr acquisition is part of a larger company strategy to build stronger ties with a younger, more tech-savvy set of users.

Pandora (Pandora Internet Radio). Pandora is a music streaming service that plays songs of a certain musical genre based on the subscriber's selection of individual artists. Pandora creates an individualized radio station (or master playlist) for the user based on the kinds of songs that he/she selects. The user then provides positive or negative feedback for songs chosen by the service, which are taken into account when Pandora selects future songs. While listening, users are given the opportunity to purchase individual songs or albums at various EC site locations.

Pandora was founded in 2004 by Will Glaser, Jon Kraft, and Tim Westergren. The service is available in the United States, Australia, and New Zealand. Pandora founders believe that all listeners have a unique relationship with music. To provide a more personalized music experience, Glaser, Kraft, and Westergren developed the Music Genome Project, a highly sophisticated taxonomy of music that breaks down individual songs according to 450 distinct musical characteristics. As they point out, "these attributes capture not only the musical identity of a song but also the many significant qualities that are relevant to understanding the musical preferences of listeners."[7] The Pandora music selection is built on an algorithm that analyzes these musical characteristics in designing and developing the personalized radio station concept.

Mobility

Mobility is a signature feature of digital lifestyle and suggests that users require flexibility of movement and not be physically tied to a communication network. From architects who require broadband on the go to first responders in a crisis situation, mobility has become an essential feature of a digital lifestyle. Wireless communication users should be able to access voice, video, and information services anytime, anywhere.[8] Consider, for example, the number of stakeholders involved in a disaster relief effort. Preparing for an impending tornado or responding to a multicar collision on an interstate highway might call into play a number of different players, including: police, fire and rescue, evacuation planning and procedures group, hospital emergency personnel, first responders, and the news media. An impending crisis situation, by its very nature, creates a situation in which rumors and misinformation can pose a threat to safety and security. Mobile and wireless IT allows planners and first responders to maintain continuous communication and better manage the flow of critical information. The information should be fast, immediate, and accessible.[9]

Smartphones

The term *smartphone* describes a new generation of cellular telephones that is highly personalized and features a variety of enhanced information services. The smartphone combines the best elements of mobility, interactivity, and convergence. As Cumiskey and Hjorth (2013) write:

> Once solely a mode of telephonic communication, the mobile phone has grown to encompass numerous forms of communication and media. As an example of convergence par excellence, the mobile phone—especially in the form of the smartphone—is now ushering in new promises of seamless engagement with technology, Internet access, and everyday common experiences.[10]

The real introduction into smartphone design began in 2006 with the introduction of the Apple iPhone. The iPhone set the standard for Internet mobile phone design by using a multi-touch screen with a virtual keyboard and buttons. Since then, other companies like Samsung, Microsoft, Amazon, and others have introduced their own smartphone versions. Unlike Apple's IOS proprietary operating software, most other companies have adopted the Android open source operating software developed by Google. Today's smartphones have built in functionality that is programmable. The smartphone emphasizes the personal aspect of wireless technology by advancing a number of enhanced feature elements, including: 1) E-mail, 2) Personal planner, 3) Text messaging, 4) Camera and video camera, 5) Internet access, 6) MP3 music player, 7) Photo storage and display, and 8) GPS locator. Mobility makes possible a whole host of wireless Internet activities that range from making and receiving telephone calls to securing an airline reservation.

Some observers have called it "broadband on the go."[11] More importantly, the smartphone has become one of our essential possessions, no less important than a set of car keys or favorite article of clothing. A smartphone is digital lifestyle in its most essential form. It allows us to stay in touch with one's friends, family, and work as well as filling downtime.

Digital Mapping

Digital mapping (also called digital cartography) is the process by which a collection of data is compiled and formatted into a virtual image. The primary function of this technology is to produce maps that give accurate representations of a particular area, detailing major road arteries and other points of interest. The technology also allows the calculation of distances from once place to another.

Global Positioning System (GPS). GPS is widely used for the purpose of detecting the location of a moving vehicle or a ship at sea. GPS represents a particular kind of digital mapping system. In the GPS system, a constellation of 24 satellites circle the Earth in near-circular, inclined orbits. Each of these satellites circles the Earth in a medium-range orbit (12,000 miles), making two complete rotations every day. The orbits are arranged so that at any time, anywhere on Earth, there are at least four satellites visible in the sky. (See Figure 9.1.)[12] The original GPS concept and design was developed by the U.S. Department of Defense and has been available for civilian use since 1994. Other international GPS systems include Russia's GLONASS system, China's Compass navigational system, and the Galileo system used by the European Union.

Figure 9.1 Global Positioning System

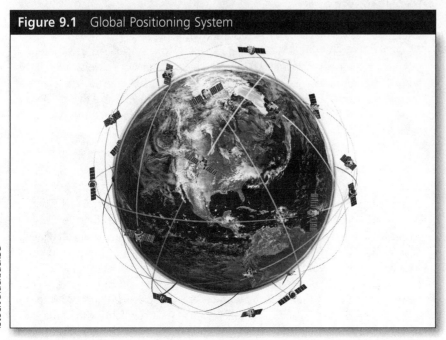

A GPS receiver is designed to read three or more of these satellites, figure out the distance to each, and use this information to deduce its own location. This operation is based on a mathematical principle called trilateration. A GPS receiver computes its position by comparing the time taken by signals from three or four different GPS satellites to reach the receiver. By receiving signals from at least three of these satellites, the receiver's position (latitude, longitude, and altitude) can be accurately determined.[13]

The primary benefit of GPS includes travel directions and location accuracy. Whether traveling locally, cross country, or globally, the user is able to access accurate directions in real time as well as being provided the constant monitoring of his/her vehicle location. GPS has become an essential navigational tool for freight delivery and courier services. Maritime users also benefit from GPS use. Ships at sea depend heavily on GPS for navigating their way across the oceans and major lakes. GPS has become a standard feature on many of today's smartphones. One important feature is the ability to track the physical location of a friend, colleague, or loved one.

Instagram. Instagram is a mobile photo and video-sharing service that enables its users to take pictures and videos, apply digital filters to them, and share them on a variety of social networking services, such as Facebook, Twitter, and Tumblr. One of Instagram's distinctive features is that it formats photos to a square shape, similar to a Kodak Instamatic and Polaroid image, in contrast to the 4:3 aspect ratio typically used by mobile device cameras. We live in a visual world. Creating a photo gallery on the web has become a mainstay of social media, EC marketing, and news information Web sites. One of the cool factors of Instagram is the ability to use one of eleven different filters to enhance particular photos. Users are also able to record and share short videos lasting for up to fifteen seconds. Instagram was created by Kevin Systrom and Mike Krieger and launched in October 2010. The service rapidly gained popularity and was acquired by Facebook in April 2012 for approximately US$1 billion in cash and stock. At the time CEO Mark Zuckerberg said, "For years, we've focused on building the best experience for sharing photos with your friends and family. Now, we'll be able to work even more closely with the Instagram team to also offer the best experiences for sharing beautiful mobile photos with people based on your interests.[14]

Snapchat. Snapchat is a photo messaging app that allows users to take photos, record videos, add text and drawings, and send them to a controlled list of recipients. These directed photos and videos are known as Snaps. Users set a time limit for how long recipients can view their Snaps (typically one to ten seconds), after which they will be hidden from the recipient's device and deleted from Snapchat's servers. The origins of Snapchat began as an earlier app known as Picaboo, developed by Stanford undergraduate students Evan Spiegel and Bobby Murphy in 2011. The original Picaboo app was designed as a solution for the problem of sending a photo that the sender later regretted sending. Picaboo solved that problem with self-deleting snaps. When sending a photo, the sender can decide how many seconds it will be viewable by someone before self-deleting. Picaboo was subsequently rebranded as Snapchat. Newer features include video as well as the ability to write messages on photos before sending them. The main appeal of Snapchat (especially among teenagers) is the ability to engage in momentary (or short-lived) messages that leave few digital tracks, specifically, the ability to send strange or embarrassing photos that might make the user uncomfortable were he/she to post them on regular social media. At a time when everything posted on Facebook and Twitter can become part of one's permanent Internet profile, a temporary moment has a value to some users. Says Spiegel, Snapchat was less about disappearing selfies and more about letting people capture a goofy, irreverent moment that they can share freely online without considering the long term consequences.[15] That said, one of the criticisms of Snapchat is that it can be used for sexting and bullying. To date, Snapchat has garnered a lot of interest from outside investors, including an offer from Facebook's Mark Zuckerberg for US $3 billion that was subsequently turned down.

Convergence

The clear lines and historic boundaries that once separated broadcasting, cable, telephony, and Internet communication are no more. A natural convergence of industries and information technologies has blurred those distinctions. The word *convergence* means the joining together of media and IT. As noted earlier, digital media represents the artistic convergence of various kinds of hardware and software design elements to create entirely new forms of communication expression.[16] Such examples might include: 1) the Internet, 2) Television and film animation, 3) Music and video streaming, 4) Digital television (including HDTV), and 5) Video game entertainment systems. There are a number of driving forces that focus public attention on the issue, including new methods and approaches to social media, cross-media ownership patterns in business, as well as continuing changes in technology; most notably the Internet.[17]

Digital media has proved to be a major game changer when it comes to the presentation and storage of information. Digital media allows for the creative handling and transformation of data. From streaming video on a Facebook posting to special effects in a hero adventure film, the combination of technology and software production can be blended to create entirely new forms of communication expression. Author Ithiel de Sola Poole (1983) describes it as a *convergence of modes*.[18] It is at the heart of digital media display and storytelling.

Digital Photography

The digital media revolution owes its beginnings to the many changes that transformed the field of photography. Digital photography has many advantages over traditional film. Digital photos are convenient and allow the user to see the results instantly. Digital photography offers the user the ability to customize one's photos, including the ability to edit and impose special effects. Moreover, digital photos don't require the costs associated with film and development time. Gone are the days of purchasing rolls of Kodak film in preparation for a vacation trip for capturing those special moments. No longer do users have to take rolls of completed film to the local supermarket or camera store and wait for prints to be developed. Instead, digital cameras allow the user to take multiple shots at no extra cost. They can be stored on a variety of digital devices, including PCs, flash drives, smartphones, computer tablets, as well as on the Internet, including social media sites as well as personal and professional Web site displays.

Today, there are numerous types of digital cameras that allow individuals to capture the events unfolding around them with varying levels of ease and sophistication. Nearly all of today's smartphones have small cameras built into the body of the camera. Those wishing for more functionality and increased resolution can opt for a point-and-shoot camera. Those wanting greater customization including the ability to modulate exposure time (with differing focal lengths) will likely gravitate toward a digital single lens reflex camera. All this points to the fact that the transition to digital cameras is no longer about a single product but, rather, a fundamental shift in thinking regarding visual display, storage, and the communication process.[19]

Filmmaking and Special Effects

The special effect scenes that appear in modern-day adventure films involve the blending of live action footage and computer-generated imagery to create environments that look realistic but would be too expensive or impractical to capture on film. Computer-generated imagery (CGI) is the art of creating moving images with the use of computers. To a creative filmmaker, nothing is impossible, whether it's monsters rising from the sea to terrorize a Japanese city or space aliens traveling to Earth to fight humans. Both CGI (special effects) and digital animation have become hallmarks of production companies like Pixar Animation, Marvel Studios, and Sony Picture Entertainment. With each film, dozens of computer animators, audio engineers, explosives experts, and makeup artists spend thousands of hours crafting these on-screen realities.

Most on-screen special effects begin as 3-D digital models. The models are first created as wire frames that establish the underlying structure of a character or object. The next step is for the animator to add realistic surfaces, skins, and textures. Facial features and clothes are moved on key frames.[20] The skilled animator can apply select mathematical algorithms to achieve detailed facial expressions or the effect of someone falling through space. The differences in appearance between key frames are adjusted automatically by the computer in a process known as morphing. The animation is subsequently rendered. Human movement also can be replicated using motion-capture technology. The technology records and captures real-life movement and then transfers it to the computer. This technique was widely used in the making of James Cameron's 3-D movie *Avatar*. Special effects design is a slow, painstaking process that requires incredible attention to detail as well as a deep understanding of building construction, landscape design, and human movement.

Pixar Animation Studios. Pixar Animation Studios is a computer animation studio originally formed when Steve Jobs purchased George Lucas's special effects computer division for $10 million in 1986. Dr. Edwin E. Catmull, who was the head of the failing Lucasfilm subsidiary, was instructed by George Lucas to find a buyer if he wished to continue his work as an animator. When Dr. Catmull was unable to lure any buyers to acquire the special effects division, he turned to Apple's Steve Jobs. After some initial hesitancy, Jobs agreed to purchase the Lucasfilm unit.[21] With Jobs acting as CEO of the newly formed Pixar Studios, Ed Catmull, who was vice president at Lucasfilm, was named president. The main thread to the Pixar story occurs with the hiring of John Lasseter. Starting as a graphic designer for Lucasfilm in 1984, he stayed with the division after it was purchased by Jobs in 1986. John Lasseter is the creative genius behind many of the colorful characters that are featured in Pixar's animated films. If Ed Catmull provided the hands-on management at Pixar, it was Lasseter who instilled the creative vision that became Pixar. Says Lasseter, "When I came into this studio, I just loved the heritage of this place. Why I do what I do for a living is because of the films of Walt Disney. When I figured out as a kid that people made cartoons for a living, that's all I ever wanted to do."[22] More than any other production studio for its time, it was Pixar that combined computer animation with the special effects lessons of Lucasfilm to create an altogether new approach to film animation. Pixar elevated computer animation to a whole new level using software technology known as RenderMan, which provides photorealistic renderings of people, objects, and landscapes.[23] Pixar's success began with the 1995 debut of Toy Story, which earned revenues of $192 million domestically and $362 million worldwide. From there, Pixar was responsible for producing an ongoing series of animated film hits, including: *A Bug's Life* (1998), *Toy Story 2* (1999), *Monsters Inc.* (2001), *Finding Nemo* (2003), *The Incredibles* (2004), *Cars* (2006), *Ratatouille* (2007), *WALL-E* (2008), and *Up* (2009). There have been numerous films beyond that including multiple sequels to some of the earlier films. Several of Pixar's films have won Academy Awards for best-animated feature film including *Finding Nemo* and *Toy Story 3,* which are among the top fifty highest-grossing films of all time. In 2006, the Walt Disney Company purchased Pixar for $7.4 billion.[24] Reflecting on Pixar's body of work, Lasseter tells a very interesting exchange that he had with Steve Jobs:

Steve Jobs and I were very close, and early on when I was making *Toy Story* we started talking and he said, "John, you know at Apple when I make computers, what is the lifespan of this product, two years, three years at the most, and then about five years, they're like a doorstop. But if you do your job right, these films can last forever." I was amazed by that statement, and I was humbled by it too.[25]

Digital Television

Digital television (DTV) represents the next generation of television capable of delivering significantly improved television pictures. DTV provides image quality approaching that of 35 mm film. DTV is considered the most significant development in television technology since color television because of features such as improved television resolution and high-quality audio. DTV sets are wider than those of earlier television. They more closely resemble a wide screen found in today's movie theaters.[26] The transition to an all-DTV environment has meant a corresponding change in aspect ratio, that is, screen width to height from 4:3 to 16:9. DTV comes in two basic formats: HDTV and standard definition television (SDTV). DTV offers certain obvious advantages when compared to analog television.

- **Improved Picture Quality.** In a digital system, images and sound are captured using the same digital code found in computers. A digital picture is more detailed and stable, offering the viewer ten times more pixels on the screen.
- **Improved Sound.** Multiple DTV speakers provide surround sound quality.
- **Computer Friendly.** DTV has become more computer friendly. Current TV monitors are able to display both television pictures as well as computer graphics and data, such as picture-in-picture Web sites.
- **More Spectrum Efficient.** DTV provides the ability to squeeze increased picture detail and higher quality surround sound into a lesser amount of bandwidth space. DTV allows for digital video compression, thus enabling television pictures to be processed, stored, and distributed with greater flexibility and ease.[27]

What makes today's DTV monitor different from earlier television monitors is the fact that they have become more multipurpose in design and application. They are designed to interface with multiple video inputs, including cable/IPTV television, digital video recorders, video game systems, Internet and streaming video, as well as video telephony (Skype, Facetime, etc.). It is the principle of convergence made practical and real.

Artificial Intelligence

Artificial intelligence (AI) is concerned with developing computer systems that are able to perform tasks that imitate human intelligence, such as visual perception, speech recognition, analytical problem study, and decision making. The study of AI owes its beginnings to British mathematician Alan Turing, the intellectual father of the modern computer, who believed that one day machines would be powerful enough that they could think like humans.[28] The term *artificial intelligence* was coined in 1956 by John McCarthy at the Massachusetts Institute of Technology. AI is closely tied to the study of decision theory in mathematics and expert systems in computer science. *Decision theory* is concerned with identifying the values, risks, and uncertainties associated with important decisions. Most decision theory tends to be prescriptive in approach. The goal is to find the best tools, methodologies, and software to help people and organizations solve problems and make better decisions. The practical application of this is called *decision analysis.* The most systematic and comprehensive software tools are called *decision support systems.*[29]

All Reasoning and Problem-Solving Features

The goal of AI is to develop new approaches to reasoning and problem solving. What all AI systems share in common is the ability to reason, problem solve, and take corrective action based on preprogrammed assumptions and information inputs.[30] There are two distinguishing features that characterize all AI systems. First, the AI system must have the ability to scan its external surroundings. Second, the AI system must have the ability to evaluate a situation and initiate an appropriate decision or response. The decision must be rational.[31] We call this adaptation.

Adaptation

The term *adaptation* is central to biology, particularly evolutionary biology. The ability to adapt enables living organisms to cope with environmental stresses and pressures. Adaptation is part of the natural selection process and increases the survival capability of the person or animal. Adaptation can be structural, behavioral, or physiological. *Structural adaptation* refers to physical body elements that help an organism to survive in its natural habitat (e.g., skin color, shape, etc.). *Behavioral adaptations* are the different ways a particular organism behaves to survive in its natural habitat (e.g., sensitivity to impending danger). *Physiological adaptations* are systems present in an organism that allow it to perform certain biochemical reactions (e.g., sweating, digestion, etc.).[32]

Adaptation, in an IT context, refers to the idea of a system that possesses self-correcting features, that is, the ability to monitor, adjust, and react to changes in the environment. Adaptation is a key element in understanding the power of AI. A simple case in point is a computer system that utilizes a type of virus protection software. As soon as the network system senses a potential virus, it automatically triggers a firewall protection to prevent the system from being corrupted. Similarly, a cellular telephone system is designed to monitor and adapt to users in moving traffic. Cellular telephone systems are organized into cell clusters or areas of coverage. Each cell is assigned a bloc of frequencies that can only be used within that designated cell. As a moving vehicle passes from one cell to another, the system must be able to determine the location of the moving vehicle and automatically switch to an available frequency as it enters the new cell. To accomplish this, a set of base transceiver stations monitor the calls in progress and can sense the signal strength of the mobile units in their own areas as well as adjoining cells. The results are sent to the Mobile Telephone Switching Office (MTSO), which determines when the telephone call should be handed off upon entering a new cell site.[33]

Neural Networks and Adaptation

An artificial neural network (ANN), or neural network (NN), is a mathematical model based on biological neural networks. An ANN is an information processing model that parallels the way biological nervous systems, such as the brain, process information. An ANN is made up of interconnecting artificial neurons (i.e., programming constructs) that mimic the properties of biological neurons. In principle, an ANN is an adaptive network system that changes its structure based on external or internal information that flows through the network during the learning phase. They can be used to model complex relationships between inputs and outputs to find patterns in data. In short, an artificial neural network, like people, learns by example.[34] In practical terms, AI systems can be both simple and complex in design. The movie rental service Netflix, for example, exhibits simple AI features to the extent that it knows how to create recommended film viewing lists based on user inputs as well as a preprogrammed algorithmic-based rating system.

Self-Driving Vehicles. At a more complex level, self-driving vehicles developed by Google and Mercedes Benz are designed to perform most of the primary driving functions. The self-driving car uses sensors that monitor traffic flow, oncoming vehicles, pedestrians, cyclists, and other moving objects. Adaptation is a key. The self-driving car must be able to safely navigate through constantly changing driving conditions. The car's intelligence center is designed to know its present geographic location as well as destination point. The car's sensors regularly monitor various objects around it according to size, shape, and movement patterns. The car must be able to differentiate between a moving vehicle, cyclist, and pedestrian. The car's algorithmic software is able to predict what these various objects are going to do next. The software then chooses a safe speed, route, and trajectory line for the car.[35] What is important to remember is the degree to which AI systems make preprogrammed choices on behalf of the user. In principle, the AI system can make faster calculations and decisions involving complex decision making and high speeds than humans as well as reacting to unexpected changes in the external environment. AI changes the nature of intelligent networks from one information repository to that of an automated decision-making support system. It is a more dynamic interactive tool that aids the user by analyzing problems, answering questions, or making automatic adjustments to a changing set of external conditions.

Social Robotics. The term *robot* refers to an artificial machine or agent that performs highly skilled tasks with a high degree of consistency. Robots are typically guided by highly sophisticated computer program software and electronic circuitry. Robots can take the place of humans in dangerous environments or manufacturing processes. They can resemble humans in appearance, behavior, and/or cognition. The branch of the field that deals with how people interact with robots is called *social robotics.*[36] We empower the robot to perform certain tasks and assignments in our stead. Robots possess AI, which enables them to learn from their environments. Part of the relationship and adaptive factor is built on the kinds of communication and information inputs designed between humans and robots.[37] Language plays an important role in how we define that relationship.[38] Giving the robot or intelligent agent a name, for example, goes a long way in personalizing that relationship whether it be the onboard computer called Hal in Arthur C. Clarke's *2001: A Space Odyssey* or the Siri voice assistant on the present-day Apple smartphone. Robots and intelligent agents are not people; they are machines or software applications. While a robot may appear personal in style and communication pattern, it remains at present a simulation.

The study of social robotics is important because it represents a natural progression in human/computer interface design. From Douglas Engelbart's original prototype of the computer mouse to modern-day social robotics, one of the promising areas of human/computer interface design can be seen in the area of intelligent agents. An intelligent agent (IA) is a software program that organizes information in support of personal and professional decision making. Think of the IA as a virtual secretary whose job is to maintain the user's calendar, organize appointments, prioritize incoming information, and scan relevant Web sites for important news and information items. In time, the IA exhibits the principles of network evolution that use knowledge and past experience as the basis for growth and improved decision making. This could include everything from highlighting a simple Amazon product alert to aiding in a complex research and design project. We already see it in separate and disparate pieces, including Google search and calendar, Facebook postings, EC shopping alerts, video game avatars, Microsoft OneNote, business and entertainment news feeds, and the like. Most promising is the ability of the individual to customize his/her IA to meet the unique personal and professional needs of the individual. In time, we will give our IAs names in addition to the ability to make select preprogrammed decisions on our behalf. This is personalization in an altogether new way. In sum, all of the essential software elements for IA presently exist. What remains is the task of making them fully integrated.

Virtual Reality

Virtual reality (VR) is the consummate form of AI. It represents a natural progression in the applied principles of adaptation, data modeling, and simulation.[39] VR involves constructing illusory realities out of data drawn from a variety of databases. It allows the user to enter into a three-dimensional space and interact with his/her surroundings. The simulated environment can be realistic (e.g., flight simulation, VR surgery, etc.) or imagined (e.g., a trip to Mars). While a video game is played on a two-dimensional screen, VR invites the user to physically enter into a three-dimensional space and engage one's opponent directly. There is a shared common space involving action and reaction to one's movements. This is interactivity in its highest form. In the television and film series *Star Trek: The Next Generation,* science-fiction writer and producer Rick Berman illustrates such an environment in the program's depiction of the holodeck.[40]

VR combines many of the feature elements found in intelligent networking, including interactivity, mobility, virtual communication, as well as AI. A properly constructed VR space elicits both physiological as well as psychological reactions on the part of the user.[41] VR can elicit changes in perceptual experiences on the part of the individual based on the realism of the simulation. A highly realistic simulation involving a sudden and dramatic increase in speed, or sense of falling, can stimulate sensory-motor reactions on the part of the individual, such as nervousness, fear, increased heart rate, and so on.[42] VR represents a unique form of AI interaction between humans and machines.

The quality, color, and realism of the simulated environments begin with the use of a head-mounted display. In a virtual environment, the visual display must change in accordance to the user's point of view and movement.[43] Some of the best work in head-mounted display is being done in the area of video game systems and design. Oculus Rift is the first in a new generation of VR headsets designed specifically for video games that create an altogether different immersion for the user in the way he/she experiences gaming. Oculus Rift allows the user to enter (albeit, virtually) into the place and setting of the gaming story line. The combination of a high-resolution display and a wide field of view takes 3-D gaming to a different level of realism. Whereas in the past, VR headgear was very expensive ($20,000+) and bulky, the Oculus Rift headgear design has ultra low latency and is more affordable.

A second feature element is the tracking system, which relays the user's position and orientation to the computer. A VR environment must give the user a realistic sense of physical touch. There must be action and reaction to the user's sense of touch and movement. Motion capture is the process of recording the movement of objects and people. It is used in the military, video games, filmmaking, sports, and medical applications. In video games and filmmaking, motion capture refers to recording the actions of human actors and using that information to animate digital characters and models onto a video monitor or screen. It is the principal technology behind gaming technology such as Wii.[44] Motion capture technology is being tested and used as a physical therapy rehabilitation treatment for older adults with disabilities.[45]

Today, VR technology is being used in a variety of settings, including aerospace, military defense, and medicine. In each case, simulation becomes an integral part of how we learn a specialized process before the fact. As the quality of the simulation becomes more realistic, it becomes increasingly difficult to distinguish between mediated communication and the actual process or event.[46] As an example, U.S. pilots during the Persian Gulf and Iraq Wars have commented on how eerily similar an actual bombing run was to their flight simulation exercises. What is clear, however, is the speed at which we are moving in the direction of AI-based simulated realities used in both professional settings as well as personal entertainment.

Discussion

Predicting the future, as any technology futurist can attest, is a risky business. One of the underlying assumptions in technical forecasting is the ability to recognize the natural patterns and trajectories of technology development over time. The seeds of the technology future are in the present. In short, if we want to understand the future, then we have to understand current trends and design practices. Such design practices can be thought of as innovation links that when strung together along a continuum, guide us toward understanding the future. AI continues to advance at an ever-increasing pace of change in what some researchers describe as the *singularity principle* first identified by Vernor Vinge (1983) and later popularized by Ray

Kurzweil (2000, 2005).[47] Technological singularity is the law of accelerating returns, not unlike Moore's law.[48] Singularity can be thought of as a theoretical future point of unprecedented technological progress caused by the ability of machines to improve themselves using AI. As technology becomes more cost-effective, added resources are deployed toward its advancement so that the rate of exponential growth increases over time. As Kurzweil (2000) points out, "Once machines achieve the ability to design and engineer technology as humans do, only at far higher speeds and capacities, they will have access to their own designs (source code) and the ability to manipulate them."[49]

Endnotes

1. Ithiel de Sola Poole, *Technologies of Freedom* (Cambridge, MA: Harvard University Press, 1983), 8.
2. Phil Napoli, "The Audience Product and the New Media Environment: Implications for the Economics of Media Industries," *The International Journal of Media Management* 3, no. 2 (2001): 66–73; John Dimmick, *Media Competition and Coexistence: The Theory of the Niche* (Mahwah, NJ: Lawrence Erlbaum Associates, 2003).
3. Richard Gershon, *Media, Telecommunications and Business Strategy,* 2nd ed. (New York: Routledge, 2013).
4. Richard Gershon, "Business Process Innovation and the Intelligent Network," in *Managing Media Economy, Media Content and Technology in the Age of Digital Convergence,* eds., Z. Vukanovic and P. Faustino (Lisbon, Portugal: Media XXI/Formal Press, 2011), 59–85.
5. Chris Anderson, *The Long Tail: Why the Future of Business Is Selling Less of More* (New York: Hyperion, 2006).
6. Sylvia Chan-Olmsted, *Competitive Strategy for Media Firms* (Mahwah, NJ: Lawrence Erlbaum Associates, 2006).
7. Pandora, "About the Music Genome Project," last modified, January 23, 2015, http://www.pandora.com/about/mgp
8. L. Leung and R. Wei, "More Than Just Talk on the Move: Uses and Gratifications of the Cellular Phone," *Journalism and Mass Communication Quarterly* 77, no. 2 (2000), 308–320.
9. M. Palenchar and K. Freberg, "Conceptualizing Social Media and Mobile Technologies in Risk and Crisis Communication Practices," in *Mobile Media Practices, Presence and Politics,* eds. K. Cumiskey and L. Hjorth (New York: Routledge, 2013), 15–29.
10. K. Cumiskey and L. Hjorth, eds., *Mobile Media Practices, Presence and Politics* (New York: Routledge, 2013), 1.
11. Gerard Goggin, "The Mobile Turn in Universal Service: Prosaic Lessons and New Ideals," *Journal of Policy, Regulation and Strategy for Telecommunications, Information and Media,* 10, no. 5–6 (2008), 46–58.
12. Gershon, *Media, Telecommunications and Business Strategy.*
13. Ibid.
14. "Facebook buys Instagram for $1 billion," *New York Times,* Apr. 9, 2012, http://dealbook.nytimes.com/2012/04/09/facebook-buys-instagram-for-1-
15. Brad Stone and Sarah Frier, "Interview with Evan Spiegel," *Bloomberg/Businessweek,* June 1, 2015, 42–46.
16. Richard Gershon, "Media Convergence," *Oxford Bibliography Series on Communication—Online,* last modified June 26, 2012, http://www.oxfordbibliographies.com/view/document/obo-9780199756841/obo-9780199756841-0026.xml

17. Lucy Kung, *Strategic Management in the Media* (Los Angeles, CA: Sage, 2008); Gracie Lawson-Borders, "Integrating New Media and Old Media: Seven Observations of Convergence as a Strategy for Best Practices in Media Organizations," *International Journal of Media Management* 5 (2003): 91–99.

18. Ithiel de Sola Poole, *Technologies of Freedom.*

19. Yue-Ling Wong, *Digital Media Primer* (Upper Saddle River, NJ: Pearson Prentice-Hall, 2009); H. Lucas and J. Goh, "Disruptive Technology: How Kodak Missed the Digital Photography Revolution," *Journal of Strategic Information Systems* 18 (2009): 46–55.

20. Richard Rickitt, *Special Effects: The History and Technique* (London, UK: Aurum Press, 2006).

21. David Price, *The Pixar Touch* (New York, Vintage Books, 2009).

22. Stephanie Goodman, "Pixar's John Lasseter Answers Your Questions," *New York Times,* Nov. 1, 2011, http://artsbeat.blogs.nytimes.com/2011/11/01/pixars-john-lasseter-answers-your-questions/?_r=0

23. RenderMan has been used in creating digital visual effects for major films such as *Toy Story, Finding Nemo, Jurassic Park, Titanic,* the Star Wars prequels, and *Lord of the Rings.*

24. Claudia Eller, Kim Christensen, and Dawn C. Chmielewski, "Disney Pins its Digital Future on Pixar Deal," *Los Angeles Times,* Jan. 25, 2006, A-1.

25. Goodman, "Pixar's John Lasseter Answers Your Questions."

26. Pete Seel, *Digital Universe: The Global Telecommunication Revolution* (Malden, MA: Wiley-Blackwell, 2012).

27. Gershon, *Media, Telecommunications and Business Strategy,* 2nd ed.

28. Walter Isaacson, *The Innovators* (New York: Simon & Schuster, 2014).

29. Stuart Russell and Peter Norvig, *Artificial Intelligence: A Modern Approach,* 2nd ed. (New York: Prentice-Hall, 2003).

30. Ray Kurzweil, *The Age of Intelligent Machines* (Boston, MA: MIT Press, 1990).

31. Russell and Norvig, *Artificial Intelligence: A Modern Approach.*

32. John Holland, *Hidden Order: How Adaptation Builds Complexity* (New York: Helix Books, 1995).

33. Adaptation and cellular telephone networks: a cellular telephone system is designed to service customers within a specified geographical area, known as a Cellular Geographic Service Area (CGSA). The CGSA is designed as an interlocking grid of cell sites (or coverage areas). The CGSA is often visually depicted as a series of hexagonal zones or circles. Each cell has its own base transceiver station (BTS) and a dedicated set of over-the-air frequencies. Areas of coverage overlap at the outer boundaries. The cell size depends on population density (including expected number of users), physical terrain, and traffic. The MTSO is the radio equivalent of a Class 5 telephone switch and oversees the primary switching and control functions for the cellular system. Each BTS is connected via landline to the MTSO. The MTSO is designed to interface with the public switched telephone network.

34. Richard Gershon, "Intelligent Networks and International Business Communication: A Systems Theory Interpretation," *Media Markets Monographs, No. 12* (Pamplona, Spain: Universidad de Navarra Press, 2011).

35. A collision avoidance system (CAS) is designed to react to an impending car accident. The CAS will automatically initiate stability control including the use of antilock braking and sensory systems to determine the optimal requirements to support driver safety and prevent accidents. The CAS uses front and rear millimeter wave detection radar to detect vehicles and obstacles on the road. The system automatically engages seatbelts and warns the driver when it determines that a high probability of a collision might occur. If the driver does not brake, the precrash brakes are applied to reduce collision speed.

36. M. A. Goodrich and A. C. Schultz, "Human-Robot Interaction: A Survey," *Foundations and Trends in Human-Computer Interaction* 1, no. 3 (2007): 203–275.

37. Cynthia Breazeal, "Toward Social Robots," *Robotics and Autonomous Systems,* 42 (2003): 167–175.

38. Mark Coeckelbergh, "You Robot: On the Linguistic Construction of Artificial Others," *Artificial Intelligence & Society* 26, no. 1 (2011): 61–69.

39. Any discussion of VR begins with an understanding of the principles of data modeling and simulation. The term *data modeling* can be defined as the creation of a replica or simulated project design, process, or experience. Data modeling is at the heart of today's computer-aided design (CAD) and manufacturing processes. CAD enables engineers to design and draft products in two dimensions using color and shading. CAD provides realistic simulations of how a design might appear before it is manufactured. This, in turn, allows for the making of blueprints, schematic diagrams, multilayer drawings, and so on.

40. A holodeck is a VR facility located on a star ship or starbase. The holodeck was first seen in the pilot episode of *Star Trek: The Next Generation* "Encounter at Farpoint." In later episodes, the holodeck is used for research, combat training, as well as entertainment. The holodeck is depicted as an enclosed room in which objects and people are simulated.

41. Frank Biocca and Mark Levy, eds., *Communication in the Age of Virtual Reality* (Hillsdale, NJ: Lawrence Erlbaum & Associates, 1995).

42. M. Slater and M. Usoh, "Modeling in Immersive Virtual Environments," in *Virtual Reality Applications,* eds. R. Earnshaw, J. Vince & H. Jones (San Diego, CA: Academic Press, 1995).

43. Jean-Claude Heudin, ed., *Virtual Worlds: Synthetic Universes, Digital Life, and Complexity* (Reading, MA: Perseus Books, 1999).

44. W. Zhu, A. Vader, A. Chadda, M. Leu, X. Liu, and J. Vance, "Wii Remote-Based Low-Cost Motion Capture for Automated Assembly Simulation," *Virtual Reality* 17, no. 2 (June 2013): 125–136.

45. D. Rand, R. Kizony, and P. Weiss, "The Sony Playstation II EyeToy: Low-Cost Virtual Reality for Use in Rehabilitation," *Journal of Neurologic Physical Therapy* 32, no. 4 (2008): 155–163.

46. Ken Hillis, *Digital Sensations* (Minneapolis, MN: University of Minnesota, 1999).

47. Vernor Vinge, "Signs of Singularity," *IEEE Spectrum* (June, 2008): 77–82; Ray Kurzweil, *The Singularity is Near: When Humans Transcend Biology* (New York: Viking Press, 2005).

48. Moore's law describes a long-term trend in the history of computing hardware. Since the invention of the integrated circuit in 1958, the number of transistors that can be placed inexpensively on an integrated circuit has increased exponentially, doubling approximately every two years. The trend was first observed by Intel cofounder Gordon Moore in a 1965 paper. Moore's law is now used as a kind of general metric in evaluating the exponential growth of other digital devices, including processing speed, core memory, and so on.

49. Ray Kurzweil, *The Age of Spiritual Machines: When Computers Exceed Human Intelligence* (New York: Penguin, 2000): 17.

CHAPTER 10

Smart Cities and the Common Good

I will take a backseat to no one in my commitment to network neutrality because once providers start to privilege some applications or Web sites over others, then the smaller voices get squeezed out, and we all lose. The Internet is perhaps the most open network in history, and we have to keep it that way.

—Barack Obama, 2007

Introduction

The 21st-century knowledge economy stands in marked contrast to the very assumptions and technology patterns of the industrial age. The industrial age gave us the concept of mass production that relied heavily on centralized manufacturing facilities, where the methods of assembly were highly routinized and standardized.[1] In contrast, the 21st-century knowledge economy celebrates the entrepreneur and the power of a good idea. The Internet has become the great equalizer in terms of affording increased opportunity for the person who wants to advance a creative idea or an innovative solution to a problem. The Internet is an example of a common good. The term *common good* has time-honored philosophical roots dating back to the time of Aristotle. It is a utilitarian ideal and should be thought of as representing the best possible good for the greatest number of people. Today, the principle of common good can be seen in such things as national parks, interstate highways, and the electromagnetic spectrum. The goal is to provide the maximum value and benefit for the greatest number of people.[2]

In this chapter, we explore the growing importance of smart cities and the role of IT and broadband delivery in helping to advance community development. In addition, we consider two important legal and policy issues that will directly impact the future of smart city development. They include net neutrality and digital rights management. They represent two of the most salient topics related to the business of digital media and innovation. Two important themes emerge in this chapter. First, the Internet and broadband delivery should be considered a common good. Second, the very notion of what it means to own a software product is undergoing a major redefinition as to design and purpose.

Smart Cities

Smart cities are communities that utilize communication and IT for the purpose of managing people and resources in highly efficient and sustainable ways. Today, more than half of the world's population now lives in urban areas. There is a major shift underway, whereby an ever-increasing number of working professionals are consciously choosing to live in the downtown urban centers of major cities.

This shift from primarily rural areas to cities or megacities is projected to continue for decades to come, increasing the need for urban reform. By the year 2025, China alone will create an additional 81 cities due to population growth and migration.[3] As more and more people continue to cluster into larger urban centers, city planners will be faced with a number of emerging problems, including resource management, business development, education, telecommunications and IT support, public safety, and so forth. Additional and less obvious are the unique challenges associated with city planning and environmental sustainability.

The goal of smart city technology is to leverage the collective intelligence of the city and its major constituents by coordinating community resources and skill sets.[4] A smart city is comprised of various stakeholders, including but not limited to government, business, education, public safety, health care, energy and utilities, religious centers, transportation, as well as parks and recreation. The word *smart* refers to a new generation of integrated hardware, software, and advanced analytics that provide real-time information that helps decision makers involved with strategic and operational planning activities.[5]

Geographic Information Systems

One such technology is GIS, which involves electronic mapping and database management. GIS can be used to identify underground utility lines (gas, water, and electric) as well as constructing residential and commercial survey maps. The ability to capture, manage, and display various kinds of geographical (and spatial) data provides obvious benefits when it comes to land use planning, conducting an environmental impact study, or contemplating disaster evacuation scenarios. The use of GIS technology reduces the amount of time necessary for planning improvements while helping to avoid costly mistakes. The demand for accurate geographical information is especially important during a crisis situation. GIS allows for database modeling in which different emergency scenarios are considered in planning for natural and man-made disasters before they occur. Database modeling, for example, can prove highly useful for those communities vulnerable to flooding. City planners can use that information to predict where a river is most likely to crest while recognizing the preparations needed to minimize its impact.

Historic Preservation and Smart Cities

Creating an environment for industrial development is pivotal to a smart and sustainable city life. The potential economic benefits include enhancing the city's historic look and natural landscape, workforce development, cleaner environments, and improvements in organizational productivity.[6] The obvious challenge is how to advance city development while decreasing the carbon footprint of that community. Further complicating the problem are the legacy costs associated with buildings that were developed decades ago and represent the city's past. While these buildings may have historic significance, they were not built efficiently by today's standards. By the year 2050, 60 percent of the buildings currently in use will still be in operation.[7] This begs the question: How do we make such buildings of the past smarter and more efficient going forward? Constructing new buildings and remodeling old ones that are sustainable are major environmental challenges of the 21st century. The use of broadband delivery and well-designed energy management systems are essential to making such buildings cost-effective. Developing the right approach to historic preservation has a role to play in helping to advance the smart city concept.

While everyone has their own idea of what the city of the future should include, it's important to point out that not all systems have to be high-end technical solutions. Even strategies as basic as a well-designed community Web site or a 211 directory that provides contact information for vital, citywide services (i.e., food, housing, and health care) are in keeping with the smart city concept. Whether it's GIS or an Internet web directory, the goal of smart city thinking is to centralize key information elements for the purpose of promoting positive economic development and social growth opportunities.

Broadband Delivery and Smart Cities

The term *broadband* refers to high-speed Internet access using the power of intelligent networking. Broadband is the great infrastructure challenge of the early 21st century. It has sometimes been compared to developing the U.S. interstate highway system in the 1950s. Like electricity a century ago, broadband is a foundation for economic growth, job creation, global competitiveness, and a better way of life. It is enabling entire new industries and unlocking vast new possibilities for existing ones.[8] It is changing how we educate children, deliver health care, manage energy, ensure public safety, engage government, and access, organize, and disseminate knowledge. In February 2009, as part of the American Recovery and Reinvestment Act, the U.S. Congress directed the Federal Communications Commission (FCC) to develop a plan to ensure that U.S. citizens have clear and equitable access to broadband capability.

Broadband Delivery and Community Development

Designing a high-speed broadband delivery network is at the heart of community development and economic planning. It is central to the principle of smart cities of the future. The future design and development of a broadband community network has to be understood in the larger context—that it is providing an electronic gateway for a whole host of entertainment, utility, and value-added services. Both cable television system operators and telephone carriers are the new architects of tomorrow's smart city grids. The proposed solutions will have a long-term effect on all aspects of telecommunication services for business and residential users alike, including 1) Education, 2) Geographic information services, 3) Smart grids and energy management, 4) Emergency communication and medical services, and 5) Business communication. The business community, for its part, needs broadband to compete on a global level. More and more, they seek out forward-thinking *smart cities* when choosing to grow their business.[9] When it comes to finding jobs, or applying for jobs, high-speed Internet access is essential. The FCC estimates that 80 percent of Fortune 500 companies only advertise for positions online.

The Role of Public-Private Partnerships

Broadband delivery has become an important symbol of national development. Internationally, the best examples of broadband development and delivery rely on some kind of public-private partnership. A *public-private partnership* can be defined as a contractual agreement between a public agency (federal, state, or local) and a private-sector entity. Through this agreement, the skills and assets of each sector (public and private) are shared in delivering an important service or facility for the general public's use. In addition to the sharing of resources, each party assumes both the risks and rewards in providing such services or facilities.[10] Examples of public-private partnerships can be seen in transportation (airport and highway construction) as well as energy (gas and electric utilities, advancing fuel efficiency, etc.).

Broadband delivery is considered a critical planning piece in helping to accelerate business development while providing new opportunities for innovation, expansion, and EC. Most countries of the world place a high priority on Internet delivery speed, as evidenced in Table10.1. The global average is 18.4 Mbps. The best examples include countries like Hong Kong, Japan, and South Korea, where government and business have partnered to create high-speed Internet delivery standards.

The Internet internationalizes the scope of business, trade, and communication, thereby underscoring the principle of the common good, albeit on a global level. Internet governance and copyright law established by one country can have a cascading effect on both media and information content providers as well as neighboring countries.[12] United Nations regulatory agencies like the International Telecommunications Union (ITU) are responsible for setting technical standards and ensuring cooperation among member nations when it comes to international spectrum use as well as other technical matters. Similarly, the World Intellectual Property Organization (WIPO) is one of 17 specialized agencies of the United

Table 10.1 International High-Speed Internet Delivery

Country Delivery Time	Estimated Speed
1. Hong Kong	63.6 Mbps.
2. Japan	50.0 Mbps.
3. Romania*	47.9 Mbps.
4. South Korea	44.8 Mbps.
5. Latvia*	44.2 Mbps.
6. Singapore	41.1 Mbps.
7. Switzerland	40.3 Mbps.
8. Bulgaria	38.2 Mbps.
9. Netherlands	38.2 Mbps.
10. Belgium	38.0 Mbps.
11. United States	36.6 Mbps.
12. United Kingdom	36.3 Mbps.
13. Hungary	35.9 Mbps.
14. Israel	35.9 Mbps.
15. Czech Republic	35.5 Mbps.

SOURCE: Adapted from information presented by Bloomberg.com.[11]

* It should be noted that smaller countries like Romania and Latvia are easier to blanket with high-speed Internet, which is one reason they consistently rank high on the global list of high-speed Internet delivery.

Nations tasked with promoting the protection of intellectual property throughout the world. WIPO provides a global forum for intellectual property services, policy, information, and cooperation. Both the ITU and WIPO are premised on the value of treating international spectrum use and intellectual property protection as examples of a common good as all countries are legitimate stakeholders in their proper management and use.

The principle of the common good takes on a different meaning when it comes to Internet governance. The Internet is less regulated when compared to other forms of electronic communication. That said, the Internet Corporation for Assigned Names and Numbers (ICANN) is a nonprofit organization responsible for the registry and coordination of Internet protocol identifiers (including both top-level domain names and IP addresses).[13] ICANN is somewhat more politicized and controversial than their ITU counterparts because not everyone believes that the Internet should be governed. In March 2014, the United States withdrew its membership from ICANN.

Two of the most salient questions now facing the future of digital media and innovation pertain to net neutrality and digital rights management. Both sets of issues consider, in varying forms, the need to preserve the common good for the greatest number of people. Such policy questions and legal requirements challenge all countries of the world to consider their respective approaches to Internet governance and copyright law.

Net Neutrality

The term *net neutrality* refers to the basic freedom that all users of the Internet enjoy in terms of accessing and providing content. Net neutrality presupposes a neutral and steady playing field with easy on-ramps. It prevents cable operators, telephone carriers, and other Internet service providers (ISPs) from blocking content or deliberately slowing down any part of the network for business reasons. In sum, all Internet traffic should be treated equally regardless of that information's point of origin or destination.[14] At the same time, the Internet faces serious congestion issues that will only get more serious with time given the rapid increase in users engaged in music and video streaming, massive e-mail campaigns, and the playing of online video games. The nation's Internet Service Providers (ISPs), for their part, would like to sell multitiered service plans to heavy users. This raises three important questions. First, should certain Web sites (i.e., Apple, YouTube, and Netflix) that generate massive amounts of data traffic have access to high-speed delivery lanes? In turn, is it reasonable to create a system that would allow such companies the ability to pay higher fees for the privilege? Second, do the nation's ISPs have the right to restrict certain types of content perceived to be injurious to the proper functioning of the network's design and operations?

Third, what is the proper role and responsibility of government (specifically the FCC) for ensuring fairness on the Internet? At issue is who owns the Internet? The idea of the common good figures prominently in any and all discussions pertaining to the Internet and broadband delivery. This becomes especially important for smart city planners who have an obvious stake in the outcome from a planning and design standpoint. The principle of net neutrality goes to the heart of promoting business and individual user access as well as entrepreneurial opportunity.

Net Neutrality: Framing the Debate

Consumer Advocate Position. Net neutrality presupposes a level playing field for information and entertainment transport. A neutral network ensures that users face no conditions limiting access to applications and services.[15] Related to this same argument are First Amendment considerations. One of the implied rights of the First Amendment is the right to receive information. A basic assumption of the Internet is that all Web sites (and the ability to access all sites) should be treated equally. There is no place for the censoring of information or the deliberate slowing down of content delivery. Both are considered a form of prior restraint and are contrary to the principles of the First Amendment. This was affirmed in *Reno v. ACLU,* where the U.S. Supreme Court effectively recognized the value of preserving free expression on the Internet and saw the unique technological challenges in trying to enforce program restrictions on the Internet.[16]

Internet Service Provider Position. Cable operators and telephone carriers see the issue differently. For companies like AT&T, Verizon, and Comcast, net neutrality is not a content issue but rather a maintenance and cost of service delivery question. They make the analogy between maintaining the U.S. interstate highway system and the Internet. In the case of the nation's interstate highways, trucks and major freight carriers pay higher tolls than individual cars. Major freight carriers, so the argument goes, potentially do more damage to highways than individual cars and therefore should assume a greater cost for maintenance and road repairs. How does this apply to the Internet? The nation's ISPs are responsible for building and maintaining the electronic highways that have become the Internet. There is a price to be paid for maintaining such highways. America's cable operators and telephone carriers want to establish different pricing levels for Internet speed and quality of service. As they see it, the Internet faces serious congestion issues that will only get more serious with time. The issue is especially problematic when dealing with wireless communication and limited spectrum availability. Both telephone carriers and ISPs would argue that restricting information content is not their primary concern. There is little business incentive to do so.

Comcast and BitTorrent

In October 2007, cable multiple system operator Comcast was discovered blocking (or delaying) peer-to-peer technology BitTorrent, an open-source protocol used to facilitate the exchange of large files between users, including both music and videos. BitTorrent had previously been cited as a major contributor to Internet music piracy. Comcast users reported a significant decrease in download speeds and were often unable to establish file downloads. Comcast argued that it delayed BitTorrent file transfers to alleviate network congestion. On August 1, 2008, the FCC ruled that Comcast had violated the FCC's Internet Policy Statement by selectively blocking "peer-to-peer connections in an attempt to manage its traffic."[17]

The FCC declared that Comcast had violated federal policy by impeding consumer access to an online technology. The FCC concluded that the company had "unduly interfered with Internet users' rights to access the lawful Internet content and to use the applications of their choice."[18] No financial penalty was imposed on Comcast, but the company was ordered to discontinue any further interference with the BitTorrent software protocol. However, the BitTorrent case raised a number of concerns about cable operators who are willing to engage in restraint of trade for business reasons. For net neutrality advocates, this case clearly demonstrated the need for some kind of regulation to offset the possibility of future prior restraint abuses by cable operators and telephone carriers.

Comcast v. FCC, 2010

Comcast challenged the FCC ruling by appealing the commission's decision to the U.S. Court of Appeals for the District of Columbia. In this case, the court was asked to consider whether the FCC has the right to exercise "ancillary authority" over ISPs by trying to advance net neutrality policies involving openness on the network. The court issued its opinion on April 6, 2010. In a unanimous decision by a three-judge panel, the U.S. Court of Appeals declared that the FCC lacked the authority to censure Comcast for interfering with subscribers' Internet traffic. This decision sidetracked the commission's attempt to establish binding net neutrality guidelines and policies, absent a legislative mandate from the U.S. Congress.[19] The D.C. Circuit Court vacated the FCC's ruling against Comcast based on the court's refusal to accept the commission's claim of ancillary jurisdiction. The court said that the FCC lacked an explicit mandate to regulate the broadband delivery of services to the home, previously established in the 1980 Computer II decision. It should be noted that the D.C. Circuit Court chose to ignore earlier legal precedent where the Supreme Court affirmed FCC ancillary authority when it came to the regulation of new media technologies such as cable television.[20] The case of *Comcast v. FCC* also spelled out the relationship between basic telephone service versus enhanced information services. Basic service was understood to mean traditional telephone communication where the basic message is not changed or altered during the communication process. In contrast, enhanced information services (i.e., data communication) would be unregulated.[21]

NCTA v. Brand X Internet Services

While the Computer II decision established the distinction between basic versus enhanced information services, the actual provision of high-speed Internet delivery was still years away for all practical purposes. One of the obligations of a telephone common carrier is the requirement to sell one's services on a nondiscriminatory basis to any and all users. This includes so-called *telephone resellers* who do not own their own network infrastructure. Instead, a telephone reseller sells voice communication services under their own brand name but uses the facilities of an existing carrier. The established telephone carrier is placed in the odd position of having to sell voice communication services to a would-be competitor. The issue becomes all the more complicated when that same reseller wants to enter into the delivery of advanced information services in direct competition with the ISP. The 9th Circuit Court of Appeals was asked to consider whether telephone carriers should be obligated to sell information services to resellers as well.

Case Description. Brand X Communication and Earthlink were ISPs that relied on dial-up, cable modem services and DSL as the basis for reselling their own Internet access service, albeit at a reduced rate. The local cable operator refused to sell them Internet service capability for the purpose of reselling it to the general public. The FCC was asked to consider whether cable television operators are obligated to provide carriage to an external service provider under a traditional common carrier model?[22] At issue is the proper regulatory classification of a broadband cable modem service under Title II of the Communications Act of 1934 as amended by the Telecommunications Act of 1996.

On March 14, 2002, the FCC adopted a Declaratory Ruling and Notice of Proposed Rulemaking. In its declaratory ruling, the FCC classified cable modem delivery as an information service and not as a telecommunications service. They concluded that cable modem service, as currently offered, is properly classified as an interstate information service, not as a cable service, and that there is no separate offering of telecommunications service.[23] Brand X, EarthLink, the State of California, and others sought review of the FCC's declaratory ruling in various federal circuit courts. The petitions for review were assigned to the 9th Circuit by lottery. The petitioners argued that cable broadband delivery is both an information and a telecommunications service and subject to common carrier regulation. In sum, they argued that the cable television operator should be required to let other ISPs use their facilities.

Outcome. On October 6, 2003, the U.S. Court of Appeals (9th Cir.) ruled in favor of Brand X Internet Services, thus vacating the FCC's 2002 Declaratory Ruling. The case was appealed to the U.S. Supreme Court. In a highly controversial 6–3 decision, the U.S. Supreme Court ruled on June 27, 2005, in favor of the FCC's position to exempt cable modem service from common carrier regulation. The U.S. Supreme court concluded that cable companies that sell broadband Internet service do not provide "telecommunications service" as the Communications Act defines that term and are exempt from mandatory common-carrier regulation under Title II. The Supreme Court determined that cable broadband is an information service, thus reversing the judgment of the U.S. Court of Appeals (9th Cir.).

The FCC's Internet Policy Statement, 2005

On August 5, 2005, the FCC issued an Internet policy statement designed to foster the open and interconnected nature of the public Internet. One of the important objectives of this policy statement was to extend the same regulatory guarantees to the telephone industry that was outlined in *NCTA v. Brand X Internet Services* (2005). Henceforth, neither cable companies nor telephone carriers offering broadband services would be required to adhere to the more strict regulation associated with common carriage delivery. Specifically, the delivery of high-speed Internet service to the home by the nation's telephone companies was to be classified as an information service.[24]

The Federal Communications Commission Open Internet Order, 2010

Under the terms of the Open Internet Order, 2010, America's ISPs are prohibited from blocking content and prioritizing certain kinds of information traffic. The order imposed stricter rules on wired Internet services than mobile services. Consumer rights advocates criticized the rules for being too weak because they did not cover mobile web providers. In contrast, telecommunications companies like Verizon and AT&T felt that the rules were too strong. At the time of the FCC ruling, America's ISPs were legally classified as "information services."[25] As such, the FCC lacked the proper authority to regulate those services, though the commission did have indirect authority to regulate interstate and international communications.

After the FCC released its Open Internet Order, Verizon filed a lawsuit against the FCC claiming that the commission does not have the authority to make those rules or enforce them over ISPs like itself. In *Verizon v. FCC*, the D.C. Court of Appeals agreed with Verizon and said that the FCC can't stop ISPs from blocking or discriminating against Web sites or any other Internet traffic unless the Internet is reclassified as a public utility.[26] But the court also said the FCC does have some authority to implement net neutrality rules insofar as it promotes broadband deployment across the country.[27]

Net Neutrality: FCC Open Internet Ruling, 2015

From its very beginning, the Internet was designed as a neutral network so that no one person or organization could exercise disproportionate control over its design and evolution. The Internet was intended to be an open system that would enable highly creative people to contribute to its growth and development (i.e., permeability principle). Today, we have witnessed the exponential growth of the Internet due to the many contributions of its users, including powerful search engines, unique Web site design, aggregation of content, and increased delivery speed, to name only a few. The Internet has transformed the world's business, education, and social environments.

On February 26, 2015, the FCC issued a new set of net neutrality rules designed to ensure that ISPs treat the delivery of information content equally and fairly. In a historic 3–2 vote, FCC Commissioner Thomas Wheeler indicated that broadband communication will now be regulated as a utility under Title II of the Communications Act.

> Today, the commission—once and for all—enacts strong, sustainable rules, grounded in multiple sources of legal authority, to ensure that Americans reap the economic, social, and civic benefits of an open Internet today and into the future.[28]

These rules contain the following features:

- ISPs shall not block lawful content, applications, services, or non-harmful devices.
- ISPs shall not impair or degrade lawful Internet traffic on the basis of Internet content, application, or service, or use of non-harmful devices.
- ISPs shall not engage in paid prioritization where paid prioritization is defined as arrangements that directly or indirectly favor some traffic over other traffic.

- ISPs shall not unreasonably interfere with or unreasonably disadvantage end users' ability to select, access, and use broadband Internet access service or the lawful Internet content, applications, services, or devices of their choice.[29]

The most important features of the new rules are the proposed changes in classification, whereby the FCC reasserts its ancillary authority by making broadband delivery services (both fixed and mobile) subject to Title II common carrier regulation. Under this approach, broadband communication will now be regulated more like a utility. That said, Commissioner Wheeler is quick to point out that only select provisions of the Communications Act will be enforced. The goal is to provide a "modernized version of Title II" and not "old-style 1930s monopoly regulation." The new rules are an attempt to strike up a balance by adhering to the principle of the common good while recognizing that such rules cannot and should not interfere with entrepreneurship and media innovation.

Digital Media and Intellectual Property

Intellectual property is any innovation, commercial or artistic, that provides economic benefit and value to the public. Intellectual property is protected by patents on inventions, trademarks on named brand products, and copyrights on software-developed products and services. Copyright is a form of protection provided by law to the creators of original literary, music, television, film, video game, and computer software products. The law provides a copyright holder with designated rights to determine how or when such works can be used or reproduced.[30] A violation of copyright law is called *infringement.*

Stealing intellectual property is simple and inexpensive. Once software content is digitally formatted, it becomes easy to make perfect copies as well as to shift content from one format to another. Why is this important? Piracy is a very real threat to the livelihoods of not only music and video artists but also the thousands of less-celebrated people in the entertainment industries, including video editors, sound engineers, and other technicians. The same problem holds equally true for those professionals working in computer and video game software. The problem at the international level is even worse. International software piracy costs software makers an estimated $15 billion annually. The cultural environment is a major factor in terms of software piracy. The percentage of software piracy varies by geographic location.[31] Countries like China, India, the Russian Federation, Pakistan, and Venezuela have been placed on a special watch list maintained by the International Intellectual Property Alliance for routinely violating international copyright law.[32] The continuing lost sales create a formidable problem for the information and entertainment industries. The Microsoft Office suite of products is one of the most pirated software products in the world. The powers of enforcement at the international level are limited. As a consequence, there has been a big push in recent years to ensure better copyright protections leading to an important legal principle known as *digital rights management* (DRM).

Digital Rights Management

Digital Rights Management (DRM) refers to a mixture of legal and technological tools designed to give intellectual property owners greater control over how creative works are used in a multimedia environment. DRM designates what rights consumers have in the use of such software products once they are purchased.[33] DRM has become especially important given the growing importance of music and video delivery services like iTunes and Netflix. The technology is clearly moving in the direction of music and video platforms, whereby access is steadily shifting away from a channel- or medium-specific process to a platform-based system capable of providing consumers access to a variety of news and entertainment content via the Internet.

Sony Corporation of America v. Universal Studios (1984)

Case Description. The origins of DRM date back to an important legal case entitled *Sony Corporation of America v. Universal Studios* (1984).[34] In 1975, the Sony Corporation introduced the Betamax videotape recorder, which gave television users the ability to record programming directly from one's television set. The case eventually made its way to the U.S. Supreme Court. The Supreme Court was asked to consider the following questions: 1) Does the use of the Sony Betamax videotape recorder constitute a violation of U.S. copyright law, and 2) Does the home recording of television constitute a fair use application of media software according to the terms of the 1976 U.S. Copyright Act?

Outcome. The U.S. Supreme Court in a 5–4 decision ruled that videotaping for personal use does not violate federal copyright law. In writing for the Supreme Court's majority opinion, Justice Stevens makes clear:

> Moviemakers do not have complete control over their films under copyright law. Any individual may reproduce a copyrighted work for fair use—the copyright owner does not possess exclusive right to such use.[35]

It was further argued that Sony could not be held accountable for all the possible applications (both legal and illegal) of the videotape recorder and playback.

Significance. The Sony case provided the legal basis for personal recording of television as an example of fair use. This case would be cited when it came to the personal recording of music as well. One of the unintended consequences of the Sony case was that it made possible the launch of videotape rental stores like Blockbuster, Hollywood Video, and later by extension, companies like iTunes, Netflix, and so on. Curiously enough, companies like Universal Studios and the Walt Disney Company were the direct beneficiaries of this new digital media rental and sales environment.

Digital Recording and Software Ownership

While the Sony case addressed the question of personal recording of television and fair use, it did not address the future of digital recording. During the next several years, advancements in computer and digital media technology would make it easier and more efficient to copy and reproduce information and entertainment goods. The term *copyright,* with its emphasis on "copies" was becoming more and more problematic in a world of digital works. It was increasingly unclear how copyright protection would be enforced for the owners of intellectual works in the face of continuing digital media innovation.[36]

Nowhere was this more evident than in the rise of the music service known as Napster. The launch of Napster in June 1999 created a legal controversy given the company's stated mission to make copyrighted music free and accessible to its users. Shortly after its introduction, Napster was downloaded by more than 10,000 people. Napster was subsequently accessed by an estimated 60 million people worldwide. In 2000, the U.S. music recording industry (in conjunction with the Recording Industry Association of America) filed a massive lawsuit against Napster claiming copyright violation.[37] At issue was the future of music copyright and licensing. The U.S. 9th Circuit Court was asked to consider whether the Napster service is a violation of copyright law or is an example of fair use based on a new business model. In 2001, the 9th Circuit Court of Appeals found Napster to be in direct violation of U.S. copyright law. The court rejected Napster's contention that music sharing should be considered a fair use application. This, in turn, cleared the way for U.S. District Court Judge Marilyn Patel to place severe restrictions on Napster in the area of music sharing. From there, it was only a matter of time before companies such as Grokster, Limewire, and MegaUpload would try and make the same fair use argument citing the Sony case. In each instance, the courts (both federal and district) have sided with the copyright holder.

Designing the Protections

A DRM scheme operates on three levels: 1) Establishing the proper copyright protection for a piece of software content, 2) Managing the distribution of that software, and 3) Controlling what a consumer can do with that software once it has been distributed. To that end, DRM defines three entities in the process of copyright enforcement: the user, the content and usage rights, and the relationship between them.[38] As noted earlier, DRM relies on a combination of legal and technical protections. It should be understood that there are costs associated with any attempt at legal and technical enforcement. Just as digital media technology permits easy copying, successful DRM can occur only if it is consistent and transparent to the user.

Encryption. Early attempts at DRM focused on security and encryption as a means of solving the issue of unauthorized copying. The software developer would construct an encryption system. The user could only access the software content by paying for the use of a decoder. The problem with this approach was that it did not address future restrictions on the use of the decoded content. An early example of an encryption approach was the DVD Forum's Content Scrambling System (CSS). The forum organized film producers to agree on a common encoding system for movies on DVD. While achieving its primary goals, the CSS system did little to prevent piracy and was able to be bypassed when an open source decoder (called DeCSS) was developed. Therein lies one basic problem with the containment approach, namely that the same technologies can be used to bypass or invalidate the protection scheme.

Markers. The use of markers represents the second generation of DRM. This approach involves the encoding of markers into the digital content that can be used for purposes of protection and identification as well as specifying authorized uses of said media content. The marker approach is used by a variety of software development firms that exhibit or sell goods and services via the Internet. The software development firm will use watermarks or digital seals that specify the kinds of permitted uses. Examples using the marker approach are companies like Shutterstock or iStockphoto, which feature photographs for commercial sale but that contain the company's watermark embedded in each photo. Similarly, Adobe reader makes it difficult to cut and paste content from its PDF files.

Rights Locker. Digital rights locker involves a major shift in thinking in terms of how we define the ownership of information goods and services. The premise behind a rights locker approach is that consumers don't actually own distinct physical copies of information and entertainment goods. The focus is on uses rather than copies. Software programs and user generated content (UGC) are centrally stored on a remote digital network, namely, a cloud computer. What the consumer owns is a set of legal rights to access the content from a range of devices. This is the basic approach used by companies such as Microsoft, Apple, iTunes, Netflix, and HBO Go. Proponents of rights locker argue that it provides greater flexibility and can accommodate a wider range of uses, which in turn, adds value for the consumer. One of the important programming trends today is a move toward "television everywhere," a recognition that today's consumer of entertainment should be able to access such programming on a variety of media devices, including computers, tablets, and smartphones.

The media entertainment industries view DRM as an essential tool in protecting creative works. Given the new technology realities, software development companies have become ardent supporters of DRM with the goal of preventing unauthorized viewing, copying, or distributing of proprietary software material. At the same time, DRM has set into motion a number of unintended consequences when it comes to accessing copyrighted material and transferring ownership among multiple screen devices. Consumers sometimes become frustrated when media content providers impose arbitrary restrictions on how such content can be used and under what circumstances. They sometimes find the rules of DRM complex and difficult to navigate. For the 21st-century digital media consumer, it's all about convergence, mobility, and immediacy.

Discussion

The Internet is an example of a common good. Both government and business are important stakeholders that have vital roles to play in ensuring the web's continued success. Net neutrality presupposes a neutral and steady playing field with easy on-ramps. It prevents cable operators, telephone carriers, and other ISPs from blocking content or deliberately slowing down any part of the network for business reasons. In sum, all Internet traffic should be treated equally regardless of that information's point of origin or destination.[39] The common good, in the best sense of the term, means allowing the Internet to function like an information and entertainment grid (not unlike electricity), where no distinction is made between users and applications.

The justification for intellectual property protection is based on a labor theory of property; that is, a person (or organization) acquires property rights to something by investing time, energy, and resources into the creation of an artistic or creative work. The principle of the common good is a major consideration given the fact that intellectual property protection is only as good as the international community's willingness to recognize and enforce such protections. Hence, the creation of the WIPO and the Berne Convention for the Protection of Literary and Artistic Works.

One of the important obligations of government is to ensure protection of the common good. To accomplish that, the international community through its designated regulatory agencies have a shared responsibility to ensure that the democratic principles of the Internet and the preservation of intellectual property are not subjugated to narrow corporate, political, and personal self-interests. It requires the ability to place a periodic check on the excesses of a free market and to strive, however imperfectly, to protect the common good. The same can be said at the international level, when governing bodies like WIPO and the World Trade Organization (WTO) work to ensure intellectual property protection and fair trade. Both net neutrality and DRM have become the hot-button IT issues now facing today's governing bodies and regulators. The challenge for the future is to craft a level and fair playing field that will ensure creativity and entrepreneurship on the web. This means finding the right blend of regulatory oversight that will facilitate sustainable business growth while contributing to the common good. As *Newsweek* columnist Robert J. Samuelson (1992) wrote: "We face a choice between a society where people accept modest sacrifices for a common good or a more contentious society where a group selfishly protects their own benefits."[40]

Endnotes

1. Alvin Toffler, *The Third Wave* (New York: Bantam, 1980).
2. Antonio Argandoña, "The Stakeholder Theory and the Common Good," *Journal of Business Ethics* 17 (1998): 1093–1102.
3. Leslie Norton, "Dawn of the Smart City," *Barrons*, Oct. 3, 2011, http://online.barrons.com/articles/SB50001424052748704783104576599051649765770

4. C. Harrison, B. Eckman, R. Hamilton, P. Hartswick, J. Kalagnanam, J. Paraszczak, and P. Williams, "Foundations for Smarter Cities," *IBM Journal of Research and Development* 54, no. 4 (2010): 1–16.

5. Leslie Guevarra, "Market for Smart City Technology to Reach $16B a Year by 2020," *Green Biz,* Sept. 29, 2011, http://www.greenbiz.com/blog/2011/09/29/market-smart-city-technology-reach-16b-year-2020

6. Hafedh Chourabi et al., "Understanding Smart Cities: An Integrative Framework" (presentation, Forty-fifth Hawaii International Conference on System Sciences, Maui, Hawaii, January 2012).

7. Eduardo López Moreno, Oyebanji Oyeyinka, and Gora Mboup, *State of the World's Cities 2010–2011: Bridging the Urban Divide* (Nairobi, Kenya: United Nations Human Settlement Programme, 2010).

8. Federal Communications Commission, *National Broadband Plan,* last modified March 17, 2010, http://www.fcc.gov/national-broadband-plan

9. Pantelis Koutroumpis, "The Economic Impact of Broadband on Growth: A Simultaneous Approach," *Telecommunications Policy* 33, no. 9 (October 2009): 471–485.

10. National Council for Public-Private Partnerships, *Testing Tradition: Assessing the Value of Public-Private Partnerships* (Arlington, VA: NCPPP, 2012).

11. "Top 20: Where to Find the World's Fastest Internet," *BloombergBusiness,* January 10, 2014, http://www.bloomberg.com/slideshow/2013-07-23/top-20-where-to-find-the-world-s-fastest-internet.html#slide1

12. Milton Mueller, *Networks and States: The Global Politics of Internet Governance* (Cambridge, MA: MIT Press, 2010).

13. To surf the Net with your unique number, it helps greatly if that number hasn't already been assigned to someone else. Assign it twice, and bits can get confused as they wend their way toward you (or is it toward your doppelganger?). It's the same problem with phone numbers: they shouldn't belong to more than one organization or user at a time.

14. Wendy Boswell, "The Pros and Cons of Net Neutrality," *About Tech,* http://websearch.about.com/od/searchingtheweb/i/net-neutrality.htm

15. Christopher Marsden, *Net Neutrality: Towards a Co-regulatory Solution* (Sussex, UK: University of Sussex Law School, 2010).

16. Reno v. American Civil Liberties Union, 521 U.S. 844 (1997).

17. Federal Communications Commission, "Commission Orders Comcast to End Discriminatory Network Management Practices," last modified August 1, 2008, https://apps.fcc.gov/edocs_public/attachmatch/DOC-284286A1.pdf

18. Ibid.

19. Robert Cannon, "The Legacy of the Federal Communications Commission's Computer Inquiries," *Federal Communications Law Journal* 55, no. 2 (2003): 167–206.

20. Kevin Wilson, *Deregulating Telecommunications* (Boston, MA: Rowman & Littlefield, 2000).

21. Ibid.

22. National Cable & Telecommunications Association et al. v. Brand X Internet Services, 545 U.S. 967 (2005).

23. Federal Communications Commission, "FCC Classifies Cable Modem Service as *Information Service,*" last modified March 14, 2002, http://www.fcc.gov/Bureaus/Cable/News_Releases/2002/nrcb0201.html

24. Federal Communications Commission, "FCC Adopts Policy Statement: New Principles Preserve and Promote the Open and Interconnected Nature of Public Internet," last modified March 25, 2010, http://hraunfoss.fcc.gov/edocs_public/attachmatch/DOC-260435A1.pdf

25. L. Miranda, "The FCC's Net Neutrality Proposal Explained," *The Nation,* May 21, 2014, http://www.thenation.com/article/179934/fccs-net-neutrality-proposal-explained

26. Verizon v. FCC, 740 F.3d 623 (2014).

27. L. Miranda "Court Strikes down Net Neutrality Order," *The Nation,* Jan. 10, 2014, http://www.thenation.com/article/177916/court-strikes-down-net-neutrality-order

28. Federal Communications Commission, "FCC Adopts Strong, Sustainable Rules to Protect the Open Internet," last modified Feb. 26, 2015, http://www.fcc.gov/document/fcc-adopts-strong-sustainable-rules-protect-open-internet

29. Gerald Brock, "Keynote Address" (presentation, 2015 ITERA Academic Conference, Washington, DC, March 28, 2015).

30. World Trade Organization, "Intellectual Property: Protection and Enforcement," https://www.wto.org/english/thewto_e/whatis_e/tif_e/agrm7_e.htm

31. Oliver Bremer and Willms Buhse, "Standardization in DRM—Trends and Recommendations," in *Digital Rights Management: Technological, Economic, Legal and Political Aspects,* eds. E. Becker, W. Buhse, et al. (Berlin, Germany: Springer-Verlag, 2004), 334–344.

32. International Intellectual Property Alliance, *Country Reports,* http://www.iipa.com/countryreports.html

33. Eberhard Becker, Willms Buhse, Dirk Gunnewig, and Niels Rumps, eds., *Digital Rights Management: Technological, Economic, Legal and Political Aspects* (Berlin, Germany: Springer-Verlag, 2004).

34. Sony Corporation of America v. Universal City Studios, Inc., 464 U.S. 417 (1984).

35. Ibid.

36. Lawrence Lessig, *The Future of Ideas: The Fate of the Commons in a Connected World* (New York: Vintage, 2002).

37. A&M Records, Inc. v. Napster, Inc., 239 F.3d 1004 (2001).

38. Julia Layton, "How Digital Rights Management Works," *How Stuff Works,* http://computer.howstuffworks.com/drm.htm

39. Christopher Marsden, *Net Neutrality: Towards a Co-regulatory Solution* (London, UK: Bloomsbury Academic, 2010).

40. Robert Samuelson, "How Our American Dream Unraveled," *Newsweek,* Mar. 2, 1992, http://www.newsweek.com/how-our-american-dream-unraveled-195900

CHAPTER 11

Facebook: Social Media and Business Strategy

Our whole theory is that people have real connections in the world. People communicate most naturally and effectively with their friends and the people around them.

—Mark Zuckerberg, Facebook

Introduction

Facebook is the world's largest social network, with more than 1.5 billion active users around the world. An estimated 82.8 percent of those users reside outside the United States and Canada.[1] In a few short years, Facebook has become one of the principal giants of the digital age, challenging companies like Google and Amazon with its vision of the Internet tied together by personal relationships and recommendations. The Facebook experience is built around the people you know. Facebook users flood the social network with their thoughts, commentaries, and photos on a daily basis. While Facebook is first and foremost a social medium, it also has become an important business tool. Facebook has proved to be an essential communication and marketing strategy for those organizations that operate in a world of high-speed information and entertainment. Central to this idea is that social media like Facebook provides low-cost platforms with which to market and promote a company's brand. Second, it provides an excellent way to recommend products, services, and ideas based on advice and support coming from someone the user knows. This chapter provides an inside look at Facebook with special attention given to the power of intelligent networking and social media.

Author's Note: The information contained in this chapter is based on a previous chapter that was part of an edited works collection: Richard Gershon. "Facebook: A Business Perspective on the Power of Intelligent Networking and Social Media." In *Handbook of Social Media*, edited by M. Friedrichsen & W. Muhl-Benninghaus, 375–389. Berlin, Germany: Springer, 2013.

Facebook Today

Today, Facebook claims an international workforce of more than 10,000 employees. In December 2011, Facebook moved into a new corporate space in Menlo Park, California. The fifty-seven-acre campus formerly belonged to Sun Microsystems. The new Facebook headquarters building is set up very openly, reflecting the core philosophy of sharing and openness. There are no private offices or cubicles to divide coworkers. Instead, software designers and engineers occupy rows of shared desk space. Even CEO Mark Zuckerberg's desk resides on the main floor. Facebook has become one of the most sought-after high-tech companies to work for in Silicon Valley. From a simple Boston dorm room at Harvard, Facebook has dramatically grown into a worldwide presence.

Historical Overview

The story of Facebook begins with Mark Zuckerberg, who launched his Web 2.0 venture from a Harvard dorm room. Zuckerberg grew up in Dobbs Ferry, New York, and took up writing software programs as a hobby in middle school. His father taught him BASIC and later hired software developer David Newman to tutor him privately. Newman later described Zuckerberg as a "prodigy," adding that it was "tough to stay ahead of him."[2] Zuckerberg later attended Phillips Exeter Academy, where he excelled in classic literature and fencing. His computer skills were noteworthy even then, and he was offered job opportunities at both Microsoft and AOL. He declined both offers and chose instead to attend Harvard University, where he majored in computer science and psychology.

During his time at Harvard, Zuckerberg began coding multiple Web sites including CourseMatch and Facemash. CourseMatch was a simple online tool used by students at Harvard that recommended which courses to take based on what their friends were enrolled in. Zuckerberg's second and more controversial software program, Facemash, was a rating system that evaluated Harvard female co-eds based on their relative attractiveness.[3] According to the Harvard Crimson, Facemash used photos compiled from the facebook network of nine residence houses, colocating two women next to each other at a time and asking the user to choose the "hotter person." To accomplish this, Zuckerberg hacked into the protected areas of Harvard's computer network and copied the houses' private dormitory ID images. The idea of rating one's classmates quickly proved to be a viral sensation and spread among friends and classmates. Zuckerberg's creation achieved 20,000 page views from more than 400 visitors around campus and was reported to have crashed Harvard's computer network. The site was promptly shut down, and Zuckerberg was reprimanded by Harvard's senior administration. The university initially was prepared to file charges against Zuckerberg for infiltrating the university's online campus directory and for privacy invasion. The charges were later dropped.[4] Shortly thereafter, Harvard classmates Cameron and Tyler Winklevoss brought Zuckerberg in to help finish a new social networking project they were working on.

Instead of completing the project, Zuckerberg started a separate Web site called Thefacebook.com. He registered the domain name in January and launched the Web site on February 4, 2004. In February 2007, both Zuckerberg and Facebook were the target of a major lawsuit initiated by the Winklevoss brothers and partner Divya Narendra, who claimed that Zuckerberg had taken their idea in the making of Facebook.[5]

The newly launched Facebook was an overnight sensation. More than 1,200 Harvard students had signed up after the first day. By month's end, more than half of Harvard's undergraduate population had a Facebook profile. The diffusion process was immediate. The Facebook network quickly grew to include other Boston universities, later all Ivy League schools, and eventually all U.S. universities. More than a year later, Facebook began to spread worldwide. During this time, the Facebook Photos application was implemented, quickly becoming one of the most popular photo sharing services on the Internet. Facebook's dramatic rise owes a lot to the fact that it began in a college setting where student social activity is both constant and dynamic. Facebook's origins on the campus of Harvard also lent the project an elitist aura that gave it a unique status for early users.[6]

Facebook's early success captured the interest of venture capitalist Peter Thiel, one of the cofounders of PayPal, who provided a beginning investment of $500,000 in the summer of 2004. Zuckerberg had also made friends with Napster entrepreneur Sean Parker, who became the company's first president. Zuckerberg eventually dropped out of Harvard and made the decision to move the company to Palo Alto, California, home to a number of well-known Silicon Valley IT companies. Facebook's meteoric rise gained the attention of some very large media companies, including Viacom's MTV networks as well as search engine giant Yahoo. Both companies offered to purchase Facebook. Zuckerberg rejected both offers, including a $1 billion bid from Yahoo. According to Peter Thiel, Zuckerberg was said to have remarked, "I don't know what I could do with the money. I'd just start another social networking site. I kind of like the one I already have."[7]

Worldwide Active Users

By 2008, Facebook was able to claim more than 100 million users. Two years later, that figure grew to nearly 600 million users worldwide. The success of Facebook was evidenced when *Time* magazine selected company founder Mark Zuckerberg as *Time* magazine's 2010 person of the year. Zuckerberg's selection was the result of his having established the world's largest social network.

> For connecting more than half a billion people and mapping their social relations among them (something that has never been done before); for creating a new system of exchanging information that has become both indispensable and sometimes a little scary; and finally for changing how we all live our lives in ways that are innovative and even optimistic.[8]

Today, Facebook reaches more than 1.5 billion active users around the world.

A Business Perspective on the Power of Social Media

Social media represents a category of Internet-based activity where a virtual community of users share information through the use of individual profiles, contact information, personal messages, blogs and commentary, and videos. The operative word is "social" because it involves reaching out and sharing of one's ideas, thoughts, and experiences to a common community of users. Simply put, social media is about the power of networking and relationship building.[9] There is a clear recognition that most businesses need to have a social media strategy, even if they don't fully understand how it works. While many such companies have succeeded in generating many friends and followers on Facebook, LinkedIn, and Twitter, few fully understand the potential of social media as a business strategy.[10] As Tabernero et al. (2013) point out, social networking sites present both a challenge and an opportunity. On the one hand, social media gives its users a public voice that bypasses the traditional media intermediaries, including the regular news outlets as well as corporate and political communication specialists. Social media disrupts the one-way flow of such information by giving the general public an opportunity to comment and react in more direct ways. Dissatisfied audiences can sometimes undermine even the most well-constructed communication campaigns. On the other hand, social media provides business marketers with an altogether new tool for engaging one's audience in a more personalized way.[11]

The power of social media makes it possible to communicate in real time regardless of time zones, geographical borders, and physical space. Social media has proved to be a major game changer when it comes to the diffusion of new ideas. From product launches to mobilizing people to attend a street rally, social media has redefined the principle of opinion leadership in the 21st century. Opinion leadership takes on a whole new meaning given power and persuasion techniques such as blogs, social media postings, as well as ratings and evaluation comments on EC sites. Nowhere is this more evident than when something goes viral on Facebook or when topics begin to trend on Twitter.

In this next section, we consider seven communication goals of social media (See Table 11.1). First, social media provides a low-cost platform for enhancing brand awareness. A highly successful brand is one that creates a strong resonance connection in the consumer's mind and leaves a lasting impression.[12] Branding includes a number of key elements, including brand loyalty, brand awareness, perceived quality, and brand associations.[13] Global media brands, like Pixar, Disney, and HBO use the power of social media to cultivate brand awareness by developing ongoing relationships with their audiences involving specific television and films, characters, and story lines. Second, social media provides a platform for giving both companies and individuals alike the ability to provide their audiences (or contacts) periodic news and information updates. Television services like NBC (United States), BBC (UK), RTL (Germany), Telecinco (Spain), and NHK (Japan), to name only a few, regularly use social media as a way to engage their viewing audiences with information regarding upcoming programs and/or special event features as well as provide opportunities to comment afterward. Similarly, other business

Table 11.1   The Seven Communication Goals of Social Media
1. Provides a low-cost platform for enhancing brand awareness
2. Provides a platform for periodic news and information updates
3. Provides an opportunity to meet new friends, colleagues, or clients
4. Makes recommendations based on the experiences of friends and acquaintances
5. Provides opportunities for crowdsourcing as well as testing customer reaction to proposed concepts or product ideas
6. Can perform an important gatekeeping role by highlighting select news and video items for general distribution
7. Mobilizes people to action by providing information about events, times, and locations

enterprises routinely give their followers news updates concerning product introductions or special event happenings. Third, social media allows individuals to
meet new people as well as strengthen existing relationships.[14] From personal
friendships to professional contacts, social media utilizes the power of intelligent
networking to make communication easy and accessible. To that end, one of the
important features of social media is the ability to add friends and acquaintances to
one's contact list. LinkedIn, in particular, has become the modern-day equivalent of
a Rolodex, complete with contact information, résumé, and the power to organize
professional contacts. For job seekers, LinkedIn is an essential first step as it allows
users to organize information according to various categories like profession, geography, professional skills, university, and so on. For recruiters, it provides the same
opportunities in reverse. Both Facebook and LinkedIn use a specialized algorithm
that generates a list of potential friends using a friend-of-a-friend reference matrix
system (i.e., common index naming points) based on two or more name listings.

Fourth, social media facilitates comments and recommendations on a wide variety of topics based on the experience of friends and acquaintances. Facebook Chief
Operating Officer Sheryl Sandberg makes the point that marketers are always looking for the person who's not just going to buy a certain product, but will likewise
spread the word to their friends.[15] This is word-of-mouth advertising in its purest
form. Word-of-mouth communication is more persuasive then general advertising.
At issue is a question of trust. Most consumers approach the general advertiser with
a certain degree of wariness. After all, it's the advertiser's job to persuade us with
claims of a product's superiority. In contrast, our friends will tell it like it is. The
sense of raw honesty is far more credible when it comes to a purchasing decision.
Whereas, the general advertiser is trying to reach the largest audience possible,
word-of-mouth communication is more directed toward an audience that is already
interested in the topic being discussed.[16] Fifth, social media provides opportunities
for a new kind of market research, that is testing customer reaction to a proposed
concept or product idea. The term *crowdsourcing* is used to describe the practice of

obtaining needed ideas or feedback by soliciting contributions from an online community of users. From designing ad campaigns to vetting new product ideas to solving difficult technical problems, chances are that people outside one's organization can make useful contributions in terms of providing helpful information or timely feedback.[17] Netflix uses crowdsourcing techniques to improve the software algorithms used for making film recommendations to customers. Similarly, improvements made to Linux open source software were the result of engineers and other tech professionals who added to the collective wisdom of the software design. In return, most participants simply appreciate having some form of recognition and/or desire to be part of the larger community of users.

Sixth, social media aids the agenda-setting process when individuals comment on stories and/or share a news item for general distribution.[18] Given the ease and efficiency of Internet news, readers now go the additional step of commenting and/or passing along a news item that is of particular interest to him/her. In journalism parlance, that means keeping the story alive. Researchers Berger and Milkman (2012) found that two features predictably determine an article's success: how positive the message is and how much it excites the reader.[19] Facebook, in particular, is an important driver to online news sites. It encourages the uploading and distribution of unique specialty news items that are of interest to the user. Many well-established news media sites like *The New York Times,* BBC News and CNN receive a significant amount of their traffic from Facebook links and referrals. All this points to the fact that users are especially interested in the news items shared by friends.[20]

Seventh, social media plays a critical role in helping mobilize people to action by providing information about events, times, and locations. The lessons from the 2011 Arab Spring in Tunisia, Egypt, and Yemen demonstrated the important role that social media like Facebook and Twitter played in helping to mobilize street demonstrations. While Facebook did not create the revolutions that took place in these countries, it did play a major role in helping organize large public demonstrations. The power of instantaneous communication made it possible to mobilize large numbers of people in just days and sometimes hours—simply because someone knew someone on Facebook, and the word spread from there.[21] Facebook in combination with cell phones, video cameras, blog posts, as well as traditional media outlets like *Al Jazeera,* set into motion a flood of inflammatory information and images. Facebook provided a common space where people were able to watch shocking pictures and sometimes gruesome videos of fellow protesters being brutalized by police and military authorities. Facebook and its numerous special interest sites provided a political platform for people to express their solidarity, both within the country and beyond.[22]

Facebook: Business Model Innovation

Facebook, first and foremost, is the world's leading social networking site. It is also one of the most complex intelligent networks ever designed. What gives a network its unique intelligence are the people and users of the system and the value-added contributions they make via critical gateway points (e.g., laptop computers, smartphones, and computer tablets).[23] This is especially true when it comes to Facebook, which utilizes the power of the Internet to enable users to communicate with one's friends, family, colleagues, and acquaintances. Facebook allows individuals to present themselves and maintain connections with others. The goal is to make the exchange of information easy and accessible.[24] Facebook has been described by its founder and CEO, Mark Zuckerberg, as a "mathematical construct that maps the real-life connections between people. Each person is a node radiating links to other people they know.[25] As friends and acquaintances join Facebook, they become part of a larger social grid that matters to the individual. It creates value to the individual by adding to one's social capital.[26] By social capital, we mean a network of users tied together based on shared norms, values, and understanding that facilitate cooperation between or among groups.[27] Since that person's friends are connected to other friends on the network, there is the opportunity to virtually expand one's circle of friends and acquaintances.[28] Each new person and extended link adds value and dynamism to the overall network.

Facebook Tools

The profile page features a combination of biographical information and photos that help tell the user's story. Located in the upper left-hand corner is the user's profile photo. The profile photo often says a lot about the individual. It sets the tone for the rest of the page. The profile photo can be professional, playful, adventurous, or simply in the moment. A micro representation of the profile picture appears each time the user interacts with others, such as posting comments or sending messages. The same profile image appears on the user's contact list. The profile photo is set within a larger cover photo. The cover photo speaks to the spirit of the individual by displaying an image that has some kind of personal or symbolic meaning. In addition to the profile and cover photo is an about section, which contains relevant background information such as place of birth, schooling, current location, marital status, and so on. The about section provides greater detail in terms of work and education, family and relationships, and so forth. Also featured on the profile page is the *user's wall*. It acts as a public bulletin board where any of the user's listed friends can write short public messages. These comments can be viewed by anyone with access to the user's profile. The user's wall functions as a public writing space where friends and contacts can post comments, observations, or criticisms about a particular posting.[29] The *photos* section is also an important Facebook tool, which enables the user to post photos in real time as well as locating them in various albums. The posting of photos represents an important part of the user's personal narrative and storytelling. It provides a good way to celebrate a special event or momentary happening. The photos section also allows the user to pass along photos (or videos) of other people and events. Within the photos application, there is a useful tag function, which allows the user to identify and attach their friends to pictures. Once someone is tagged in a picture, the picture will be linked to that person's profile for easy sharing. Videos function in much the same way as photos.

The posting of photos on average get 50 percent more impressions than any other type of Facebook activity as well as engendering so-called "likes," which is one of the top ways in which users interact with Facebook.

In 2012, Facebook introduced a new service called Timeline. According to Facebook, Timeline is simply another way for the user to tell his/her story. Timeline provides the user with an expanded set of formatting tools to provide a more detailed narrative of one's personal history. Timeline provides a running chronology of both past and current events, including the ability to highlight important personal moments, stories, and events. The addition of Timeline moves Facebook one step further in the direction of narrating real-time linkages between people and their activities on the web. Facebook provides a number of additional software tools such as status updates, news feeds, opinions and commentary postings, chat (instant messaging), as well as electronic mail. The various Facebook tools share the common goal of enabling the user to maintain a virtual, real-time conversation with those individuals who comprise the user's list of friends.[30] Being part of a social network allows individuals to present themselves and maintain connections with others. Researchers Nadkami and Hofmann (2012) believe that the public's fascination with Facebook is motivated by an intrinsic human need to belong and gain social acceptance by one's peers. This, in turn, is followed by the need to regularly update and manage one's social identity.[31] As the user's social capital increases, so does the power of information. This forms the basis for the Facebook business model; the more people are willing to share personal information (and by extension provide demographic data), the more advertisers are willing to pay for such direct access.[32]

Facebook as a Business Strategy

Facebook exhibits a kind of dual identity. On the one hand, Facebook is a highly engaging medium of communication for personal expression. On the other, Facebook is a for-profit business that is advertiser driven. Facebook's claim that it has 1.4 billion active users says a lot about the power of human connection. It has gained the attention of major companies around the world. From the very beginning, Facebook strategists understood that advertising was going to play a central role in any business strategy going forward. The attraction to advertisers is obvious. Facebook users willingly volunteer enormous amounts of personal data that can eventually be leveraged into targeted advertisements toward the individual user. By "liking" a certain advertisement, the user is giving his/her personal endorsement for a product or service, which may appear in a friend or colleagues' news feed. As Grossman (2010) points out,

> Looked at one way, when a friend likes a product, it's just more sharing, more data changing hands. Looked at another way, it's your personal relationship being monetized by a third party.[33]

Early on, the challenge for Facebook was how to introduce advertising into the social networking mix without being overly intrusive and, thereby, destabilize the social network's growing momentum. The concern was that highly intrusive ads would impede the user experience. The decision was made to scale back the size and location of banner ads. By opening up one's user profile, what becomes immediately observable are the advertisements that appear along the right side of the screen. The placement of ads is based on the principle of micromarketing, whereby the ads correspond to the stated interests of the user on his/her profile page. The Facebook computer server is designed to track the regular posting history and status updates of the user. It utilizes a set of highly sophisticated data mining algorithms.[34] Facebook ads are designed not to be overly intrusive. The user is invited to give a thumbs-up or thumbs-down to the ad. The thumbs-down will permanently remove the ad from future viewing. Alternatively, a thumbs-up (or stated like preference) can change the ad from a simple billboard display into a casual buzz inside the user's news feed and, thereby, into the newsfeed of the user's friends. A stated like preference becomes part of the conversation among friends, colleagues, and family members. Says Zuckerberg, "The whole premise of Facebook is that everything is more valuable when you have a context about what your friends are doing." That's true for advertising as well.[35]

From a marketing standpoint, the goal isn't necessarily for the user to go out and immediately buy the advertisers' product or to click through to their Web site. Rather, the goal is to quietly locate the advertiser's message into the user's thinking and elicit a future purchase. The "Like us on Facebook" feature becomes a simple and effective way to garner approval and help establish a relationship between the user and the advertiser. For business, the power of social media to provide a ready-made source of referrals and word-of-mouth marketing is virtually impossible to duplicate using traditional media.

Marketers like this approach. It costs them nothing to build a long-term relationship with the user via his/her news feed once the user has indicated a preference for a certain product, service, or cause. The marketer's goal is to find creative ways to extend brand awareness and help facilitate long-term relationships with prospective customers. They should quietly become part of the social conversation. It often becomes the catalyst for a future purchasing decision or mobilizing a group of people to action.

Facebook's Business Performance

In May 2012, Facebook completed a highly anticipated initial public offering (IPO) that was expected to place the company's valuation at more than $100 billion. Facebook hoped to raise $15 billion from its IPO. At $100 billion, Facebook would rank second only to Google in terms of Internet company valuation. The 2012 IPO offering, however, proved to be a spectacular failure. While the offering reached a high of $38 dollars per share, the stock closed flat after the first day of trading. Both investors and the media began to speculate whether Facebook's initial offering price was too high. Others argued that part of the first day's momentum was damaged by NASDAQ's technical difficulties, which caused half-hour delays in buying as well as mistakes executing purchase orders at the correct price.

Reuters later reported that Morgan Stanley, the lead underwriter on Facebook's public offering, told its top clients that the bank's analysts were cutting their revenue forecasts for the company just days before the IPO. This, in combination with trading glitches on the NASDAQ, contributed to a lessening in demand for Facebook stock, which proved much weaker than was originally expected.[36] The IPO was supposed to be a shining moment for Facebook and its major investors. Instead, it proved to be a debacle of epic proportions. In the three months that followed, Facebook investors saw the value of their shares drop nearly in half, wiping out some $50 billion in shareholder value. Since the May 2012 IPO, Facebook has seen a steady increase in revenues, which can be seen in Figure 11.1. In 2013, the company achieved revenues of $7.8 billion, and in 2014 that figure climbed to $12.5 billion.

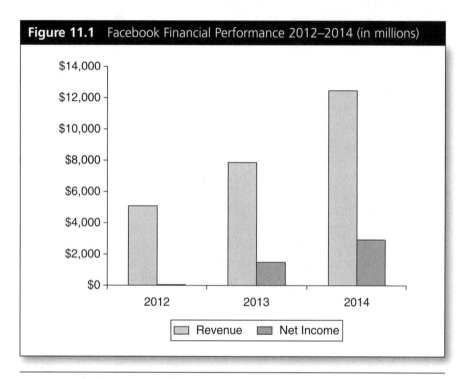

Figure 11.1 Facebook Financial Performance 2012–2014 (in millions)

SOURCE: Facebook, Inc., 2014 Annual Report.

Privacy Concerns

Privacy worries have been a source of major concern for Facebook since the company's very beginning. The problem is understandable. To have a true social network, the user must be willing to share select details of his/her personal life. If there is a single distinguishing feature that separates young people in their teens and 20s from previous generations, it is a willingness to broadcast the details of their private lives to the general public. The give-and-take exchange between Facebook and its users over privacy is gaining importance as the company's growth continues unabated. From

London, UK, to the Brazilian rain forest, Facebook's 1.5 billion worldwide users vary in their degree of knowledge about what it means to be a part of a social network.

As the world's leading social media site, Facebook more than any other company is helping to define privacy standards in the Internet age. The issues vary in size and complexity from personal, demographic data being shared with third-party advertisers to the set of facial recognition technology to identify people in photographs. Implicit in these discussions are the challenges brought on by the company's success. Facebook routinely struggles to find the right balance between giving users too little privacy control versus giving them too much while risking that such individuals will be less forthcoming in the information that they share. As part of that effort, Facebook has steadily introduced a set of changes designed to help user privacy. Every time a Facebook user makes a comment, adds a picture, or initiates any other change to their profile page, the user can specify who can see the information, whether it's specific Facebook friends or the public's general access to the Internet.[37]

Political Activism and the Power of Social Media

If Facebook was a country, it would have the second-largest population in the world, trailing only China by a slight amount. Facebook estimates that one out of every eight people around the world has a Facebook profile. The challenge, of course, is that not all countries, and by extension, political power structures are equally enamored by Facebook's grassroots mobilizing capability. It is not surprising, therefore, that countries like China see Facebook as a major threat to preserving political stability.

In 2008, Facebook established a presence in China, gaining a small number of users. The Chinese government soon thereafter made the determination that Facebook was an undesirable site. Today, Facebook operates outside the country's strictly guarded network known euphemistically as "The Great Firewall." Says Facebook's Zuckerberg, "How can you connect the whole world if you leave out 1.6 billion people?"[38] Facebook is not alone. Two other major Internet companies, most notably, Google and Twitter, face similar issues when dealing with authoritarian regimes in places like China, Russia, and Iran. China, for its part, has developed its own Facebook equivalent, called Tencent, which is used by an estimated 500 million Chinese users. As revolution sweeps through the Middle East and elsewhere, Google, Facebook, and Twitter are confronting a whole host of political and ethical problems that most business start-ups try to avoid. There are no easy solutions.

While Facebook has proved to be a remarkable organizing tool, the company itself, exhibits a kind of ambivalence when it comes to supporting political and social causes. Facebook (and its numerous special interest sites) played a critical role in bringing about the downfall of Egyptian prime minister, Hosni Mubarak. It was Wael Ghonim's Facebook page "We Are All Khaled," created to memorialize a young Tunisian businessman who died in police custody, that became the epicenter of the revolution.[39] After Ghonim was released from Egyptian police custody after 11 days of captivity, he spoke to CNN about the role of social media in the Egyptian revolution:

I want to meet Mark Zuckerberg one day and thank him. . . . I'm talking on behalf of Egypt. This revolution started online. This revolution started on Facebook. This revolution started in June 2010 when hundreds of thousands of Egyptians started collaborating content. We would post a video on Facebook that would be shared by 60,000 people on their walls within a few hours.[40]

With Facebook playing a major role in the events that led to the downfall of the Tunisian and Egyptian governments (including the personal endorsement of Google's Wael Ghonim), it might be expected that Facebook's senior management would have used this opportunity to highlight its role as being a major catalyst for democratic change. Instead, the company stays silent on the topic. At issue, is the fact that Facebook is trying to balance competing pressures from both activist groups as well as host nations that it seeks to do business with. Facebook does not want to be seen as picking sides for fear that countries like China, Russia, and Saudi Arabia will impose restrictions or closely monitor their activities. Simply put, political revolution is bad for business. A related problem is that Facebook does not want to alter its stated policy of requiring users to sign up with their real identity. Various human rights groups, however, take issue with this argument. They point out that the listing of one's true identity puts some people at risk from governments looking to target political dissenters.

Discussion

The Future of Internet Search

Facebook and Google are on a collision course with each other. Though fundamentally different, Google and Facebook overlap in a few crucial areas, including how people search for information. Google is the world's leading Internet search company. Google's principle advantage is its ability to gather and analyze vast amounts of data. The company's highly sophisticated search algorithm prioritizes a set of web pages out of a known universe of possibilities by listing information links that best correspond to the user's query. Google has steadily improved the search engine's design capability by adding a variety of enhanced features, including the Google Directory, expanded language versions, key word searches, YouTube, and Gmail.[41]

Facebook is the world's leading social network. It is the quintessential example of an intelligent network. Facebook is the sum total of user-generated content, including postings, photos, videos, comments and reactions, and so on. The information is made publicly available via a whole host of computer and portable devices. Facebook's stated mission is to give people the ability to share information and to make the world more open and connected. As part of that effort, Facebook has created a platform that knows the identities, activities, and general interests of more than 1.4 billion users worldwide.

Both Google and Facebook are jockeying for position in terms of controlling the future of Internet search. Both companies want to be the user's first destination point. The stakes are very high. By becoming the principal gatekeeper of people's online experiences and information searches, both Google and Facebook expect to lay claim to an expanding market share of loyal users who will rely on them not only to help navigate the Internet but to utilize them for trusted advice and guidance.[42] Both companies hope to influence the user's web browsing and viewing experience. Equally important, both Google and Facebook are well positioned to capitalize on various kinds of advertising opportunities. The launch of Google's key word search advertising program in 2001 helped establish the basic business model that provides most of the company's revenue. Google adheres to the principle of micromarketing, whereby the advertising corresponds to the user's query. In contrast, Facebook's approach relies more on making the connections between potential advertisers and what it knows about the users' backgrounds and general likes. Facebook's increasing sophistication allows it to know with greater certainty what its customers are really interested in.

Social Utility

Facebook has become a kind of social utility. Social media is different from other kinds of marketing channels. Social media is an "always-on" 24/7 medium of communication. Social media content must be readily available, and it must align with the customers' personal narrative and stated interests.[43] Facebook is first among equals when it comes to hosting always-on conversations among its users. The speed and efficiency of always-on conversations has been greatly aided in recent years given the explosion in mobile devices. Smartphones have been a major contributor to the growth in social media. To that end, providing mobile access has become a major Facebook strategy imperative going forward. In practical terms, Facebook continues to expand the definition of what it means to be part of a social network.

Endnotes

1. Facebook Investor Relations, "Facebook Stats," accessed April 22, 2015, http://newsroom.fb.com/company-info/
2. Jose Antonio Vargas, "The Face of Facebook," *The New Yorker,* September 20, 2010, pp. 54–63.
3. Vargas, "The Face of Facebook."
4. David Kirkpatrick, *The Facebook Effect* (New York, Simon & Schuster, 2010).
5. Following the launch of Facebook, both Zuckerberg and Facebook have been the targets of several intellectual property disputes. The 2010 Academy Award-nominated film *The Social Network* dramatized these events. The film suggests that Zuckerberg had stolen the original idea of Facebook from Harvard classmates, Cameron and Tyler Winklevoss. The Winklevoss brothers had brought Zuckerberg in to help finish a new social networking project that they were working on. Instead of completing the project, Zuckerberg started a separate Web site called Thefacebook.com. Before the Winklevoss brothers could take action, Facebook had already been launched and become an overnight sensation. The brothers filed a lawsuit against Facebook accusing Zuckerberg of using the idea from their project. Eventually, an out-of-court settlement was reached for a reported 1.2 million shares in Facebook stock (worth $300 million).

6. Kirkpatrick, *The Facebook Effect.*

7. Issie Lapowsky, "Happy Birthday Facebook: A Look Back at 10 Years," *Inc.,* http://www.inc.com/issie-lapowsky/happy-birthday-facebook.html

8. Richard Stengel, "The 2010 Person of the Year," *Time.* December 27, 2010, p 43.

9. Alan Albarran, *The Social Media Industries* (New York: Routledge, 2013).

10. Andreas Kaplan and Michael Haenlein, "Users of the World Unite! The Challenges and Opportunities of Social Media. *Business Horizons* 53, no. 1 (2010): 59–68.

11. A. S. Tabernero, J. Villanueva, and J. L. Orihuela, "Social Networks as Marketing Tools for Media Companies," in *Handbook of Social Media,* eds. M. Friedrichsen & W. Muhl-Benninghaus (Berlin, Germany: Springer, 2013), 161–178.

12. Zvezdan Vukanovic, "New Media Business Model in Social and Web Media," *Journal of Media Business Studies,* 8 no. 3 (2011): 51–67.

13. David Aaker, *Managing Brand Equity: Capitalizing on the Value of a Brand Name* (New York: The Free Press, 1991).

14. Mikotaj Piskorski, "Social Strategies That Work," *Harvard Business Review,* November 2011, pp. 117–122.

15. "How Powerful Is a Facebook Like for Advertisers?" *CBS News,* last modified May 17, 2012, http://www.cbsnews.com/news/how-powerful-is-a-facebook-like-for-advertisers/

16. Jonah Berger, *Contagious: Why Things Catch On* (New York, Simon & Schuster, 2013).

17. "What Is Crowdsourcing?" *CBS* Money Watch, last modified March 7, 2007, http://www.cbsnews.com/news/what-is-crowdsourcing/

18. Agenda setting involves the ability of the news media to focus public attention on certain issues. First proposed by Maxwell McCombs and Donald Shaw in 1972 in *Public Opinion Quarterly,* the authors suggest that the traditional news media sets the public agenda in terms of what is to be considered newsworthy. The stories that the media covers can often shape public attention and opinion in terms of what is important in day-to-day news affairs.

19. Jonah Berger and Katherine L. Milkman, "What Makes Online Content Viral?" *Journal of Marketing Research* 49, no. 2 (2012): 192–205.

20. Agnes Urban and Tamas Bodoky, "The Impact of Facebook on News Consumption," in *Handbook of Social Media,* eds. M. Friedrichsen and W. Muhl-Benninghaus (Berlin, Germany: Springer 2013), 805–818.

21. Richard Gershon, "Facebook: A Business Perspective on the Power of Intelligent Networking and Social Media," in *Handbook of Social Media,* eds. M. Friedrichsen and W. Muhl-Benninghaus (Berlin, Germany: Springer, 2013), 375–389.

22. Jose Antonio Vargas, "Spring Awakening," *New York Times,* Feb. 17, 2012, http://www.nytimes.com/2012/02/19/books/review/how-an-egyptian-revolution-began-on-facebook.html?_r=0

23. Richard Gershon, "Intelligent Networks and International Business Communication: A Systems Theory Interpretation," *Media Markets Monographs, No. 12* (Pamplona, Spain: Universidad de Navarra Press, 2011).

24. Laura Locke, "The Future of Facebook," *Time,* Jul. 17, 2007, http://content.time.com/time/business/article/0,8599,1644040,00.html

25. "Most Innovative Companies," *Businessweek,* May 14, 2007, p. 60.

26. N. Ellison, C. Steinfield, and C. Lampe, "The Benefits of Facebook Friends: Social Capital and College Students' Use of Online Social Network Sites," *Journal of Computer Mediated Communication* 12, no. 4 (2007): 1143–1168.

27. The concept of social capital dates back for more than a century, while the ideas behind it are older still. Tightly knit communities, such as some immigrant groups, have strong social bonds, with individuals relying heavily for support on relatives or people who share their ethnicity. See Organization for Economic Co-operation and Development (OECD) Insights: Human Capitol, "What Is Social Capital?" http://www.oecd.org/insights/37966934.pdf

28. Lev Grossman, "Person of the Year," *Time,* Dec. 27, 2010, pp. 44–75.

29. Tharyn Taylor, "Facebook: A Case Study Analysis of Telecommunications and Business Strategy" (presentation, 2011 ITERA Conference, Indianapolis, Indiana, April 11, 2011).

30. Taylor, "Facebook: A Case Study Analysis."

31. Ashwini Nadkami and Stefan Hofmann, "Why Do People Use Facebook?" *Personality and Individual Differences* 52, no. 3 (2012): 243–249.

32. Gershon, "Facebook: A Business Perspective."

33. Grossman, "Person of the Year," 58.

34. Jiawei Han, and Micheline Kamber, *Data Mining: Concepts and Techniques* (San Francisco, CA: Elsevier, 2006).

35. "Sell Your Friends," *Bloomberg Businessweek,* Sept. 27, 2010, pp. 63–72.

36. "Facebook Lessons: What Not to Do When Planning an IPO," *Reuters,* last modified May 24, 2012, http://www.reuters.com/article/2012/05/24/facebook-lessons-idUSL1E-8GOEI220120524

37. "New Control Over Privacy on Facebook," *New York Times,* Aug. 23, 2011, http://www.nytimes.com/2011/08/24/technology/facebook-aims-to-simplify-its-privacy-settings.html

38. Philip Caulfield, "Facebook's Mark Zuckerberg Kicks Off Trip to China," *New York Daily News,* Dec. 20, 2010, http://articles.nydailynews.com/2010–12–20/news/27084933_1_baidu-kaiser-kuo-robin-li

39. Jacob Weisberg, "Tech Revolutionaries," *Slate,* Feb. 24, 2011, http://www.slate.com/articles/news_and_politics/the_big_idea/2011/02/tech_revolutionaries.html

40. "Freed Google Exec Ghonim Thanks Facebook for Role in Egyptian Revolution," *The Inquisitr,* Feb. 11, 2011, http://www.inquisitr.com/98197/wael-ghonim-thanks-facebook/

41. Ken Auletta, *Googled: The End of the World as We Know It* (New York: Penguin Press, 2009).

42. Gershon, "Facebook: A Business Perspective."

43. Steve Kerho, "Social Utility: A New Imperative for Social Content," *Fast Company,* Mar. 28, 2012, http://www.fastcompany.com/1826401/social-utility-new-imperative-social-content

CHAPTER 12

Digital News Reporting, Computer Tablets, and the New Journalism

If I'd asked my customers what they wanted, they'd have said a faster horse.

—Henry Ford

It's really hard to design products by focus groups. A lot of times, people don't know what they want until you show it to them."

—Steve Jobs

Introduction

In his book, *Megatrends,* author John Naisbitt (1982) said that the problem with the 19th-century train industry was a failure to ask the question: What business are you really in? Naisbitt contends that many industrialists at the time incorrectly saw themselves in the train business rather than the future of transportation.[1] Today the question for journalists and newspaper managers is the same. What business are you really in? If the answer to that question is newspapers, then the road ahead will be formidable. One of the great paradoxes of the newspaper industry is that while circulation and advertising levels are in decline, readership levels are up as a whole. Newspapers have more readers than ever, especially among young people. The problem, however, is that most of these people get their news online for free rather than pay for it by purchasing a newspaper or magazine.[2]

Disruptive Technology and the Changing Newspaper Environment

Before the era of digital communication, the gathering and presentation of news was relatively simple and straightforward. In getting the day's news, one had only to buy a paper, listen to the radio, or watch television. All that has changed. Today the international newspaper industry is feeling the full effects of creative destruction. The combination of news information on the Internet coupled with the ease and access of posting news information and blog commentary has fundamentally challenged the economic business model for newspaper and magazine production on a worldwide basis.[3] According to Mark Perry of the American Enterprise Institute,

> The dramatic decline in newspaper ad revenues since 2000 has to be one of the most significant and profound Schumpeterian gales of creative destruction in the last decade, maybe in a generation.[4]

At issue is the loss of in-depth news reporting that provides quality information, investigation, and analysis of both national as well as local news events.

The New Journalism

During the 1960s and 1970s, the term *new journalism* was used to describe a first-person narrative style of writing where the author often immerses himself/herself into the story itself. One of the original proponents of this type of writing was author Tom Wolfe, who edited an anthology of writing in 1973 titled *The New Journalism*. That book featured writers such as Truman Capote, Normal Mailer, Gay Talese, Joan Didion, and Hunter Thompson, to name only a few. Since then, many of the writing techniques associated with this period have been adopted by present-day authors. It has become especially pronounced among writers who post their work online in the form of personal blogs and commentary. We could, of course, debate the quality and depth of current writing when compared to the aforementioned writers. Nevertheless, digital storytelling and online news reporting represent today's version of the new journalism, albeit version 2.0. This chapter will look at the state of the newspaper industry and consider the role of the Internet and the new journalism. Special attention is given to the design and development of the computer tablet. Since the introduction of the Apple iPad in 2010, a growing segment of the world's newspaper readers now own a computer tablet. More to the point, there are any number of mobile devices that are capable of receiving news, including laptop computers, tablets, computer hybrids, and smartphones.

Digital news reporting in combination with the computer tablet presents both the problem and solution for the challenges now faced by today's newspaper industry. The computer tablet is the quintessential disruptive technology knocking at the gate. This juncture represents what former Intel CEO Andy Grove refers to as a strategic inflection point; a time when a triggering event in the competitive marketplace requires new solutions or face the prospect of business extinction.[5] There is no going backwards. Digital news reporting and the computer tablet present a unique and historic opportunity to reconsider the meaning and purpose of news delivery.

The Causes and Consequences of Newspaper Circulation Decline

Starting in 2008, the world's newspaper industry entered into an unprecedented period of decline. Facing what former *Chicago Tribune* Chairman Sam Zell called a "perfect storm" of forces roiling the media industry and the broader economy, the company filed for Chapter 11 bankruptcy protection from its creditors in December 2008.[6] It was emblematic of the problems faced by other notable U.S. newspapers as well, including the *Minneapolis Star Tribune, Boston Globe,* and *Philadelphia Daily News.* Nor was the problem confined to the United States. International newspapers face declining circulation and advertising revenues as well, including diverse countries such as the UK(*The Daily Mirror, The Guardian*), Spain (*El País, El Mundo,* and *La Vanguardia*),[7] China (*Guangzhou Daily* [广州日报], *People's Daily* [人民日报], and *Reference News* [参考消息]), and Australia (*Sydney Morning Herald, The Daily Telegraph,* and *The Age*), to name only a few.[8]

What is the "perfect storm" of forces roiling the media industry? In short, what are the triggering events that are contributing to circulation decline? The causes of newspaper circulation decline are well documented. A number of media research studies and authors have identified five major causes. They include the following:

- The availability of good substitutes in obtaining news information
- The loss of advertising dollars due to information available on the Internet
- A change in readership demographics among younger audiences
- The high cost of newspaper production and distribution
- The failure to fully appreciate the importance of digital lifestyle[9]

The move from print to digital media has been a difficult transition for newspaper and magazine publishers. Readers have been reluctant to pay for content on the web. Likewise, companies are unwilling to pay as much for online advertisements. The field of journalism is threatened by the sheer quantity of free news in a variety of formats ranging from radio, television, and cable to multiple Internet, newspaper, and magazine Web sites that provide varying degrees of free news information.[10] Such changes have affected the quantity and quality of news information now available to the public. The real issue is that many of today's newspapers have become less substantial in their news coverage. They lack the depth, size, and quality of information to satisfy those readers still willing to pay good money for a print newspaper.[11] As circulation continues to decline, they lose value to advertisers. The solution for many newspapers is to scale back the number of print publication days to three while simultaneously producing a daily electronic version.[12]

Few papers today offer the same level of news coverage of its cities and surrounding communities that was once provided in the past. Instead, the shift is toward regional newspapers that provide general news reporting with some local coverage. The regional news service is no substitute for the once highly valued local paper. It's now possible to contemplate a time when some major cities will no longer have a newspaper and when magazine and broadcast news operations will employ no more than a handful of reporters.[13] According to Picard (2010), we are in danger of moving toward a system in which social elites have access to high-quality news and information because they can pay for it, and the rest of the public is left with a poorer news selection.[14] Therein, lies the challenge. Specifically, how does one turn an audience that appreciates news, but undervalues it, into paying customers? To better understand the full measure of such changes, we need to be able to reverse engineer; that is, look more specifically at the process of news selection from a user's perspective and work backward toward the news source. The computer tablet presents us with such an opportunity.

The Computer Tablet

The computer tablet is a multimedia platform that can support books, newspapers, movies, music, games, and web content. The computer tablet's multimedia platform provides users with the capability of experiencing information and entertainment on multiple levels, including one or more combinations of text, audio and video. This is the very essence of convergence.[15] Moreover, the computer tablet allows the user to customize one's reading and media experience.

The Apple iPad

The Apple iPad was introduced on January 27, 2010, by Apple's then CEO Steve Jobs. The debut of the iPad was greeted with a great deal of public anticipation. The *Economist* magazine featured Steve Jobs on its cover, hooded, robed, and holding what was dubbed "the Jesus Tablet" because of the quasi-religious fervor with which it was greeted by consumers worldwide.[16] Similarly, the *Wall Street Journal* took a similar tone by noting, "The last time there was this much excitement about a tablet, it had some commandments written on it."[17] Apple sold 3 million iPads in 80 days.[18] Most importantly, the iPad, more than any device of its kind, pointed the way to the future of journalism.

Technical Design Features. The Apple iPad runs on the same operating system as the iPod Touch and iPhone. And like both devices, the iPad is controlled by a multi-touch GUI display, which represents a significant departure from earlier versions of tablet computers, which used a pressure-triggered stylus. The iPad is managed and synced by the Apple iTunes media center. iTunes serves as the basic platform for downloading music, photos, and other software.[19] The iPad's software integration with Apple's online app store is designed to make downloading books, newspapers, and magazines as easy and popular as downloading music.[20] Apple's third-generation iPad (or iPad 3) was released in March 2012. It features a retina display and the Siri voice recognition system that is part of Apple's newest generation of computer tablets and smartphones.

Throughout its history, Apple has a long history of approaching product design by paying close attention to detail. This is reflected in a striving for perfection in both product design as well as looking for new ways to make products more user-friendly. For Steve Jobs, one way to accomplish this was to have end-to-end software and hardware control for every product that Apple makes. Taking an integrated approach was a central tenant to Apple's basic design philosophy. Says Jobs,

> We do these things not because we are control freaks. We do them because we want to make great products, because we care about the user and because we like to take responsibility for the entire experience rather than turn out the crap that other people make.[21]

A second important principle is that aesthetics in design should be as important as the product's function. Apple was not the first to design a computer tablet. Apple did not invent the computer tablet so much as reinvent it. Apple reinvented the computer tablet by focusing on ways to improve the user experience.[22] But in doing so, it helped redefine the newspaper screen.

The Computer Tablet and Digital Lifestyle

Central to any discussion related to computer tablets is understanding the importance of software applications (or apps). The term *app* refers to a software program used on a mobile device such as a smartphone or computer tablet. This is reflected in various computer tablet commercials where the focus is not on the device but instead on what you can do with it. A second important aspect of digital lifestyle can be seen in the area of mobility. From laptop computers to smartphones, mobility has become an important requirement for people whose personal lifestyle or professional work habits require greater portability and flexibility of movement.[23] As a device, the computer tablet most closely simulates the traditional newspaper readership experience in terms of portability and ease of use.[24] Research performed by the Pew Research Center indicates that tablet users prefer the computer tablet over other sources of news delivery, including regular computers, print publications, and/or television as a way to obtain quick headlines as well as longer articles. Tablet users are more likely than the general public to follow the news frequently. They also turn to the Internet as a main source for news more so than the general public. In sum, tablet users appreciate having access to multiple news sources from one convenient and portable location.[25]

In looking to the future, the computer tablet and hybrid versions including tablet PCs and smartphones will become a primary means by which consumers get their news. In 2012, Apple dominated the business of computer tablet manufacturing by claiming an estimated 61.4 percent international market share. This was followed

Table 12.1 International Computer Tablets (Current and Projected Market Share)

	2012	2016
Apple iPad (IOS)	61.4%	28.7%
Google Android	31.9%	63.1%
• Samsung		
• Amazon		
• Lenovo		
• Asus		
• Barnes & Noble		
Microsoft Windows	4.1%	8.2%
Other	2.6%	5%

SOURCES: Adapted from Statista, Inc. and Gartner Group.

by the Google Android system used by Samsung, Amazon, Lenovo, Asus, and Barnes & Noble, which captured a combined 31.9 percent of international market share.[26] This is expected to change in the years to come. Statista projects that by 2016, those manufacturers that use the Google Android and Microsoft Windows RT operating systems will have increased their international market share to 63.1 and 8.2 percent, respectively.[27] (See Table 12.1)

Digital News Reporting

The Internet has transformed the reading of news into a multimedia event, including text information, embedded video, as well as hyperlinks to related stories. Moreover, the very concept of a daily news digest (or once-a-day news presentation) is no longer a valid premise.[28] Readers have now come to expect regular news updates to existing stories as well as the inclusion of late-breaking stories as part of the overall news Web site composition. Part of this same news presentation includes a running history of the stories' evolution as well as blogs and commentary that consider what different readers have to say about an ongoing story. The computer tablet has made the reading of news a more interactive and less passive experience.

Reframing the Question

The first rule of technology diffusion is that once you go forward, there's no going backward. We cannot disinvest what we already know how to do. Both the Internet and the computer tablet are here to stay. We should, therefore, reframe the question. How does the news media industry combine the best practices of traditional journalism with the best tools available in the digital world in which we live? According to Arianna Huffington (2013), cofounder of the *Huffington Post,*

> Though the distinction between new media and old has become largely mean-ingless, for too long the reaction of much of the old media to the fast-growing digital world was something like the proverbial old man yelling at the new media kids to get off his lawn. Many years were wasted erecting barriers that were never going to stand. The future will definitely be a hybrid one, combining the best practices of traditional journalism—fairness, accuracy, storytelling, deep investigations—with the best tools available to the digital world—speed, transparency, and, above all, engagement.[29]

Today, we have before us an opportunity to move the conversation away from the future of newspapers to the future of journalism. In this next section, we consider four perspectives on digital reporting and the new journalism.

Perspective 1: News Presentation, Format, and Delivery

Digital news reporting operates in real time. The challenge is no longer about meeting an 11 p.m. deadline for tomorrow's paper delivery. Instead, the goal is to provide ongoing news coverage that includes both direct reporting as well as regular news updates. A digital news room presupposes greater flexibility in terms of digital news story technique, which may include a combination of direct reporting, video inserts, blogs, and news commentary or simply providing a helpful URL link. Among the benefits the Internet brings to an emerging news story is the ability to stay fully committed to an investigative piece well after the traditional news media has moved on. There is a running history of the news event, containing past links that keeps the story fully accessible to the reader. Internet-delivered news allows the reader to grow with the story over time.

Digital news reporting and the computer tablet have forced a fundamental change in the economics of news delivery. Computer tablets and other mobile devices force us to rethink how we receive news. Historically, newspapers and magazines have been very costly to produce and distribute. Both are subject to two serious disadvantages when compared to electronic media. First, newspaper and magazine production do not realize the inherent economies of scale typically associated with radio and television broadcasting. Rather, there is an incremental cost associated with each newspaper and magazine produced, distributed, and sold. There is an environmental cost as well for any and all publications not sold, thrown away, or recycled. All this points to the mechanics of news delivery.[30]

Newspapers, today, still adhere to news delivery methods that are more typically associated with early 20th century practices; specifically, the newspaper carrier and the newspaper stand. Digital publishing releases the publisher or owner from the fixed costs associated with the publication and delivery of news. Specifically, it levels the news delivery playing field by offering the same economy-of-scale advantages usually associated with the broadcast and cable television industries. Add to this the importance of portability and digital lifestyle, and one gets a very different perspective on the future of news delivery. Publishers recognize that computer tablets and other mobile devices have become the 21st-century equivalent of the printed page, offering up new ways to present news and entertainment content as well as the ability to charge for it.[31]

Perspective 2: Understanding the Importance of Digital Lifestyle

We are witnessing the demassification of media and entertainment product made possible by the Internet and the power of intelligent networking. Broadcast television and large-circulation newspapers are no longer seen as the primary means of delivering news information. Traditional mass-circulation newspapers and television broadcasting are examples of push technology, whereas the Internet is a decidedly pull technology. Broadcast television and large-circulation newspapers take a one-size-fits-all approach, hence the idea of push technology. In contrast, Internet-delivered news gives consumers the ability to compile, edit, and customize the information they receive.

Internet Narrowcasting. If the cable television industry brought us narrowcasting, that is, specialized television programming (i.e., ESPN, the Food Channel, Black Entertainment Television, etc.), so too has the Internet become highly specialized in terms of news, arts, and entertainment coverage. Today's journalist is competing for the time and attention of readers who are regularly exposed to a whole host of Web sites and specialty blogs on most any subject. The audience has become fragmented in terms of its interests.[32] The new journalism features a wide variety of digital storytelling capability to meet the unique interests of its readers. Table 12.2 provides a select sampling of some of today's best-known specialty news Web sites and blogs.

News Aggregators. Visiting multiple Web sites to receive information can be a very time-consuming process. News aggregators help to consolidate many Web sites into a more customized approach for the user. A well-constructed news aggregator enables the user to customize his/her reading with select news items from multiple information and entertainment sites. This, in turn, makes for creating a unique information space or personal newspaper. Examples of news aggregators include Flipboard, Google News Reader, News360, Feedly, Pulse, and Fark. Aggregators also reduce the time and effort needed to regularly check Web sites for updates. One of the benefits of a news aggregator is the ability to receive news feeds and updates directly onto one's tablet or smartphone.

Perspective 3: Digital Opinion Leaders

The term *opinion leadership* is a principle idea found in the classic theory of two-step flow of communication first proposed by Elihu Katz and Paul Lazarsfeld in

Table 12.2 The New Journalism: Specialty News Web Sites and Blogs

BuzzFeed

BuzzFeed was founded in 2006 by Jonah Peretti and Kenneth Lerer, both of whom helped create the *Huffington Post*. BuzzFeed offers its readers brisk, entertaining news that includes teasing headlines, topical lists, as well as engaging visuals (brief animated clips).While BuzzFeed covers the same kinds of stories as regular news, its writing style and format is very tabloid like. BuzzFeed features a trending section; that is, what's hot and moving up in the news (http://www.buzzfeed.com).

The Huffington Post

The *Huffington Post* is an American online news Web site founded by Arianna Huffington, Kenneth Lerer, Andrew Breitbart, and Jonah Peretti. It was launched on May 10, 2005. The site covers a wide variety of topics, including general news, business, politics, entertainment, popular culture, and so forth. In February 2011, the *Huffington Post* was acquired by AOL for $315 million. Arianna Huffington was made editor in chief of the Huffington Post Media Group. In 2012, the *Huffington Post* was the first U.S. digital media enterprise of its kind to win a Pulitzer Prize. Celebrating its 10th anniversary, the company now has an editorial staff of about 50 in its New York headquarters as well as a staff of 40 in its Washington office, plus 13 international editions (http://www.huffingtonpost.com).

TechCrunch

TechCrunch (TC) is an online publisher of technology industry news. TC was founded by Michael Arrington and Keith Teare in 2005. TC primarily covers businesses ranging from small start-ups to established companies in the field of media and telecommunications and features major stories concerning new IT as well as product announcements. TC also offers its readers newsletters as well. One of the highest-read technology start-up news sources available on the Internet, TC has more than 35 million readers per month (http://techcrunch.com).

Politico

Politico is a political news organization that is based in Arlington, Virginia, that specializes in U.S. politics and policy making. Politico's primary focus includes the U.S. Congress, the presidency, lobbying, and governmental policy making. *Politico* magazine was created in November 2013 by Susan Glasser, a former editor at the *Washington Post*. She was later named editor in chief. Politico now has an online magazine version that features a daily mix of reports, analysis, and opinion (http://www.politico.com).

Business Insider

Business Insider is an American business, celebrity, and technology news Web site launched in February 2009 and is based in New York City. It was founded by Doubleclick founder and former CEO Kevin Ryan. The site provides and analyzes business news and acts as an aggregator of top news stories from around the web. Business Insider covers both national and international business news stories (http://www.businessinsider.com).

Slate

Slate is an online news magazine that covers politics, business, technology, and the arts. It was founded by former New Republic editor Michael Kinsley in 1996. While initially owned by Microsoft's MSN group, it was later sold to the Washington Post Company in 2004. The news site provides commentary and analysis with a style of writing that is both crisp and entertaining (http://www.slate.com).

FastCompany

FastCompany is an online magazine that specializes in innovation and design. The focus of the site is on artistic and creative people as well as business and technology design issues. Fast Company magazine was launched in November 1995 by Alan Webber and Bill Taylor, two former editors of the Harvard Business Review and publisher Mortimer Zuckerman (http://www .fastcompany.com).

Quartz

Quartz is an international business news magazine and is owned by Atlantic Media. It was launched in September 2012. Quartz serves business professionals who travel the world, are focused on international markets, and value critical thinking. Atlantic Media chose the Quartz name because it embodies the new brand's essential character: global, disruptive, and digital. Quartz, the word, is bookended by two of the rarest letters in the English language, Q and Z, an easy-to-remember contraction (http://www.qz.com).

1957. It describes select individuals who wield considerable influence on the people and members who comprise different kinds of social systems. The opinion leader is typically someone who is well respected and embodies the cultural norms of that social system.[33] Over time, opinion leadership has taken its place as one of the signature theories in the field of communication. Opinion leadership in the 21st century takes on a whole new meaning given such power and persuasion techniques as special news Web sites, blogs, and social media postings as well as ratings and evaluation comments on EC sites.

Today's digital opinion leaders are looking to influence the social conversation about a particular topic whether it be politics, technology, entertainment, and so forth.[34] There is no shortage of opinions or consumers willing to comment. Digital opinion leadership can take a variety of forms from the amateur observer to the professional expert. According to Nisbet and Kotcher (2009), there are several important factors that distinguish the amateur from the genuine expert, including identification, professional training, message development, and coordination.[35]

Blogs. A blog is a Web site that features the opinions and observations of a particular writer or set of writers. News media Web sites and the specialty blog have created an altogether new type of opinion leader. Message development in the hands of a skilled professional writer can very directly influence the social conversation. A successful blog helps to build communities with common interests. They tend to focus on a specific set of interests, thereby prioritizing ideas and reaching audiences who are already engaged in a particular issue. The reader sometimes enters the conversation with strongly held views and opinions. The audience composition is relatively homogenous, which makes them all the more engaged with the topic. Blogs can provide an opportunity to reach out in a more personal way, thereby bringing readers together in a way that is more genuine and productive in purpose.[36] In the best sense, it can provide meaningful dialogue.

Ratings Systems and Customer Comments. Internet and EC sites like eBay, Netflix, and TripAdvisor (to name only a few) offer consumers practical and applied ways to evaluate the quality and worthiness of a potential purchase or product use. Ratings systems and customer comments represent a different kind of digital opinion leadership. Who better than one's friends and peers to recommend a particular product or service, albeit digitally using a rating system or customer comments section. As noted earlier, TripAdvisor provides its readers with a general comments sheet as well as standardized rating system per hotel. Therein lies the real power and appeal of TripAdvisor—the ability to provide firsthand observations and experience from those travelers who have stayed at a certain hotel now under consideration by a prospective visitor. It is digital opinion leadership in its most essential form.

Amateur Observation versus Expert Opinion. There is, of course, a potential downside with the Internet being as publicly accessible as it is. Not all self-appointed digital opinion leaders are equal to the task. As Keen (2007) points out, our present-day Internet culture has succumbed to the "law of digital Darwinism, the survival of loudest and most opinionated":

> What the Web 2.0 revolution is really delivering is superficial observations of the world around us rather than deep analysis, shrill opinion rather than considered judgment. The information business is being transformed by the Internet into the sheer noise of a hundred million bloggers all simultaneously talking about themselves.[37]

As Dylan Byers, a media reporter for Politico, observed in 2014, "the appeal of the blog in [Andrew] Sullivan's heyday, was that if you were smart enough or provocative enough, you could cover whatever you wanted. The truth is, people want breaking news from well-sourced reporters or smart analysis from experts who know what they're talking about. Sensibility is cheap."[38]

A similar toxicity has seeped into readers' comments sections. When first introduced, most journalists found readers' comments to be a thoughtful and useful form of feedback. As Michael Massing (2015) points out, it didn't take very long before the sections became inundated with insults and mean-spirited attacks posted by "trolls hiding behind the anonymity of the Internet."[39] More and more news organizations have decided to either rigorously vet them or drop them altogether. Artist Nicola Formichetti (2011) writes that "the dark side of social media is that within seconds, anything can be blown out of proportion and taken out of context. And it's very difficult not to get swept up in it all."[40] The Internet has become the public battlefield in which users have to routinely differentiate between the marketer's well-crafted message, the journalist observer, the expert opinion, and the amateur writer who engages in speculation and frivolous comment.

Perspective 4: Business Model Innovation—News Delivery and Value Creation

The major test ahead for the modern newspaper owner and publisher is finding the right combination of news gathering, writing, and technology delivery efficiencies that is both cost-effective and sustainable over time. Resistance to change, however, has proved particularly salient for the newspaper industry, where executives acknowledge the difficulty in altering the behavior of writers and editors who were trained to write for mature and well-established newspapers. Newspaper executives describe an industry still caught between the gravitational pull of the past and the need to create a faster and more efficient digital future.[41] In 2014, the *New York Times* performed an internal study of its organization, referred to as the New York Times Innovation Report.[42] The *New York Times* has steadily come to realize that a standing reputation and past success can sometimes be a liability. One of the issues cited in the report is the problem that many of the paper's writers and editors see the paper as a final destination point, all the while neglecting the need for social engagement with its readers. One of the major conclusions of this report is that the newspaper needs to embrace its digital future:

> But at *The Times*, discovery, promotion and engagement have been pushed to the margins, typically left to our business-side colleagues or handed to small teams in the newsroom. The business side still has a major role to play, but the newsroom needs to claim its seat at the table because packaging, promoting and sharing our journalism requires editorial oversight.[43]

The New York Times Innovation Report asks the kinds of questions that newspapers from around the world are considering. How does the newspaper industry leverage quality journalism and the principles of digital lifestyle and turn it to an advantage? Today's news media operate in a world where news competes against any number of free and available news and social media Web sites. The challenge, of course, is nothing beats free. The problems facing both print newspapers and magazines are analogous to the music industry in the early 21st century, when illegal music downloads threatened to tear the music industry apart. There are essentially three ways to finance the cost of production in the field of media and communication. They include advertising, subscription, and governmental/ foundation subsidies or a combination of the above. Some newspapers and magazines like the *Wall Street Journal, New York Times*, and the *Economist* magazine have adopted the HBO model of creating a premium service, including electronic access to the said publications.

The challenge for most other news publications is to change public perception about the nature of news information and delivery. In 2010, HBO embraced the principle of digital lifestyle by introducing its HBO Go service. The new single subscription fee approach allows those users with mobile devices to access a virtual storehouse of HBO programming on demand. The company recognizes that the modern digital consumer is just as likely to watch television on his/her iPad or laptop computer as on a television set. What do companies like Apple, HBO, and Amazon.com have to teach us about the future role of the news media and their readership? If newspapers are indeed in the information and entertainment delivery business, then the future of newspapers will be about uniquely customized reading experiences and smart advertising. Such newspapers are effectively providing their readers with a news service rather than a newspaper. The operative word is *service*.

One important change that is emblematic of the new journalism and the principle of service was the decision by Amazon's Jeff Bezos to purchase the *Washington Post* newspaper. *Washington Post* columnist David Ignatius remarked that once the shock of the sale wore off, *Post* staffers began to feel the excitement:

> And when we picked ourselves off the floor and began thinking about this, it began to dawn on people that having someone with $25 billion of net worth acquire your paper, and also to have that person be a proven disrupter of technologies, somebody who made it easy to read print, to read print content (books, magazines, newspapers) on the Kindle, which I think really preceded the tablet as a new way of reading, that's pretty exciting. So by the end of the week, people were thinking, "How do we go on the offensive? How does this dynamic new owner take us into a space where we're going to be more exciting?"[44]

One important quality Bezos possesses is his understanding of the power of engagement. Engagement is about relationship building. Amazon.com's entire business model is based on delivering fast and efficient service to its customers. All this presupposes a willingness to engage one's customers using the power of personalization. Amazon.com is also the same company that introduced readers to its Kindle e-reader and digital books. This becomes especially important as the field of journalism transitions from a model of mass media presentation to one focused on interactivity and participation. News is now an ongoing two-way conversation. Bezos is convinced that the *Washington Post,* which he called a "national institution," can be brought into the digital age by leveraging Amazon.com's technical expertise with the journalistic strength and capability of its news organization.[45]

The lessons of iTunes and Amazon.com have clearly demonstrated that consumers want to customize their music listening and shopping experiences. The same principle can apply to news readers as well.[46] The success of PressReader and Flipboard application sites are indicative of the move toward news customization.[47] If the purpose of journalism is to give people information about their world and thus more power to control it, Bezos's commitment to engagement shows obvious potential for journalism. The Internet's interactive capability changes the basic relationship between the individual and news media, challenging managers and news editors to shift their emphasis from mass media distribution to relationship building and customization.

Discussion

Today's newspaper should be simultaneously national and international in perspective while at the same time hyper-local. It should provide a central linking point for a community and its residents. The community newspaper has to be everything local and foster a sense of common ownership in the paper itself. It should be viewed as a community resource in which everyone has a stake in its success. Whereas the paper may be owned and published by a group publisher or individual, the newspaper franchise belongs to the community and its citizens. Names like the *Boston Globe* (Boston, United States), *Yomiuri Shimbun* (Tokyo, Japan), and *El Pais* (Madrid, Spain) are part of the cultural fabric of their respective communities.[48] In contrast, amateur journalism, blogs, and commentary do not carry the same weight and authority as a well-established newspaper with a history and a past.

Newspaper Brand and Authority

There is no substitute for the newspaper brand and authority. Quality journalism is best exemplified by those news organizations that have both the resources and the courage to defend their work when it challenges powerful institutions and individuals. The public may perceive journalism as an enterprise comprised of individual reporters, but this is rarely the case. The best work is usually done by a team that has the backing of an organization committed to the highest standards of news reporting. As Downie and Schudson (2009) point out, "There is a need not just for news but for newsrooms. Something is gained when reporting, analysis, and investigation are pursued collaboratively by stable organizations that can facilitate regular reporting by experienced journalists."[49] News credibility is everything. The 21st-century newspaper should fully understand the importance of its established brand and leverage both its name and position as a starting point for delivering multiple forms of information and entertainment content and to charge a set fee for a combined news service.

Digital news reporting creates both a challenge and an opportunity for the modern newspaper. If newspapers are going to survive the current business and technological climate, the industry will have to let go of some traditional assumptions about news format, presentation, and methods of delivery. "What business are you really in?" has never become a more pressing question. Today, the Internet has become steadily woven into all aspects of work and leisure. It has become the all-important network engine that drives globalization forward, making instantaneous communication possible for business and individual users alike. The Apple iPad evokes Naisbitt's (1982) principle of "high tech—high touch."[50] The emergence of the computer tablet does indeed change the newspaper reading experience.

But it does not have to mean the end of quality journalism.

The task before us is to transform the current moment into a redesign of modern journalism by combining the best practices from the past with new possibilities for the future. One can envision a scenario whereby the busy working professional gets his/her daily news by subscribing to a newspaper's online edition during the week. The subscriber may supplement his/her reading with a news aggregator like Flipboard (or the equivalent), including information on news, sports, business, and the arts. The same individual may desire a hard-print copy of the same paper for Sunday morning over a cup of coffee. This is digital lifestyle in practical terms. It speaks to the future of the 21st-century newspaper and is at the heart of high tech—high touch. While the technology of delivery may change, the need for talented reporters and writers remains the same. The newspaper's brand and authority must remain constant over time.[51]

Endnotes

1. John Naisbitt, *Megatrends* (New York: Grand Central Publishing, 1982).

2. R. Nielsen and D. Levy, eds., *The Changing Business of Journalism and its Implications for Democracy* (Oxford, UK, The Reuters Institute for the Study of Journalism, 2010), 3–16; F. Esser and M. Bruggemann, "The Strategic Crisis of German Newspapers," in *The Changing Business of Journalism and its Implications for Democracy*, eds. R. Nielsen and D. Levy (Oxford, UK, The Reuters Institute for the Study of Journalism, 2010), 39–54.

3. Robert McChesney and Victor Pickard, eds., *Will the Last Reporter Please Turn Out the Lights: The Collapse of Journalism and What Can Be Done to Fix It* (New York: The New Press, 2011); Robert Kaiser, "The Bad News about the News," *Brookings Essay*, last modified October 16, 2014, http://www.brookings.edu/research/essays/2014/bad-news

4. Jordan Weissmann, "The Decline of Newspapers Hits a Stunning Milestone," *Slate*, Apr. 28, 2014, http://www.slate.com/blogs/moneybox/2014/04/28/decline_of_newspapers_hits_a_milestone_print_revenue_is_lowest_since_1950.html

5. A. Webber, "The Apple Effect," *The Christian Science Monitor*, Sept. 19, 2011, 26–31.

6. "Tribune Co. Files for Chapter 11 Protection," *Chicago Tribune*, Dec. 9, 2008, http://www.wsj.com/articles/SB122876270495988567

7. "Shadows Creep Across Face of European Newspapers," *Financial Times*, Sept. 21, 2014, http://www.ft.com/cms/s/0/49cf1598-3e56-11e4-b7fc-00144feabdc0.html#axzz3goQHNy6w

8. Nic Newman, "Digital News Report 2014: Executive Summary," *The Reuters Institute for the Study of Journalism*, accessed July 22, 2015, http://www.digitalnewsreport.org/survey/2014/executive-summary-and-key-findings-2014/; "Media Watch," *The Daily Telegraph*, Feb. 14, 2014, http://www.abc.net.au/mediawatch/transcripts/1403_mumbrella.pdf; "Data Watch: Global Newspaper Circulation in Decline," *The Media Briefing*, Feb. 11, 2013, http://www.themediabriefing.com/article/datawatch-circulation-decline-developing-economies

9. Robert Picard, "A Business Perspective on the Challenges Facing Journalism," in *The Changing Business of Journalism and its Implications for Democracy*, R. Nielsen and D. Levy, eds. (Oxford, UK: The Reuters Institute for the Study of Journalism, 2010), 17–24; Ramon Salaverría and J. A. García Avilés, "La Convergencia Tecnológica en los Medios de Comunicación: Retos para el Periodismo," *Trípodos* 23 (2008): 31–47.

10. Pippa Norris, *A Virtuous Circle: Political Communications in Post-industrial Societies* (New York: Cambridge University Press, Fall 2000), 63–90.

11. McChesney and Pickard, *Will the Last Reporter Please Turn Out the Lights*.

12. "The Search for a New Business Model," Pew Research Center, last modified March 5, 2012, http://www.journalism.org/analysis_report/search_new_business_model

13. Richard Gershon, "Digital Media Innovation and the Apple iPad: Three Perspectives on the Future of Computer Tablets and News Delivery," *Journal of Media Business Studies* 1 (2011): 41–61.

14. Picard, "A Business Perspective on the Challenges Facing Journalism."

15. Gracie Lawson-Borders, "Seven Observations of Convergence as a Strategy for Best Practices in Media Organizations," *International Journal of Media Management* 5 (2003): 91–99.

16. "The iPad (and Steve Job's) Second Coming," *The Economist*, May 2, 2011, http://www.economist.com/blogs/babbage/2011/03/tablet_computers?page=2

17. Walter Isaacson, *Steve Jobs* (New York: Simon & Schuster, 2011), 493.

18. "Apple Sells Three Million iPads in First 80 days," *Los Angeles Times*, June 22, 2010, http://articles.latimes.com/2010/jun/22/business/la-fi-ipad-20100623

19. Adam Lashinsky, *The Legacy of Steve Jobs 1955–2011* (New York: Fortune Books, 2011), 10–15.

20. Apple's second generation computer tablet, the iPad 2, was introduced on March 2, 2011. The iPad 2 was about 33 percent thinner than its predecessor, a reduction in thickness from 13.4 mm to 8.8 mm. The iPad 2 features front and back cameras that support the device's FaceTime video calling application. FaceTime is Apple's telephone videoconferencing answer to Skype.

21. Isaacson, *Steve Jobs*, 35.

22. Adam Lashinsky, *Inside Apple* (New York: Business Plus, 2012).

23. Gershon, "Digital Media Innovation and the Apple iPad."

24. In a survey conducted by the Boston Consulting Group (BCG), more than 80 percent of American respondents said being able to access content from anywhere would be an important factor in their choice of a computer tablet ("The iPad and Steve Job's Second Coming," 2011).

25. "The Tablet Revolution," *Pew Research Center*, last modified October 25, 2011, http://www.journalism.org/2011/10/25/tablet/

26. "Gartner Sees Microsoft Stealing Market Share from Apple," *Fortune*, June 20, 2012, http://tech.fortune.cnn.com/2012/06/20/gartner-sees-microsoft-stealing-market-share-from-apple/

27. Statista, "Global Tablet Operating System Market Share Forecast 2013–2018," http://www.statista.com/statistics/272446/global-market-share-held-by-tablet-operating-systems/

28. Salaverría and Avilés, "La Convergencia Tecnológica en los Medios de Comunicación."

29. Arianna Huffington, "Bezos, Heraclitus and the Hybrid Future of Journalism," *Huffington Post*, Aug. 14, 2013, http://www.huffingtonpost.com/arianna-huffington/future-of-journalism_b_3756207.html

30. Gershon, "Digital Media Innovation and the Apple iPad."

31. "The Tablet Revolution," *Pew Research Center*.

32. Michael Massing, "Digital Journalism: The Next Generation," *The New York Review of Books*, June 25, 2015, http://www.nybooks.com/articles/archives/2015/jun/25/digital-journalism-next-generation/

33. Elihu Katz, "The Two-Step Flow of Communication: An Up-to-date Report on a Hypothesis," *Public Opinion Quarterly* 21, no. 1 (1957): 61–78; Elihu Katz and Paul Lazarsfeld, *Personal Influence* (New York: Free Press, 1957).

34. S. Segev, M. Villar, and R. Fiske, "Understanding Opinion Leadership and Motivations to Blog: Implications for Public Relations Practice," *Public Relations Journal* 6, no. 5 (2012), http://www.prsa.org/Intelligence/PRJournal/Documents/2012Segev.pdf

35. M. Nisbet and J. Kotcher, "A Two-Step Flow of Influence? Opinion-Leader Campaigns on Climate Change," *Science Communication* 30, no. 3 (2009): 328–354.

36. Michael Kent, "Critical Analysis of Blogging in Public Relations," *Public Relations Review* 34, no. 1 (2008): 32–40; Robert Scoble and Shel Israel, *Naked Conversations:*

How Blogs Are Changing the Way Businesses Talk With Customers (Hoboken, NJ: John Wiley & Sons, Inc., 2006).

37. Andrew Keen, *The Cult of the Amateur* (New York: Random House, 2007): 15–16.

38. Michael Massing, "Digital Journalism: How Good Is It?" *The New York Review of Books,* June 4, 2015, http://www.nybooks.com/articles/archives/2015/jun/04/digital-journalism-how-good-is-it/

39. Massing, "Digital Journalism: The Next Generation."

40. Nicola Formichetti, "Merging Physical and Digital in Fashion," *Huffington Post,* Jul. 15, 2011, http://www.huffingtonpost.com/nicola-formichetti/merging-physical-and-digi_b_900049.html

41. T. Rosenstiel, M. Jurkowitz, and Hong Ji, "The Search for a New Business Model," *Pew Research Center,* last modified March 5, 2012, http://www.journalism.org/analysis_report/search_new_business_model

42. "New York Times Innovation Report," *New York Times,* Mar. 16, 2014, http://mashable.com/2014/05/16/full-new-york-times-innovation-report/

43. "New York Times Innovation Report," 23–25.

44. NBC Universal, "Meet the Press Transcript," last modified August 11, 2013, http://www.nbcunicareers.com/news-feed?id=23838

45. M. Isaac, "Amazon's Jeff Bezos Explains Why He Bought the *Washington Post,*" *New York Times,* Dec. 2, 2014, http://bits.blogs.nytimes.com/2014/12/02/amazons-bezos-explains-why-he-bought-the-washington-post/

46. It is interesting to note that the prospect of an iTunes approach to news delivery was actually discussed in February 2010 when Steve Jobs and a group of Apple senior managers met with Arthur Sulzberger from the *New York Times,* Rupert Murdoch from News Corporation Ltd., and Jeff Bewkes from Time Warner Inc. Jobs floated the idea that iTunes could serve as a basic platform for the delivery of news content, charging subscribers a suggested fee of $5 a month. It was proposed that Apple would receive 30 percent of all revenues derived from the sale of news and information content. The critical issue for most of the publishers was not the 30 percent. Rather, it had to do with Apple's unwillingness to share circulation or subscriber data with the publishers.

47. PressReader allows the reader to access more than 2,000 newspapers or magazines from 95 countries in 51 languages available through a large, online newspaper and magazine kiosk. With PressReader, the user is able to acquire a complete digital copy featuring articles, photographic displays, advertisements, and commentary in their original form. Flipboard is a news aggregation software application that collects information from other news information Web sites and presents it in magazine format. It allows the user to select topical areas according to personal interest.

48. Gershon, "Digital Media Innovation and the Apple iPad."

49. Leonard Downie and Michael Schudson, "The Reconstruction of American Journalism," *Columbia Journalism Review* (November/December, 2009), http://www.cjr.org/reconstruction/the_reconstruction_of_american.php

50. In his book, *Megatrends,* author John Naisbitt (1982) coined the phrase "high tech—high touch" as a way to describe the importance of finding the right balance between technology and the softer, aesthetic aspects in the way we live.

51. Gershon, "Digital Media Innovation and the Apple iPad."

CHAPTER 13

Hacker Culture

Redefining Creative Work Space

Our greatest weakness lies in giving up. The most certain way to succeed is always to try just one more time.

—Thomas Edison

If something is important enough you should try, even if the probable outcome is failure.

—Elon Musk

Introduction

From the original AT&T Bell Labs to the modern-day Googleplex, the history of innovative discovery is really the study of how organizations set out to problem solve. The best moments in innovation seldom follow a predictable path. What is sometimes underappreciated is that great innovators like Akio Morita (Sony), Steve Jobs (Apple), and Jeff Bezos (Amazon.com), to name only a few, are the faces of a team of engineers, marketers, and designers who spend thousands of hours creating the breakthrough products and services that have become real game changers. They, better than anyone, understand that great discoveries are seldom achieved quickly. Rather, greatness is achieved over time through patience and perseverance. It requires hard work and a willingness to take the long-term view toward project success. In 1997, the year Amazon.com went public, company CEO Jeff Bezos wrote in the company's report to stockholders:

We believe that a fundamental measure of our success will be the shareholder value we create over the long term. This value will be a direct result of our ability to extend and solidify our current market leadership position. The stronger our market leadership, the more powerful our economic model. . . . We can't realize our potential as people or as companies unless we plan for the long term."[1]

Every year since then, Bezos has ended his shareholder letter by attaching the original 1997 essay with a reminder of the importance of thinking long term. As a company, Amazon.com has helped define the field of EC. Still, the challenges remain persistent. Bezos gets routinely challenged by investors looking for immediate results. Says Bezos,

If everything you do needs to work on a three-year time horizon, then you're competing against a lot of people. But if you're willing to invest on a seven-year time horizon, you're now competing against a fraction of those people, because very few companies are willing to do that.[2]

Great innovation is also the story of the lone maverick who imagines an idea that heretofore did not exist. What people like Alexander Graham Bell, Gordon Moore, Tim Berners-Lee, Steve Jobs, and Jeff Bezos share in common is an insatiable curiosity. It starts with a compelling idea. What if we did . . . ? Business author Jim Collins makes the argument that "when you combine a culture of discipline with an ethic of entrepreneurship, you get the magical alchemy of great performance."[3] The best companies have both a culture of disciplined behavior as well as a latitude for individual action. Such companies create a space where risk and experimentation are encouraged. In this chapter, we consider the organizational backdrop and culture that enable creativity to flourish.

A Culture

A culture of self-discipline is critical because it creates an environment where creative people work within a defined system. Knowing the organizational boundaries gives the individual more freedom to act within that system. Highly motivated people are self-motivated. Their sense of mission and purpose is personally driven. The need for enforced rules and structure is secondary. Success is rarely achieved in a sudden flash of insight. There is no magic formula or defining moment that brings about great product transformation. Rather, greatness is achieved over time through a constant, deliberative effort. It's not dramatic, revolutionary change but rather a passion and dedication to hard work. Momentum is built a little bit at a time. This was certainly the case with the development of the transistor and other research projects at AT&T's Bell Labs. Goals were carefully set and reached by a process of hypothesis, testing, and experiment. As Mervin Kelly, former research director of Bell Labs, liked to say, "Bell Labs is no house of magic. There is nothing magical about science. Our research people are following a straight plan as part of a system and there is no magic about it."[4] Fast-forward some 60 plus years later, and Apple co-founder Steve Wozniak similarly writes,

> Innovation is 99% perspiration. Hard work beats flashes of genius, and it is the only way that fresh ideas can evolve into lasting change. The easy first idea that comes into your head as a designer is not always the best. If you work and work, you can come up with a much better approach.[5]

Having the Right People

Great innovation also means having the right people. Putting the right structures, people, and processes in place should occur as a matter of course—not as an exception. Collins (2001) makes the point that one of the most important decisions for a senior leader is to clearly assess the performance capability of key professional staff during the start-up of that company or organization. He refers to it as "getting the right people in the right seats on the bus and the wrong ones off it."[6] When thinking about the important positions within an organization, formal titles become less important than the tasks and responsibilities that need to be performed. This is very much in keeping with the principle of hacker culture. People don't have jobs; they have responsibilities. For Collins, there are two important essentials:

> First, if you begin with *who,* rather than *what,* you can more easily adapt to a changing world. Second, if you have the right people on the bus, the problem of how to motivate and manage people largely goes away. The right people don't need to be tightly managed or fired up. They will be self-motivated by the inner drive to produce the best results and to be part of creating something great.[7]

Having the right people means making the hiring and recruitment of professional staff one of the most important responsibilities for a CEO or senior manager. Having the right people also means not settling for those individuals who may be wrong for the organization. In practical terms, that may mean parting ways with a longtime traveling companion who needs to step off the bus in order for the vehicle to move forward.[8] Apple's CEO Steve Jobs makes a similar point about the importance of finding the right people. For Jobs, putting together the right project team was every bit as important as the project design itself.

> I noticed that the dynamic range between what an average person could accomplish and what the best person could accomplish was 50 or 100 to 1. Given that, you're well advised to go after the cream of the cream. . . . A small team of A+ players can run circles around a giant team of B and C players.[9]

Recognizing and Valuing Talent

Is there a certain litmus test in determining who are the A people for an organization? No. It would be more accurate to say that there are certain truisms that apply in helping to advance highly successful project teams. Among the questions to consider are the following:

1. Does the person share the organization's core values? Part of the success of any business start-up (or project group) is a sense that the person knows that he/she is engaged in some unique work.

2. Does this person possess some exceptional ability? Does this person have the potential to be one of the best in his/her field?

3. Does this person possess a sense of ownership in the work that has to be performed? Is this person willing to take responsibility (i.e., going the extra mile) for ensuring that a job gets completed correctly? This stands in marked contrast to the person who is simply holding down a job.

There is very little sentimentality in Steve Job's thinking.

I've learned over the years that, when you have really good people, you don't have to baby them. By expecting them to do great things, you can get them to do great things. The original Mac team taught me that A+ players like to work together, and they don't like it if you tolerate B grade work.[10]

Mavericks Often Lead the Way

It takes a unique person in a leadership role to appreciate the talent factor when it comes to understanding the role of the maverick within an organization. Mavericks are often some of your best examples of A+ people. They stand apart from the rest of the group. It is almost an article of faith that such individuals are often eccentric, rude, and annoying. They are all too willing to challenge the system by asking tough questions. Mavericks often lead the way when it comes to experimentation. They are fully focused on developing their ideas at the expense of everything else.[11]

As sometimes happens, the maverick will leave the familiarity of his/her home in search of independence and a better place to apply his/her ideas. As an example, Tony Fadell was a vice president at Philips when he left to develop a digital music player. Steve Jobs recruited him to Apple, where he codeveloped the iPod. John Warnock left Xerox PARC to cofound Adobe because Xerox would not commercialize the InterPress graphics language he codeveloped. Gordon Moore and Robert Noyce left Fairchild Semiconductor to cofound Intel because Fairchild was not willing to implement their ideas. Smart, innovative companies recognize talent when they see it. They give such individuals the freedom and creative space to test out new ideas and working concepts.

Hacker Culture

One of the most interesting trends of the early 21st century has been the emergence of hacker culture located throughout the workplace of today's best-known media and IT companies. From Apple and Facebook to the small, five-person start-up company, there is a common element of behavior that is distinctly present-day IT. By hackers, we don't mean people who pose security threats to computer networks. Rather, *hacker* refers to media and IT-savvy people who are focused on the power of IT. Hacker culture is very hands-on and applied. Hacker, in the Facebook sense, means building something quickly or testing the boundaries of what is possible. It's an approach that involves constant refinement. Says Zuckerberg,

> Hackers believe that something can always be better, and that nothing is ever complete. They just have to go fix it—often in the face of people who say it's impossible or are content with the status quo. Hackers try to build the best services over the long term by quickly releasing and learning from smaller iterations rather than trying to get everything right all at once. To support this, we have built a testing framework that at any given time can try out thousands of versions of Facebook. We have the words, *Done is better than perfect*, painted on our walls to remind ourselves to always keep shipping.[12]

One of the core values of hacker culture is a belief that talent and dedication reign supreme. The best ideas should prevail. To encourage this approach, Facebook periodically hosts so-called hackathon sessions, where designers are encouraged to build prototypes for new ideas they have. At the end, various design teams get together and look at what has been built. Many of Facebook's most successful products were the direct result of hackathon sessions, including Timeline, chat, video, the Facebook mobile development framework, as well as important infrastructure, like the HipHop compiler.

In contrast to previous generations, hackers tend to be more casual in dress: T-shirts, jeans, and running shoes. They are less concerned about the traditional representations of professional success (e.g., business attire, professional title, or a corner office). Instead, the focus is on being smart and creative and making really great products. The best companies also attract smart, likeminded people. As one Google employee noted,

> We are surrounded by smart, driven people who provide the best environment for learning I've ever experienced. I don't mean through tech talks and formal training programs, I mean through working with awesome colleagues—even the non famous ones.[13]

Implicit in hacker culture is a belief that work should be fun and challenging. If work is fun, then you don't mind working long hours to see a project through to its completion. But working long hours comes at a cost to the individual and his/her family. Today, there is a growing recognition that companies need to provide workers with support services and amenities that make it easier to balance work and family life issues at a time when there are few stay-at-home spouses and work demands a constant effort. The motivation is also financial. High taxable incomes can be partially offset by offering amenities that take the place of spendable income. A number of employee benefits are tax free.[14]

At one end of the spectrum are companies like Google that provide free food to their employees. Google employees take their meals in what are referred to as cafés, not cafeterias or dining halls. Before Google, food at IT companies was similar to a college cafeteria. It is a well-known fact that the cafés on Google's Mountain View campus serve some of the best food in Silicon Valley. Google also has a health club facility as well as a free dry cleaning services. Not to be undone, Facebook offers a different set of enticements that include $4,000 in baby cash for those employees having children and reimbursement for day care and adoption fees. Similarly, Facebook employees can take home a free dinner, or if working late, families can join the company employee—leading to a regular sight of children in the campus cafeteria.[15] Both companies have set the standard for how the modern-day company should function, including good health-care benefits as well as food, day care, and exercise facilities.

At the other end of the spectrum is the small, five-person start-up company. This is hacker culture in its most essential form: a strong dedication to the work and no frills. Instead of high-end, open-space architecture, it may be a one-room office over a dry cleaning store. Or it may be the 130-person organization that occupies a set of offices that are part of an incubator program at a university. Instead of gourmet food, it's pizza all the way or at least a sandwich from home. What levels the playing field for both kinds of start-up groups is the power of a good idea and a core group of people who are fully committed to seeing it succeed. The people who work for such companies have a strong sense of purpose. They are committed and willing to work the long hours to make things happen. Team members want to know that their work matters to the overall success of the company. Hacker culture means giving team members a real sense of ownership in the process and outcomes for which they are committed.

Risk and Experimentation

Successful businesses with proven track records find it hard to change. There is a clear pattern of success that translates into established customer clients, sales volume, and public awareness for the work that has been accomplished to date. A variety of commitments have been made in terms of people, manufacturing, production schedules, and contracts going forward. Such commitments to ongoing business activities have an established trajectory. As researcher Rosabeth Moss Kanter (1989) points out, "Mainstreams have momentum. Their path is established, the business flow is already developed."[16] At issue is the fact that most managers are unable or unwilling to sacrifice a successful product in favor of a new, untested one. Instead of blue ocean thinking, managers become preoccupied with fine-tuning and making slight adjustments to an existing product line rather than preparing for the future.[17] There is a tendency toward playing it safe by focusing on present customers and what works (i.e., the innovator's dilemma). New product development and innovation carry with them uncertainty and risk. The commitment to advance a new technology or service requires large start-up costs, with no guarantees of success:

. . . and the newer it is, the more likely that there will be little or no precedent, little or no experience base to use to make forecasts. Timetables may prove unrealistic. Anticipated costs may be overrun. Furthermore, the final form of the product may look different from what was originally envisioned.[18]

A related problem is the self-imposed limitation of sunk costs, that is, investments in research and technology, construction of production facilities, education and training, contract obligations, and so on. Companies feel they can't afford to change given the amount of time and investment spent in the current research or project design. The difficulty, however, is that mainstream technology can become steadily obsolete. It is only when faced with a rival product or a disruptive technology that the same set of managers feel the urgency to adapt and innovate. By then, it may be too little too late. Response time is critical. Those companies whose response time is slow pay a heavy price in terms of revenue decline, lost market share, and missed opportunity. As was discussed earlier, companies like Kodak, BlackBerry, and Blockbuster were slow to react. Such companies did not anticipate a time when a substitute product (or changing market conditions) might come along and dramatically alter the playing field.

The Testing of New Ideas

Experimentation lies at the heart of every company's ability to innovate. The most successful companies are those that are willing to experiment and not rest on their past achievements. Accordingly, the CEO and senior leadership team help set the tone by putting their full weight behind such experimentation. Such companies create a culture of innovation where experimentation and mistakes are an understood part of the process of testing new ideas and boundaries. As Thomke (2001) points out,

> The systemic testing of ideas is what enables companies to create and refine their products. In fact, no product can be a product without having first been an idea that was shaped, to one degree or another, through the process of experimentation.[19]

Most companies like to talk a good game about being innovative. But in practical terms, many such organizations are not comfortable with change. They are not inclined to take risks (and stand outside themselves) when things are going well (i.e., the innovator's dilemma). They are risk averse and want to avoid failure at all costs. David Kelley, founder of IDEO, believes that it is important to rethink the role of failure in the design process. When a novel idea fails in an experiment, the failure can expose important knowledge gaps.[20] But such efforts can also reveal unique ways of looking at the problem. It can refocus the group's efforts in more promising areas. A culture of innovation means taking risks and, with it, the very real possibility of product failure. It's part of the DNA of what it means to be innovative.

Creating the Proper Work Space

Creating a culture of innovation presupposes having the right work environment with which to develop and implement great ideas. From the corner office to the nondescript cubicle, there are considerable differences of opinion as to what makes for a successfully creative work space. There are, however, certain truisms in terms of what makes for a creative work space. Innovation needs a place to flourish and grow. The creative office should function like a well-designed stage or movie set, thereby contributing to great performance. Good design space creates opportunities for prototyping new ideas.[21]

Many of today's more innovative companies are abandoning the very notion of the corner office. Certainly, within media and IT circles, the private office is considered a relic of the 20th century.[22] Gone are the immense executive desks from the past symbolizing power and authority as well as trophy-laden walls. Large drawers and closet space for storage are steadily being deemphasized, reflecting the shift away from paper and more toward cloud computing and the electronic storage of information.[23] More and more of today's media and IT executives are giving up the private office to sit with employees, thereby improving overall communication and collaboration.

At the same time, there is still a very obvious need for privacy. Working professionals still need to be able to have quiet, deliberative time to think and work without interruption. The more demanding the task, the more individuals need punctuating moments of private time to think or recharge. The challenge is that critical thinking time is hard to come by when one is faced with constant interruptions. As Congdon, Flynn, and Redman (2014) write,

> The increased focus on collaborative work means we're rarely alone, and the ubiquity of mobile devices means we're always accessible. In light of these pressures, it's not surprising that the number of people who say they can't concentrate at their desk has increased.[24]

Privacy versus open work space is not a zero-sum game. Rather, it's about finding a balance between the work that needs to get accomplished and creating the proper work space that will enable that to occur. James Ludwig, head of design for U.S.-based Steelcase Corporation writes, "My work space should reflect the way I work."[25] *New York Times* writer Allison Arieff (2011) concurs and argues that furniture is not the problem. Rather, it has more to do with understanding how people really work in a fast-paced business environment. The key design principle is sustainability, where the emphasis is on energy efficiency and economy of space. The designers of the 21st-century office recognize the importance of creating work zones, that is, areas where specific types of tasks get accomplished.[26]

Mobility and Intelligent Work Space

Another consideration is the importance of building intelligence into the design of the modern office work space. The combination of computer and telecommunications technology has had a major effect on the spatial design and activity of the modern organization. The buildings and office space that we occupy are not nearly as important as the tools we use to get work done. The blending of powerful communication tools with flexible work space can greatly enhance productivity and innovation.[27] Related to this idea is the importance of mobility, which recognizes that business professionals and creative teams need greater flexibility of movement. In previous chapters we have used the term *virtual communication* to describe the artificial space and network linkages connecting a decentralized group of users using a variety of communication and IT. Today's business professional needs to be able to access the Internet anytime, anywhere. Location should never be an obstacle.

Serendipitous Connections

One of the important lessons in innovation is that some of the greatest discoveries occur as a result of a chance encounter: "I was sitting next to this guy on an airplane, and he said . . . I met this woman at a conference, and she told me . . . " As mentioned in Chapter 1, Alexander Graham Bell's invention of the telephone was the unintended consequence of working on a device called the harmonic telegraph, which would allow multiple telegraph messages to be shared on a single transmission line. The pacemaker was invented by an electronics technician who happened to have lunch with two heart surgeons; Starbucks became a national chain after salesman Howard Schultz stopped by the original single store in Seattle's historic Pike Place Market and realized that his future lay in cafés and fresh-roasted, whole-bean coffee.

As Steven Johnson points out, some of the best discoveries occur when different people with diverse backgrounds and skill sets find themselves in a common space sharing their ideas.[28] The unfiltered exchange of a chance idea can sometimes spawn a radically new working concept. And so it is that some of today's most innovative companies create spaces for chance encounters—enabling good ideas to move freely—making connections in unexpected ways.

Disney's Pixar and the Serendipitous Encounter

At Pixar, employees are encouraged to be creative. There is a lot of wide-open space that greets a visitor when arriving at Pixar's football-sized atrium. Pixar cofounder and CEO Steve Jobs wanted to design a building where people would interact naturally. He positioned the mailboxes, meeting rooms, cafeteria, and most importantly, the bathrooms in the center atrium. He wanted to avoid people going off to the separate silos of software coding, animation, or production. This would ensure little or no interaction with people from other areas of the organization. Pixar's current design makes the serendipitous encounter with employees from other departments a mainstay of the Pixar organizational culture. Jobs believed that when people casually interact and have fun, good things can sometimes happen.

Décor also contributes to a playful, fun atmosphere. The atrium at Pixar is decorated with larger-than-life statues of Pixar characters, concept paintings on the walls, and storyboards and color scripts in clear view. Pixar's rolling, sixteen-acre campus also includes offices, studio and sound rooms, screening rooms, a lap pool, volleyball courts, and a soccer field (which is being sacrificed for a new four-level building to provide expanded work and play space)—all of which makes for a welcome escape from the daily grind. Says Pixar artist Nate Wragg, "It's the freedom and encouragement to relax between deadlines and to take fun breaks when you are feeling tired that I feel really creates that fun atmosphere at work that most businesses lack."[29]

The Googleplex

Over the years, Google has evolved a unique business culture. The company's headquarters, referred to as the *Googleplex,* is an informal, highly charged atmosphere that encourages collegiality and innovation. Adam Lashinsky (2006) refers to it as *chaos by design.*

> The 1.3 million square foot headquarters is a mélange of two-story buildings full of festive cafeterias (yes, they're all free), crammed conference rooms and hallway bull sessions, all of it surrounded by sandy volleyball courts, youngsters whizzing by on motorized scooters . . . and anything goes spirit. It's a place where failure coexists with triumph, and ideas bubble up from lightly supervised engineers, none of whom worry too much about their projects ever making money.[30]

Google is planning a major expansion of the Googleplex. Plans are underway to take sixty acres of land in an area called North Bayshore (adjacent to the Googleplex) and build a facility that can be likened to a human terrarium. The proposed design represents a major rethinking of professional work space. Instead of solid buildings, the plan calls for a series of rising, tentlike structures with canopies of translucent glass. Beneath each of the major canopies are lightweight, modular structures that can be moved and repurposed to accommodate different types of spaces and projects. The new campus includes neatly developed parks, bike paths, and restored coastal wetlands that will be available to the public.[31]

Google's 20% Time. Google famously has a unique incentive program that allows employees to spend 20% of their time to work on a project that is company-related or that is of personal interest to the individual. In its earliest form, the Google 20% time rule was the quintessential innovation incubator program. Introduced in 2004, such projects fell outside the employee's regular job description. Several important projects were the direct outgrowth of the 20% time rule, including Gmail, AdSense, and Google Books quick-scanning technology. Google's 20% time incentive is not for everyone. The most promising projects usually involve a small group of individuals who are committed to an idea. Google works from the bottom up. If an engineer has a great technical idea, he/she takes it to fellow engineers and tries to convince them of the project's worthiness.[32] Good ideas spread fast. The burden falls on the individual engineer or group to convince company managers of the project's intended benefits.

To be sure, not all projects have achieved the once hoped for success. As Google has become more successful, the regular workday pressures to succeed have seen a corresponding increase as well. The difficulty is that the 20% rule is no longer sustainable given the size of the company. There was a lot of lost productivity that was starting to occur. Since Google's managers are judged on the productivity of their team, it is often in everyone's best interest that engineers and designers are fully focused on their primary work 100 percent of the time. Starting in 2011, Google began the first phase of scaling back its 20% rule. Today, the 20% rule has taken a different form. Google employees now go through a more formal process for obtaining release time to pursue individual projects.[33] Perhaps the most important takeaway has been the resulting effect of the 20% rule on other companies like Facebook, LinkedIn, and other tech companies that have introduced similar type incentive programs.

Facebook and Hacker-style Décor

Today, Facebook claims an international work force of more than 10,000 employees. In December 2011, Facebook moved into a new corporate space in Menlo Park, California. The fifty-seven-acre campus once belonged to Sun Microsystems. The new Facebook headquarters will eventually include ten planned structures. The first building, known as MPK 2, can hold up to 2,800 people and includes a nine-acre green roof roughly the size of seven football fields.[34] Perhaps it's fitting that the company's main address is 1 Hacker Way, Menlo Park, California.[35] There are no private offices or cubicles to divide coworkers. Instead, software designers and engineers occupy rows of shared desk space. Even CEO Mark Zuckerberg has a desk on the main floor. There are multiple chalkboards that line the hallways as well as glass conference rooms. The new style of office space has been described as *hacker style*.

Workers roam with laptops, meet on sofas, and scribble on walls at Facebook's Silicon Valley headquarters, where rusted steel beams, exposed heating ducts, and plywood-covered corridors are part of the decor. The office campus in Menlo Park, California, was renovated for $250 million in a hacker style intended to express the culture of the world's largest social networking company.[36] Rather than debating the merits of new ideas, the company encourages its developers to build and test prototypes. "There's a hacker mantra that you'll hear a lot around Facebook offices: 'Code wins arguments.' "[37]

Innovation Centers Within the Mainstream

It's one thing to be a Silicon Valley start-up company, but it's quite another when one is operating as a small project group that is part of a larger mainstream company. More and more companies have created so-called *innovation centers* or *incubator* programs whose goals are to develop next-generation products and services. It sometimes happens that building a new innovation center is met with a certain measure of skepticism from other divisions and groups within the company. It's not uncommon that division heads from other areas become resentful when needed resources are being diverted away from businesses with an established track record to support what appears to be a speculative project venture. This can include privileges and rewards that may exceed what other established businesses are getting at the present time. Over time, there evolves an unspoken culture clash between those who are free to experiment (and by extension—have all the fun) and the serious business enterprise that generates revenue by providing reliability and growth.

Open Communication and Keeping Everyone Involved

Innovators and project leaders should not work in isolation if they want buy-in and support from the rest of the organization. If they want their ideas to catch on, the project manager should engage in open communication by keeping the larger organization informed and involved. Open communication will go a long way in building a coalition of supporters who will provide project support both during formal meetings as well as behind the scenes. There should never be a perception that the new start-up group is off doing its own thing. Rather, the goal should be to make everyone feel that they are legitimate stakeholders in the project outcome.[38]

Core Strategy and Plan

It's important that everyone understands the proposed plan and long-term goal of the project undertaking. If the idea is compelling enough, even people who are not directly involved will feel some measure of ownership that careful thought and applied strategy are being directed toward the project start-up. One way to help define the movement is to pilot (or showcase) the project. By giving periodic demonstrations or updates, this will go a long way in helping to build support among the various departments and divisions that are part of the organization's larger mission.

Keep the Project Review Process Flexible

Another important lesson is that overly tight performance review measures can strangle innovation. There is a tendency among well-established companies to apply the same performance review metrics to new project start-ups, thus weakening the venture before it has the opportunity to get some traction. Too much emphasis on traditional performance metrics like return on investment (ROI) or risk tolerance at an early stage of development can kill a good project before it gets off the ground. Traditional demographic research reflects information that is currently available, but it cannot accurately forecast what customers want and would be willing to pay for in the future.[39] It cannot fully consider blue ocean opportunities because there is no basis for analysis and comparison. In sum, strict controls have their place, but flexibility goes a long way in ensuring that promising projects have the possibility to see the light of day.

The Value of Partnerships and Collaboration

One of the most important lessons executives have learned about innovation is that companies can no longer afford to go it alone. The traditional model of R&D is to create and manufacture products exclusively within confines of one's own company. The basic logic is that if you want something done right, you've got to do it yourself. Researcher Henry Chesbrough (2003) challenges that basic assumption and makes the argument that the not-invented-here approach is no longer sustainable. Accordingly, companies should be drawing business partners and suppliers into so-called *innovation networks*.[40] Two such examples can be seen with the partnership that was formed between Sony and Philips Corporation in the development of the CD. Similarly, Apple collaborated and eventually acquired a company called Portal Player, which led to the creation of the Apple iPod.[41] The idea behind open innovation is that there are simply too many good ideas available externally and held by people who don't work for the host company. They simply cannot be ignored. Even the best companies with the most extensive internal capabilities have to take into consideration external knowledge and information capabilities when they think about innovation. Thus, good ideas can come from outside one's company as well as internally.

The Value of Customer Insights

What is the value of one good idea or suggestion? No one knows better than one's customers what they want in terms of improved product design or service performance. Many new product development opportunities originate from customers who have difficulties with existing products or have needs that are not being fully addressed. Customers want solutions to their problems. They seek better value from the products and services they buy. Taking time to understand the behavior activities of one's customers in their daily work routine can go a long way in helping to understand the kinds of special features and benefits that may be of interest to them in the long term. The principle of engaging one's customers goes well beyond the focus group model. Instead, the emphasis should be on trying to understand the essential habits (and support technology) that drive the customers' everyday work engines.[42] This idea is in keeping with an earlier point made about Google placing a strong emphasis on understanding user intentions and then building complementary solutions.

Discussion

Companies, like people, can become easily satisfied with organizational routines that stand in the way of being innovative. Respect for past success is important. However, too much reliance on the past can make an organization risk averse. Such companies become preoccupied with fine-tuning and making slight adjustments to an existing product line rather than preparing for the future. The lessons of business history have taught us that there is no such thing as a static market. There are no guarantees of continued success for any business enterprise no matter how good its reputation or past performance. Over time, tastes, preference, and technology change. Innovative companies keep abreast of such changes, anticipate them, and make the necessary adjustments in terms of strategy and new product development. Forward-thinking companies create a culture of innovation where risk and experimentation are an accepted part of the process of testing new boundaries.

The irony, of course, is that even the best-managed companies are susceptible to innovation failure. Specifically, a company's very strengths and ongoing success can lay the groundwork for its eventual decline. This can occur at a time when the company is realizing some of its highest profits. Failure sometimes goes with the territory of introducing game-changing technologies and services. The challenge, therefore, is to develop a culture of innovation where risk and experimentation are fully supported. If innovation can be likened to the game of baseball, and more specifically being a professional pitcher, there is no such thing as a perfect 30–0 season. Rather, innovation is about putting together a winning record (perhaps 26–4) and making innovation (like games) a sustainable, repeatable process.

Endnotes

1. Amazon.com Inc., *1997 Annual Report to Stockholders,* http://www.scribd.com/doc/43386750/Amazon-Letter-to-Shareholders-in-1997
2. Steven Levy, "Jeff Bezos Owns the Web in More Ways than You Think," *Wired,* Nov. 13, 2011, http://www.wired.com/2011/11/ff_bezos/all/1
3. Jim Collins, *Good to Great* (New York: Harper Collins, 2001), 13.
4. Jon Gertner, *The Idea Factory: Bell Labs and the Great Age of American Innovation* (New York: Penguin Press, 2012), 113.
5. "Work and Work and Work, Says Woz," *Bloomberg/Business Week—Smart Brief,* Dec. 15, 2009, http://www.smartbrief.com/12/15/09/work-and-work-and-work-says-woz#.VVoIinrqK-8
6. Collins, *Good to Great,* 41.
7. "Get the Right People on the Bus," *The Wunderlin Company,* last modified August 14, 2013, http://wunderlin.com/get-the-right-people-on-the-bus-2/#.VUEaG3rqK-8
8. Jim Collins, "Do You Have the Right People on the Bus?" *Bloomberg/Business Week—Smart Brief,* Sept. 27, 2010, http://smartblogs.com/leadership/2010/09/27/jim-collins-do-you-have-the-right-people-on-the-bus/
9. Rama Jager ad Rafael Ortiz, *In the Company of Giants* (Darby, PA: Diane Pub. 1997).
10. Walter Isaacson, *Steve Jobs* (New York: Simon & Schuster, 2011), 124.
11. During the development of Playstation, Sony's Ken Kutaragi earned the moniker of Crazy Ken for his bizarre and outspoken comments during the development of Playstation 2. For a time, Kutaragi was seriously considered as a possible candidate to become the future CEO of Sony. It never came to pass. By 2005, Kutaragi had done little to prove to Sony's board of directors that he had the structured leadership style to run the entire company. When CEO Nobuyuki Idei retired that year, the company's senior

leadership promoted Sony BMG Music Entertainment's head Howard Stringer, making him the first non-Japanese person to lead the company. But what ultimately undermined Kutaragi was the launch of the PlayStation 3, which fell behind schedule, proved difficult to develop, and was vastly overpriced. Rumors at the time suggested that Kutaragi hid the enormous R&D costs of creating the PlayStation 3. Sony lost hundreds of dollars on every console sold.

Similarly, Linux software developer Linus Torvalds, for his part, really doesn't care whether people like him. Following his keynote speech at the Linux Conference in Auckland, New Zealand, Torvalds opened a question-and-answer session by fielding a question from Nebula One developer Matthew Garrett. He accused Torvalds of having an abrasive style when addressing contributors to the Linux kernel mailing list. "Some people think I'm nice and are shocked when they find out different. I'm not a nice person, and I don't care about you. I care about the technology and the kernel—that's what's important to me."

12. David Cohen, "Annual Meeting: Mark Zuckerberg Addresses Facebook's Hacker Culture, 2014-style," last modified May 23, 2014, http://www.adweek.com/social times/annual-meeting-mark-zuckerberg-hacker/435177

13. "Google Employees Reveal their Favorite Perks Working for the Company," *Business Insider,* http://www.businessinsider.com/google-employee-favorite-perks-2013–3#the-free-gour-met-food-and-snacks-are-never-ending-1

14. "Silicon Valley Employees Go Wild," *Forbes,* Oct. 30, 2012, http://www.forbes.com/sites/johngoodman/2012/10/30/silicon-valley-employers-go-wild-with-lavish-employee-benefits/

15. "Perk Wars: Facebook, Zynga, Google Jockey for Top Talent," *USA Today,* July 5, 2012, http://usatoday30.usatoday.com/tech/news/story/2012–07–04/silicon-valley perks/56021130/1

16. Rosabeth Moss Kanter, *When Giants Learn to Dance* (New York: Simon & Schuster, 1989), 175.

17. Nicholas Negroponte, "Incrementalism is Innovation's Worst Enemy," *Wired,* April 1995, 188.

18. Rosabeth Moss Kanter, *When Giants Learn to Dance,* 217.

19. Stefan Thomke, "Enlightened Experimentation: The New Imperative for Innovation," *Harvard Business Review* (February 2001).

20. Tom Kelley, *The Ten Faces of Innovation* (New York: Doubleday, 2005).

21. Ibid.

22. Allison Arieff, "Beyond the Cubicle," *New York Times,* July 18, 2011, http://opinionator .blogs.nytimes.com/2011/07/18/beyond-the-cubicle/?_r=0

23. Sue Shellenbarger, "Designs to Make You Work Harder," *Wall Street Journal,* June 22, 2011, http://www.wsj.com/articles/SB10001424052702304070104576399572462315158

24. Christine Congdon, Donna Flynn, and Melanie Redman, "Balancing We and Me: The Best Collaborative Spaces Also Support Solitude," *Harvard Business Review* (October 2014), https://hbr.org/2014/10/balancing-we-and-me-the-best-collaborative-spaces-also-support-solitude

25. Arieff, "Beyond the Cubicle"

26. Ibid.

27. Ben Waber, Jennifer Magnolfi, and Greg Lindsay, "Workspaces That Move People," *Harvard Business Review* (October 2014): 69–77.

28. Steven Johnson, *Where Good Ideas Come From: The Natural History of Innovation* (New York: Riverhead Books, 2010).

29. Bill Capodagli, "Magic in the Workplace: How Pixar and Disney Unleash the Creative Talent of their Workforce," *Effectif* (September/October 2010), http://www.hcamag .com/hr-resources/hr-strategy/magic-in-the-workplace—how-pixar-and-disney-unleash-the-creative-talent-of-their-workforce-115686.aspx

30. Adam Lashinsky, "Chaos by Design," *Fortune,* Oct. 2, 2006, 86–96.

31. Brad Stone, "Building Planet Google," *Bloomberg Businessweek,* May 17, 2015, 53–58.

32. "Google Couldn't Kill 20 Percent Time Even If It Wanted To," *Wired,* Aug., 21, 2013, http://www.wired.com/2013/08/20-percent-time-will-never-die/

33. While unique for Google and other tech companies, the granting of release time is considered standard operating procedure for a university. Release time at a major research university can take different forms from government grants (e.g., National Science Foundation, Fulbright scholarship, etc.) to university grants, government or business contracts, and so on.

34. "Facebook's Gorgeous New Campus," *Time,* Mar. 30, 2015, http://time.com/3763880/facebook-campus-grass-roof/

35. In addition to its main campus, Facebook has bought additional properties in Menlo Park, including a sixty-acre TE Connectivity campus that runs along the Bayfront Expressway, adjacent to the main headquarters building as well as the fifty-six-acre Prologis complex located nearby. While Facebook has no immediate plans to occupy the campus, both acquisitions are being done to accommodate future growth.

36. "Facebook's Cool Space Campus Points to the Future of Office Growth," BloombergBusiness, Dec. 22, 2011, http://www.bloomberg.com/news/2011–12–20/facebook-s-cool-space-campus-points-to-future-of-office-growth.html

37. "Facebook IPO Reveals Hacker Culture," *InformationAge,* Feb. 2, 2012, http://www .information-age.com/technology/applications-and-development/1689138/facebook-ipo-reveals-hacker-culture

38. Rosabeth Moss Kanter, "Innovation: The Classic Traps," *Harvard Business Review* (November 2006): 73–83.

39. Clayton Christensen, *The Innovator's Solution* (Boston, MA: Harvard Business School Press, 2003).

40. Henry Chesbrough, *Open Innovation: The New Imperative for Creating and Profiting from Technology* (Boston, MA: Harvard Business School Press, 2003).

41. Jeffrey Young and William Simon, *iCon: Steve Jobs* (New York: John Wiley & Sons, 2005).

42. David Rainey, *Product Innovation: Leading Change Through Integrated Product Development* (Cambridge, UK: Cambridge University Press, 2005).

Name Index

Organization Index

Subject Index